Heaven Therapy

INSIGHTS INTO THE AFTERLIFE

A Book for the Bereaved and the Curious

Heaven Therapy

INSIGHTS INTO THE AFTERLIFE
A Book for the Bereaved and the Curious

Ross Bartlett

FINDHORN PRESS

Findhorn Press
One Park Street
Rochester, Vermont 05767
www.findhornpress.com

Findhorn Press is a division of Inner Traditions International

ISBN 978-1-84409-697-8

Cataloging-in-Publication Data for this title is available from the British Library

Printed and bound in the United States

Edited by Michael Hawkins
Cover design by Richard Crookes
Front cover photograph by John Byer
Text design and layout by Damian Keenan

DISCLAIMER
The information in this book is given in good faith and is neither
intended to diagnose any physical or mental condition nor to serve
as a substitute for informed medical advice or care. Please contact
your health professional for medical advice and treatment. Neither
author nor publisher can be held liable by any person for any loss
or damage whatsoever which may arise from the use of this book or
any of the information therin.

Contents

Dedication

· · · · · · · · · · · · · ·

I dedicate this book to all the people on Earth
and all the people in the afterlife
who have helped me with my work.

Without you, this would have never been possible.

Introduction

· · · · · · · · · · · · ·

What is Heaven Therapy?

As far as I am aware, I'm the first person to coin the term "Heaven Therapy". I would define Heaven Therapy as an experience that appears to have any form of healing benefit through a communication or experience with a person who is considered deceased.

After death communication (ADC) can happen spontaneously or with the assistance of something or someone else, for example, a psychic medium. In this book, I will be focusing on what I consider to be the current gateway to Heaven Therapy. This gateway is an assisted ADC, with the aid of a psychic medium. Further, I will demonstrate how this form of Heaven Therapy can be a real alternative or a complementary approach to bereavement healing, and I will show how this approach can dramatically reduce grief caused by bereavement. In some cases, this approach can completely extinguish the grief and bereavement process.

Mental mediumship – the current gateway to Heaven Therapy

Mediumship is a special form of Psi phenomena performed by a psychic. If the psychic can perform mediumship consistently well, then he/she may add medium to their title. Mediumship is the area I have specialized in for the last decade. It's important to understand that not all psychics can perform mediumship, but all mediums are psychic.

Because of cultural/religious backgrounds, the medium can have a wide range of philosophies and value assumptions. In the West, mediums are commonly connected to spiritualist practice, meaning at some point they have derived their practices and philosophy from spiritualism. I would fall into this category. These mediums hold the understanding that our consciousness has a transpersonal quality, specifically that our consciousness has the ability to go beyond the brain and the physical body. Further, that upon physical death, our consciousness contained within our spirit becomes detached from the physical body. I prefer to use the term transbodily consciousness for this specific phenomena and I believe am also the first to coin it so.

This consciousness then lives on eternally, in an afterlife, and continues to take an active interest in the lives of their relatives and friends, who are still living in, what is commonly termed, a physical body on Earth. These spirit people are able to come and visit with us here to see what is happening in our lives. They also have a certain ability to be aware of our thoughts at any time, particularly if the thoughts are directed towards them. Through these means, they are often very aware of what is taking place in our life.

Mediums also hold the understanding that they are capable of, in various ways, channelling the disembodied spirit. Mental mediumship readings are one method of channelling and are the focus of this book. These readings are an activity that is commonly practised by Western mediums today.

The communication happens exclusively within the mind of the medium. This mental communication is formed through a mind-to-mind telepathic link, meaning the mind of the medium, their consciousness, is connected to the consciousness of the disembodied spirit. This process happens through a form of a connection between the medium's physical body and their energetic matrix and the energetic matrix of the disembodied spirit.

This connection can be seen as the lightest form of over-shadowing. In a way, it is an extremely light form of possession. So light that the medium remains in control and consciously aware at all times of what he or she is thinking, doing and saying. This does not require the spirit to be extensively within the body space of the medium.

Normally, the spirit will move their energy to one side of the medium, and project their consciousness from there. Space is not important here; as long as the spirit is capable of projecting their consciousness strongly enough, it could be done through any distance. Even though this connection is very light compared to other forms of channelling, the medium can still exhibit behaviours the spirit commonly did when in their physical body. This tends to occur subconsciously. For example, the medium may not even realize he or she has started to play with their hair in a very odd way that the spirit communicator did on a regular basis, or they may begin to exhibit a twitch that the spirit had when they were in their physical body. However, such occurrences are rare. I have done thousands of readings and this has happened only around five times. When they do happen, it can be great evidence for the recipient of the reading.

Generally, it is only a small part of the disembodied spirit's consciousness that is connected through the energetic matrix of the medium during a mental mediumship reading. However, the stronger the blend, the stronger the connection between the medium and the disembodied spirit will be. When this energetic blend has been reached, the communication is then commonly formulated by the medium, using a mixture of telepathic psychic senses, namely clairvoyance or clear seeing; secondly, clairaudience or clear hearing; thirdly, clairsentience or clear feeling. Those are the most important 'clairs' although there is also clairolfactory, which is clear smelling and clairgustance, meaning clear tasting.

A person will commonly go to see a medium for a mental mediumship reading after having recently experienced a bereavement, or when they find themselves several years removed from a loved one's death, but still stuck in a continual state of grief. They attend a mental mediumship reading with the hope that through the medium, they will receive messages from their loved ones who have passed over.

Their belief is that this may lead to a therapeutic benefit and ease the negative feelings they are experiencing. Although the practice of mediumship in the West commonly stems from and is often connected, to the religion of Spiritualism, in most cases the mourner does not convert to that religion. It is also becoming more common today for a person to have a reading with a non-denominational medium, than one who is officially a Spiritualist.

Whilst some persons who attend such readings for therapeutic benefit have an understanding of a transpersonal existence prior to the reading, there is a large number who do not. Those in the latter category, at some level, have a wish to have an understanding in a transpersonal existence, as they feel it will help them with a bereavement. However, based on their current life experience, they have not received an experience or set of experiences, which singularly or collectively allow for the justification of any transpersonal understanding.

To them, there is simply not enough grounding for such thoughts to be in their mind. These people can, at times, be immensely skeptical of the entire process at the beginning. Additionally, persons can feel a reading may help them in various aspects of their lives or in general.

The medium, through the reading process, lays the foundations for the grounding of the understanding in the mind of the mourner. In this way, if the needs of grounding in the mind of the recipient are met, then there is a change in their understanding of reality. This is when numerous potential benefits emerge.

Me

Ross William Bartlett

My given name is Ross William Bartlett. Except for my mediumistic ability and extensive interests in consciousness and spirituality, I'm no different than anyone else. My life started off in a way that would be considered very normal. I was born to a normal 27-year-old mother in Southampton, England, on the 31st of May 1992. Until I was five years old, there was nothing paranormal that could be said about me, and then I experienced this:

"I was lying on the bed in my mum's room, with its pink wallpaper, huge wardrobes and portable TV perched on the bedside table. There's something about your parents' bed when you're a child – it's so vast and comfortable that you can't resist rolling around on it, stretching out and not being able to touch the edges with your arms or legs. It feels huge. Lying on mum's bed made me feel closer to her and the adult world.

I switched on the TV. There were only four channels on that portable set – BBC1, BBC2, ITV and Channel 4. Changing channels, pushing buttons. Bored, bored, bored. I decided to go downstairs and see what my grandfather was doing. I switched off the TV, headed towards the door and turned off the light. As I was walking through the doorway, I stopped. Something was wrong or different. In the twilight, I saw that, behind me, the TV was still on, its fluorescent glare illuminating the room. That's funny, I thought. I know I turned it off. I scrunched up my face, puzzled.

Like most children of that age, I didn't think about the whys and wherefores. I'd simply switch it off again. Push more buttons. And if it didn't work, I'd move onto something else. But as I turned back into the room and approached the TV, I realized it wasn't showing the channel I had been watching when I'd turned it off. It was hissing-an eerie noise-and blurred black-and-white lines were running across the screen, the picture you get when you haven't selected a channel. This was odd: if I hadn't turned it off, surely it would still be on the channel I'd been watching. I stared at it for a few moments, as it hummed in its own hypnotic way, and then reached out a hand to turn it off again. I pushed the button, and the noise stopped. The TV's gone wrong. Time to go downstairs and see my granddad.

I turned away from the TV and saw a woman standing at the end of the bed, looking at me. Not in a quizzical way, or a threatening way, not even in a happy way. She was simply looking at me with a neutral expression. Now, at that stage in my life, I knew only a few women, my mum and my grandmother being the main ones, and this one, standing at the end of my mum's bed, was neither of them.

There was something about her I couldn't place and a sense that she didn't belong washed over me. Not just in our house, but in that period of time. She didn't wear the same sort of clothes as my mum wore, or any of the women I saw hurrying along the street. Her hair was different too. I'd watched enough television to know how people dressed. The white dress that woman was wearing seemed old-fashioned, with buttons right to the neckline. Her light brown hair was tied neatly in a little bun; she had a round, kind face. She looked older than my mum but younger than my grandmother, and I noticed a pretty black brooch pinned to the left side of her dress.

I had no idea how she appeared or what and who she was. When you're five, you can't explain something like that. I could have told you about the characters on TV and my mum or grandmother. Pretty. Ugly. Tall. Short. Long dress, short dress. Happy face, sad face. Yet this woman was not a ghost, or not as I imagined a ghost might look like.

This person from the afterlife for I know now that is what she was, appeared to me like a real person, with a solid form that eclipsed the wardrobe behind her. I could not see through her. Due to TV and the movies, we generally think of ghosts as shimmery, almost transparent figures. This woman was as solid as solid could be. And I wasn't frightened. Transfixed, I just stared at her staring at me. We didn't speak, just gazed at each other for what seemed like half an hour, but, in reality, was probably about ten seconds.

I remember being intrigued and open. At that age, our fears can be difficult to put into words. But I wasn't afraid: I hadn't been conditioned to fear interaction with anyone unfamiliar, including a person who had passed over. I experienced that woman as a real person, and she certainly didn't feel like a threatening presence. In fact, there was a real sense of... I couldn't put my finger on it at the time, but now I can identify it as compassion and love.

Just as I was getting used to the spirit-visitor beside mum's bed, she started to fade. There was a black coat hanging on the wardrobe behind her, and it became more and more visible. As she grew transparent, the coat and the wardrobe came more into focus until, finally, she was gone."

As time went on, experiences like this one, and others that could be classed as paranormal in nature, continued through into my teenage years. However, to me then and now, they were, and are completely normal. I became used to such occurrences and just took it as an aspect of me. An aspect that as a child, I wasn't all that interested in.

So why me? Why have I been blessed, or possibly cursed with a natural ability to contact those who have gone to heaven or any other name you care to call it? Has it been passed down from a relative or can it be blamed on me being dropped on my head as a young child?! From my perspective, we all have this connection to some degree. So, I must stress here that everyone, yes, everyone, can to some extent, do what I do. I teach others to develop their own natural abilities in workshops, and whilst few may become working mediums, many can become more sensitive human beings and gain a better perspective of who they are, and how they can live more spiritual lives.

It's just like anything else in life; some people are naturally gifted artists or musicians. Others can just naturally kick a football better. Just like most people could learn to play a few songs on a piano, not everyone is going to be Beethoven or Bach. In the case of mediums, very few people show great early promise. Those that do demonstrate this base raw ability, it all comes down to what one does with it. It can be nurtured or ignored. Developed or left stagnant. Since I was fourteen, I have been actively developing my mediumistic abilities and general spirituality.

For those of us wishing to contact this spirit world, meditation and various forms of visualization, breathing and mind-focusing techniques are, in my opinion, a vital key, and it is these skills I have practised constantly. Indeed, at one stage, to hone my skills, I meditated and prayed in a garage with no heating in January, the door closed, in total darkness and isolation for four days and four nights non-stop, nothing to eat or drink.

The techniques mentioned above are integral to my work and before a reading, I go through a visualization and breathing technique process for at least twenty minutes, sending out my intention to do the best possible reading and give the evidence that is required. This ensures that as soon as the reading starts, I am prepared and ready to bring through those from spirit wishing to contact my client. There are many techniques, all of which are important and useful, but the special one I do before giving a reading is the most powerful and most important one I ever use.

By my mid-teens, I knew without a shadow of doubt, that this was going to be my career, a lifetime of helping others connect with those they had loved and lost; a lifetime of teaching others that our consciousness contained within our spirit, does eternally survive the death of the physical body; a lifetime of helping the bereaved come to terms with a loss that is almost too unbearable to handle.

For those readers who would like to know more of my childhood and teenage years, as well as other aspects of my journey through life and the spiritual world, and further into developing my abilities up to date, you can read up on most of that through my first book, my autobiography, *Earth Angel*. It is still readily available on the Internet, as well as certain bookstores.

So, here I am at the ripe old age of twenty-four, having already written my autobiography, it could seem natural to think about slowing down, and putting my feet up more. However, that is the very last thing on my mind. I have plans for several more books, as well as to complete my Ph.D. connected to transbodily consciousness. I also plan on delving into research that I believe has the power to change the world.

I have so many plans, but this book you are reading is so very important to me! This book relates to certain phenomenological understandings, which drive my interest and understanding in all the areas of philosophy and science that I wish to work further on.

On that note, let me tell you that there is a growing amount of scientific-based research being done currently, which follows past research. This research collectively continues to validate the theory that our consciousness is transpersonal and that our individual consciousness does live on after physical death. Additionally, it validates that mediums are getting information from some form of external transpersonal source.

This source, I am certain, is most assuredly our relatives and loved ones who are now living on in heaven. Further, recent studies have shown that ADCs and assisted ADCs have short-term and long-term psychological healing benefits to those who have experienced bereavement. I would suggest these results signify that Heaven Therapy is a real-life alternative therapy for bereavement healing that can produce tremendous results.

I will show you that the dreadful pain and anguish of grief, which can sometimes be just too painful to bear, can be helped and eased. I can make no claims that grief can be completely cured on all levels in all persons, but this book certainly will show you that people can achieve a greater quality of life and that they can start to make sense of what appears to be senseless.

Moreover, those loved ones, who have left their physical bodies behind, are still alive. Most importantly, people gain the understanding that their loved ones in heaven know exactly what is happening in their lives on a daily basis: Illuminating to them the truth that one day, everything will be whole and good again.

I will discuss the phenomenological understandings I have gained, related to the many questions I'm often asked regarding subjects like, what do spirits do in heaven? How is a mediumistic connection possible? Do all people go to heaven? Do animals go to heaven? Is there a God, and if so, what is it? Etc.

At times, I will refer to scientific studies and understanding connected to these areas, but only lightly; a greater focus on the scientific material is something for another book. In this book, I will focus more on the phenomenological understandings of the process of mediumship, Heaven Therapy, and the afterlife.

My degree is a Master of Science (MSc) in Consciousness, Spirituality, and Transpersonal Psychology, and whilst the first two aspects of the degree are self-explanatory, most people would not be familiar with exactly what Transpersonal Psychology is.

To explain, Transpersonal Psychology seeks to integrate the spiritual and transcendent aspects of the human experience with the framework of modern psychology. Overall, the study of the transpersonal aims to study states or areas of consciousness that may suggest that consciousness has the ability to move beyond aspects of our personal identity, including the physical body itself.

I have no academic background in areas of quantum physics and neuroscience and mainstream areas of psychology. Although I will discuss concepts from these fields of study, my knowledge on these subjects was garnered through personal study and then writing about these topics connected to spirituality for my degree. My specific expertise is Psi phenomena meaning (psychic phenomena) and spirituality. So, when I relate to concepts outside of it, I'm taking what the experts in those fields say and relating it to my experience and expertise.

Overall, this book will focus on phenomenological understandings based on my experiences and most importantly the experiences of millions of ordinary people. This book will address, and explore the possibility of our consciousness being transbodily, meaning having the ability to move beyond and exist without our physical body, and even thrive without this aspect of our personal identity that we normally believe we are limited by.

I will take what I like to call an 'all-inclusive jigsaw puzzle' approach to the areas of consciousness, the afterlife, and the universe. I look to fill in the missing pieces of the puzzle in these areas by connecting aspects of spirituality and science together. It is my belief that this is the most advantageous approach and will eventually reveal the answers humanity needs to understand what happens after the death of the physical body.

I do not expect everyone who reads this book to believe immediately that all my truths are correct and, of course, there are many perspectives on all transpersonal concepts. However, I do hope and trust that, you, my readers will seriously consider what I say, as it is all based on extensive experience and rational thinking formed from what has presented itself to me through the phenomena. I do hope you find the answers interesting, thought provoking, as well as helpful.

My understandings of these topics are gained from my connection to the afterlife and the universe that I then related to modern scientific study and theory. These are thoughts that challenge the stagnant paradigm of thinking in the Western world. Further, it is my wish that this book instills hope and soothes the souls of all who read it. There may be parts you will need to re-

read several times in order to fully absorb and understand the information. You might feel like leaving certain sections, and when you come back and read them later it will make more sense, and that is fine.

There truly is so much to cover but let me begin by telling you about some of my clients and their stories. You see, working as a medium for a decade, the most recent years of my life have been surrounded by grief. Not of my own loss, but that of the people who come to me for healing – healing of the mind and the soul. These people come to me locked in a state of anguish and despair because of the passing of their loved one to whom they were immensely close.

They come to me with suffering that lingers in their heart, and the unfathomable pain that simply can't be put into words. They arrive before me looking for answers, looking for hope.

This book will share the journeys of some of those who found their way to me, and were reunited with their loved ones who reached out to them from the afterlife, through the power of love and the practice of mediumship. Each of them doing so to prove, not just that they survived physical death, but also to demonstrate that love transcends physical death and perhaps most importantly, they continue to take a very active interest in the lives of their loved ones left behind in the physical world; visiting with them from the other side on a regular basis.

It's not about moving on, it's about demonstrating our consciousness, with our memories, and feelings and personalities contained within it, live on eternally. Further, the bond and feelings we share with those on the other side also live on. It is that bond that continues to draw them to those that they care about in the physical world. It is that bond that drives them to try their best to let their loved ones know that they are ok and continue to be around them. It is that bond that will continue to grow and evolve into infinitum.

Come our time here, those loved ones who remain much closer to us, than many people have ever realized, will be there to welcome us in heaven. This is the set of understandings, which I know has the power to change millions of people's lives. I invite you now to read on and experience these journeys, coupled with my reflections, which will shed light on the true realities of our existence in this world and the next. This book and the amazing true stories of love, hope and healing within them will, I'm sure, touch your heart and may change your life forever.

ONE

Jack

• • • • • • • • • • • • •

"Meeting" Jack

Tanya

As I put pen to paper I am sitting on my sofa wrapped up in my quilt. My lovely Jack's clothes were sewn together after he passed into my quilt of love. With Jack symbolically comforting me, I'm hopeful I will be inspired to share part of our story.

Jack had a unique perspective on fashion and loved clothes and looking edgy and cool, he loved the Criminal Damage and Converse brands. How many pairs of Converse footwear did this boy have? Five pairs, I think at last count! I remember on Jack's prom night he was determined to wear a top hat and tails. Well, of course, you can imagine my pleading him not to do this... "You will be teased honey.... don't you just want to slip into prom with everyone else in a nice suit and your Vivienne Westwood tie?" I implored. "No!" said Jack, "I want to be me, this is my prom night, I'm going to be whatever I want and dance the night away."

I was so proud of him for this. He arrived at prom in top hat and tails, gloves, cane and to top it all off, a purple satin ribbon around his hat with a bright green feather in it!! What was I worried about? He had, he told me, the best night of his life. I think when he left senior school, it was his way of showing everyone he was unique and different, and no longer had to conform to the rules of school uniformity, he was free to express himself.

All I cared about when I was told that my son had passed over was that he was ok, wherever he was. I was sick with agonizing worry about him. I was riddled with horrendous guilt that it was all my fault. We were best friends. We experienced every emotion together. I felt like I was losing my mind. My Jack, my sensitive lad, could not possibly have taken his own life. Nothing made sense to me. At that point, I had not been able to look at recent photographs of Jack. His earlier years' photos were all around my living room. However, the minute I would choose to glimpse at one of his recent photographs, a river of tears would roll down my face.

When the first Christmas anniversary of Jack's passing came up, I chose to ignore the day, as best that I could and spent the day by myself. I remember thinking to myself, "Oh Jack, my beautiful, perfect son.... I can't believe; I really can't believe that I am still here on this earth, and have not joined you." I always used to say if anything ever happened to my boy, I would be with him, join him, and couldn't breathe without him... So why is it that I am still here?

The answer to this question begins just a few weeks after Jack left. I was given a book on spirituality and mediumship called Earth Angel. I was clinging to any kind of hope that there is an afterlife. Clinging to anything that my Jack hadn't really died, that the lights haven't gone out for him, and experiencing intense worry, as a mum still wanting to parent my child. I was hoping every single minute of every day that he is ok, not in pain and not sad but free from feeling pain. He had been so sensitive, and everything seemed to hurt him so much.

I looked at the cover of Earth Angel, and there, sitting, was a young man; low slung jeans, tattoos aplenty. I instinctively felt this would be the young man who would bring Jack to me... if anyone could do it. It was going to be Ross. I was desperate, yes, but through my desperation was a steely scepticism. I read this young man's story written at only 19 years old. He was only one year older than my Jack.

Ross spoke of his first image of a person from the afterlife at only five years old; he recounted his own childhood, his sensitivity and his beautiful, cherished relationship with his grandmother, "Nain", as he called her. Everything about this young man and his journey into mediumship resonated with me.

I clung to every single word. I cried into the pages. I read the book every single night after taking my sleeping pills. I managed five or six pages each night, as my ability to concentrate had been affected after Jack left. I thought about Jack intensely as I read, and re-read each page. I actually read the book through fully twice, before having the courage to Google Ross to discover if he had a website. He did, in fact, and still did private readings.

I had, up to this point in my life, no reason to think of mediums, psychics, spiritualists and wasn't sure exactly how things worked, but I contacted him via his website asking for a reading. On my request, he very kindly gave me his personal telephone number, and we had a telephone call to set up the meeting. I disclosed my son had died, but that was all I said, apart from explaining I wasn't too far away and travelling to him would be fine.

I remember the day of the reading so clearly, as it all felt a little surreal. That day started off like any other, I woke up and walked downstairs in my robe and put the kettle on, just as I did every morning, yet today felt different. I felt different. Today was a chance, a chance for some of the pain and hurt to go away. Perhaps, today the knot that had been forever embedded in my stomach could be unfastened. Today was the day I would be reunited with my son and a day that would again change my life forever.

The few hours I had to wait went by agonizingly slow, but then all of a sudden... ding dong... my friend was at the door and ready to drive me the hour-long travel to my scheduled reading. I recall being very distracted on the drive. My mind felt like it was racing at a hundred miles an hour. I recall feeling so terribly sad and with each passing mile, a little bit more desperate.

Up to losing my child, I had never given death much thought. Now, death had become all so real and all so morbid. I recall sitting in the car thinking, over and over, that if Jack did not come to me, then I would just go to the train station and die the same way Jack had.

I remember thinking about where Jack is exactly, and worrying so much about him being ok, wondering if I would hear from him or if I was being taken advantage of by some kind of charlatan, who preyed on grief-stricken individuals. These questions would continue spinning round and round in my head until we arrived at the location.

After settling into the room, I was left waiting for what seemed ages, but in truth, was only about 15 minutes. The woman, who had greeted me at the door, had popped in the room to tell me Ross would be down soon. He was "linking in" which having read his book, I sort of understood what she meant. I felt myself controlling my breathing as my heart was heavy, and the situation was now feeling utterly surreal. What am I doing here? My child had left me. He had left me, and I am pinning every ounce of hope I had on this young man in the next room.

Just then, Ross entered looking just as I had imagined. It was a lovely sight. Just like his pictures, a handsome young man with tattoos galore, low-slung jeans, and tousled hair. I felt instantly more at ease. In some ways, he reminded me of my Jack. Different in ways, but undeniable similarities. He began by telling me there were several relatives present, which was nice, but I only wanted to hear from Jack.

I remember telling myself sternly not to say anything that might give anything away as I was very, very wary. Ross had said at the outset he would let me know when I could ask questions, so this worked fine for me. Ross went on to say there was a younger male there with the other relatives. He told me that he must have passed very young and that he assumed it must be my son.

What then followed was a description of Jack's personality and his awareness of Jack's overwhelming remorse and regret over his decision to leave.

Ross explained that this lad was a very emotional boy and highly sensitive, quirky, edgy and different in a good way. When Ross began to describe these character traits, I knew he had my Jack. As he continued, I was trying my hardest to hold back tears that were ready to burst forth from my eyes at any moment. Not tears of sadness, but tears of relief, tears of happiness.

Ross described in detail the walk Jack took that evening and his jumbled thoughts. This was good for me to hear regarding knowing where he was prior. There were three possible options of where he could have gone, and no one knew where he went after he left the house. It was an hour plus later before he passed over, and I had wondered and worried about where he had gone. Now I knew. He went directly to the station. He took the direct route.

"Who is Steve or Stephen?" Ross asked. "Oh wow, that is Jack's father," I said. He caused me a lot of emotional grief during his visit to this country for the funeral. He verbally attacked me, blaming me. He rallied with other family members, who were projecting anger towards me. I felt it was an awful betrayal. Ross hit on this very clearly. Further, he said Jack is pained greatly by the family not handling things better and getting along. Wow, that was enormously comforting for me. To think on the other side of life, my beautiful son was my protector and my warrior, as he had been when he was physically here.

Ross told me that Jack had said he had changed his mind, but it was too late. Again, another beautiful validation for me as his mother. I did know my son. He wouldn't have wanted to leave. He was the type of kid who would knee-jerk react. I had seen him do this before. I do it, myself. Oh, how lovely it felt to realize how alike Jack and I were. No, not were – ARE. We both feel deep sensitivity, and I knew just how he could easily entwine himself in emotional feelings. Having Ross validate this as he said, "has unusual sensitivity in someone around my age", helped me then, and does to this day.

He was now, I felt, reuniting me with my beautiful son who was emotional and sensitive. No one seemed to really understand this while Jack was living in this world. It honestly felt like the two of us against the world, with Jack having to try to conform to society's rules, such as school life. I was forever fighting in his corner while he was stupidly teased and bullied. Ross spoke about these times and his hurt feelings. These words and Ross' sound description had strangely brought me closer to Jack than I could ever have hoped for. Ross "got" him, and brought my son's personality to me. Out of the blue, he chuckled and said, "Oh he's had his hair cut over there; he seems to want to tell you this." This was such a lovely "aww" moment for me. Such a simple thing but Jack's hair was always highly important to him. This did seem like Jack communicating through Ross.

Ross' next words were perhaps the most comforting of all. He said, "He is telling me about a message sent to a friend and that he is saying, he didn't mean it." At this point, I couldn't hold back the tears any longer. Jack had sent a text message to his good friend; minutes before he passed over and in part of the message, he had blamed me.

I had read the message. I saw the words. They cut my mind to shreds. He talked about being emotionally abused by me and when he saw me hurt myself (I slapped my face in front of him; out of pure frustration) that was it for him. He wasn't going to cry any more tears. The only tears he would cry would be "ghost tears".

So what Ross said was immensely healing for me to hear. It was perhaps, at that moment, a part of me began to breathe again. After allowing me to have a few seconds to compose myself, Ross continued.

"He keeps mentioning the name. Jack. This must be significant." Oh, how significant it is! I replied with vigour, "That's his name!" This was happening! My boy was here with Ross and me, and Ross was reuniting us. "He is also mentioning a Will," he said. "Yes, I know who that is," I replied. Will was one of Jack's best friends. "Also, is there a Luke?" Ross enquired; again I replied yes, Luke was Jack's best friend.

Words could not express the plethora of emotions moving through what felt like every fibre of my body. I remember feeling hot tears, rolling down my cheek, as Ross continued. "I believe I see an acknowledgment of an item that belonged to Jack, which you have given to Will, would this be possible?" "Yes, I gave him an item that belonged to Jack," I replied, now slightly struggling to get my words out. "I'm seeing a window," Ross explained. "Could this item be currently kept in a window? On the ledge inside, perhaps?"

I thought for a second, and replied, "No, I don't think it would be on a window ledge." "Well, that's what I'm seeing," Ross said after a short pause. "Jack doesn't seem to want to change the image in any way. You can perhaps ask his friend where it is." "Yes, I will do that," I replied, feeling very confused. Surely, this item isn't on a window ledge, I thought to myself.

Ross then spoke up again and said Jack has met up with a lady on the other side, who is the mother of one of his close friends. He wanted to communicate that he visits this friend often and his mother is watching over him as well.

Ross was undoubtedly talking about Jack's very close friend, Josh, whose mother passed away a number of years ago. I knew Josh would be so comforted to hear this.

Ross recapped the core themes that were conveyed by Jack and suggested if I had any questions I could now ask. My mind was a complete muddle of emotion. "Is he ok?" I remember asking. It was the first thing that came into my mind. "Yes," was the reply, calmly, and confidently. "Very much so. If he weren't, he would not be able to come through like this today."

"Yes, he has needed help from the other spirits present, but that is very common for someone who hasn't been passed very long. Even if they are quite capable in this way, often others are there to help give the main communicator energy, to ensure they can communicate as strongly as possible at that time."

I followed Ross' response with another question... "There was a word he used to call me. A little nickname he had for me. I wondered if he would be able to tell you that?" Ross paused again and asked me to give him a moment to enquire about this. After maybe 30 seconds, he looked back in my direction, and said, "I'm being shown lots of images that relate to his childhood." He mentioned a couple of them to me, and I was not sure how they might relate to my word. Ross then said, "I think this might be out of reach for today. They have told me in time it will come, though."

He explained in every reading there are things a medium will miss. The spirit communicating has to work through the subconscious mind of the medium; because of this, in his experience, even with the best readings, around 15 percent of the information might not be brought through and conveyed on that day. However, it might well come up in the next reading or after.

There are so many factors that influence what can and can't, is or is not, brought through during any reading. If it was needed and I continued wanting it, one way or another, Jack would find a way to bring it through to him. "Do you have any more questions for today?" Ross asked. "Well, I suppose I'd like to know more about what life is like over there. What's Jack doing? What do they do over there in general? I would think you couldn't answer all that today. Perhaps I could book some time to come and talk to you about this?" I queried. "Of course you can," Ross replied. "Just send me a text about it. We will finish for today then. Have a listen to the recording. It will help you take everything in from the communication today, and don't forget to ask Will about the item."

On the drive home, my mind was going round and round so fast. My head was spinning with questions. What had just happened? How did it happen? I went to Ross looking for what happened to my boy, yet somehow it was still beyond what I could have imagined. It all seemed so real. It seemed like my boy was right there next to Ross. Then before I knew it, I was back home.

I remember sitting down on the sofa and staring at Jack's pictures. Will! I must call Will! and ask about the item; one of Jack's favourite ties. I hastily flicked through the numbers on my phone. Finding Will's number, I immediately clicked call. Ring... Ring... Ring... Oh, what if he doesn't answer! Hmmmm... Ring... Ring... Ohhh, come on, Will... Ring...oh for the... "Hello Tanya. How are you doing?"

Will's voice beamed out of the phone at me. "Oh, Hi Will. You are there." "Yep I am." "I have a question to ask, which might seem a bit random," I continued. "Oh? Ok, then ask away," he replied. "The tie that I gave you which belonged to Jack, where is it?" "Um, it's in my bedroom, Tanya." "Where in your bedroom, Will?" "Well, currently it's on the window sill." My heart skipped a beat, and I went silent on the end of the phone.

"Why?" Will asked slightly puzzled. "I went to see a medium, and he said you kept an item of Jack's I gave you in a window sill. I thought it couldn't be the case, but you do!" "Yes, it's actually been there a little while," he remarked, "and a medium, Tanya? Really? That's well, pretty cool, I guess." "Yes, we will have to talk about what the medium said sometime, ok Will?" "Sounds good, Tanya." "Ok, we'll talk soon then," I said, as I hung up the phone. I sat back further in my chair, almost as if at some level I was worried I would fall off it.

I looked up at Jack's pictures again and then back at my phone. I wanted more answers to all of this. I frantically began texting Ross, saying that I certainly wished to book an appointment to go over various questions with him. Later that same night, Ross confirmed a date and time that suited.

I wondered if I would get answers to all my questions and would Ross mention the nickname, I so desperately wished to hear from my son. I didn't know, but what I did know was I so needed more answers. Answers to this miracle, that had moved me in such a deep way. It could not be put into words.

TWO

Moving Deeper

• • • • • • • • • • • • •

How different spirits communicate to mediums differently

Over the last decade I have done thousands of readings; sometimes certain things stick out in my mind when I remember back to them. For this one, it is the emotional person Jack always was and still is. You see, when a spirit communicates with a medium, that communication may happen more through feelings (clairsentience), visuals and images (clairvoyance) or words (clairaudience).

This is partly determined by the person they were and the person they continue to be. If when they were here, the person was very emotional, when they get over there, often the core aspects of their personality, their self, remains the same, providing they weren't negative aspects. In Jack's case, he remained a very sensitive and emotional person. If there were negative aspects or aspects that manifested in negative forms, then this is something the spirit will often work on in Heaven and address during the reading.

Some people, when they were here, were very visual persons who would often think more in images than feelings; some people think more with words and perhaps have a talent for them. In general, this affects what way the information is perceived by the medium, as does other aspects of their personality, and this is part of what makes every reading different from the next.

For instance, if my loud uncle, who was a very visual and outgoing person, came through he would likely communicate a lot through images (clairvoyance) and the communication would likely flow pretty easily as he was an outgoing person. If my more reserved and more emotionally based grandmother came through then, she would likely naturally communicate more with feelings (clairsentience) and the medium may have to ask more questions to get certain pieces of information, or indeed, understand certain pieces of information.

This doesn't mean over in Heaven they have trouble communicating certain things to each other, at least, no more trouble than we do here at times. *The medium is hindered by their physical brain and body.* Those who have passed over can communicate with each other telepathically or through speech, in the sense of they can talk out-loud to each other. How they can still do this without a physical body, I will address in a later chapter.

With Jack in his communication, there was so much coming through naturally on an emotional (clairsentient) level that it was like I had to move through an ocean of emotion before I could take in other parts of his personality and self. How is all this possible? How can we survive physical death and keep in touch with people on Earth?

This concept directly relates to consciousness. Increasing amounts of people both general and academic now believe in a transpersonal aspect of consciousness. Specifically, that our consciousness has an ability to go beyond the brain and the material body. Whilst many, including myself, hold that there is on various levels a link between consciousness and the brain, for me, and many others, it doesn't mean that when the brain dies, our consciousness also ceases to exist.

Consciousness being more than cerebral neuron computation

I would suggest from my experience that our consciousness has an energetic aspect of existence that is different than the physical body and world, as we know it. Further, from my understanding of what it is, how it's created, and through this, the properties that I attribute to it, there is no way our consciousness can be killed, die or cease to exist.

Here, I'm suggesting your spirit and soul, your consciousness and essence, is by nature indestructible and eternal. Regarding how such a phenomenological understanding can relate to science, there is a theory that has gained some ground recently in academia. This theory is called Orch-OR theory. Orch-OR is a theory of consciousness that allows for an eternal quantum soul. This is the transbodily form of existence I discuss in this book.

Anaesthesiologist Dr. Stuart Hameroff is one of the two creators of Orch-OR theory, the other creator is the extremely decorated and respected physicist, Sir Roger Penrose. Together Hameroff & Penrose, (1996) put Orch-OR forward in an article as a theoretical model of consciousness. Since that time, many articles have been published discussing the viability and possibilities of Orch-OR.

Hameroff & Chopra, (2012) published an article addressing the scientific hypothesis of a quantum soul related to Orch-OR, suggesting that Orch-Or theory allows for a transbodily form of existence. Hameroff has also discussed this possibility in many interviews some of which you can find online. Further, Hameroff suggested in these interviews that Orch-OR potentially explains the phenomenological data and certain experiment results in the field of parapsychology.

Transpersonal phenomena like transbodily consciousness are studied within parapsychology. For this book, I will not be going into much scientific detail. However, to summarize the Orch-OR theory, it suggests consciousness stems from deeper level quantum vibrations and information from within the microtubules of the neurons, and in my humble opinion, the theory forms a potential connection between the metaphysical and physical in a way that has not been adequately done before.

Orch-OR theory is in contrast to the more mainstream theory that consciousness derives from a certain level of complex computations performed by cerebral neurons.

Originally, it was heavily criticized and thought not to be biologically feasible because it was considered that the brain is too warm to facilitate quantum vibrations. However, more recently quantum vibrations have been discovered in microtubules at room temperature, as highlighted by Hameroff & Penrose, (2014) in their review of Orch-OR. This discovery basically debunks the concept that the brain is too warm to consistently facilitate quantum vibrations.

Whilst the theory has a way to go before establishing itself as a standard theory of consciousness, I think it is well on its way and I believe the general public will be hearing a lot more about Orch-OR theory in years to come. The biggest reason it will take a while to gain more momentum is very little moves fast in the academic world. It takes a great deal for something to gain big momentum. Perhaps, though, things will move along somewhat faster this time.

Overall, I suggest, if one reviews the data which has emerged from the study of the transpersonal, absolutely unbiased and with an open mind, one simply must conclude that there appear to be phenomena happening which go beyond the materialist understanding of mainstream areas of science.

Orch-OR theory, in my opinion, offers the first scientifically tangible explanation to these happenings. Further, the reason materialistic science provides no complete explanation of the creation of consciousness, or the phenomena that appear to be transpersonal, is because its current understanding is incomplete and potentially limited by its outlook.

I feel it is up to transpersonal-minded scientists, to gather more of certain forms of scientific evidence to further substantiate certain theories, and over time prove the transpersonal reality of life to the point that this will be accepted and become a part of mainstream science.

In time, my hope is that those working on Orch-OR and other areas related to transpersonal aspects in consciousness will eventually find ways to bring the next level of proof to the world, perhaps sooner rather than later.

What happens when your physical body dies?

From my experience, when the physical body is no longer able to continue living, the spirit and consciousness will instantaneously leave the body. As this happens, a person experiences a sensation that is sometimes coupled with a visual experience of hovering above the body. Often then, being gently pulled towards a tunnel of light, at which point, they may also see and/or hear spirits of family members and loved ones, who crossed over before them, as they come to greet them and help calm them.

These family members and loved ones further help them to begin to make their transition over to life in Heaven. During this process, the person will also often express experiencing an intense feeling of love that, from my experience, I believe to be the love of the spirits thinking of them at that time, both in the physical world and those coming to greet them from Heaven.

In the case of more violent deaths, the process still appears to follow the same pattern and overall, the experience post-death is commonly much more peaceful and soothing than we might think. What is important is that it appears that the consciousness of a person is less attached to the brain and body, depending on the condition of the brain and how much certain forms of brain processing is possible and occurring at that time.

What I'm suggesting here is that the brain is the real way to measure physical death, and if the brain is not completely functioning, then, and only then, is the consciousness completely detached. Further, it appears that if the brain regains functioning, the consciousness is instantaneously shifted back into the physical processing of the brain and body.

If, for some reason, the brain is damaged and not able to function normally, the less attached the consciousness is to the brain and body. This is also why, sometimes, people with certain forms of extensive brain damage or when their brain functioning has been drastically hindered, where they are often in a comatose state or some other non-ordinary state of being, it has been documented that they have various transpersonal experiences.

These experiences are often related to being out of the physical body. At times, these persons have been known to communicate through mediums even though they are not clinically dead.

How our quantum consciousness remains whole after the death of the physical body

This potentially supports the Orch-OR theory, as the theory notes that the more damage to the microtubules within the brain, the less consciousness would be able to function through the physical body.

This potentially causes the energy and information that remains entangled (connected and whole), to move outside the body, in a similar way to the process that appears to happen at the complete physical death of the brain and the body. The reason that our energy does not just disperse and remains eternally whole has been linked to the phenomena of quantum entanglement.

I will explain exactly what quantum entanglement is later in the book, but to summarize briefly, when quantum entanglement is related to the eternal existence of the soul, the suggestion is that the process of quantum entanglement has information that our consciousness is contained in our quantum vibrations at the sub-atomic level and is forever linked and bound together by an innate invisible energetic field.

This is a field that we have observed through experiments related to quantum entanglement. It may also be simply that our very sense of self, and observation of self, keeps the information that is our consciousness bound and whole.

Likewise, it could be the infinite flux of information and consciousness that observes you as an infinitesimally small part of the infinite whole and as a particular frequency of energy that we happen to experience as consciousness, individuality and sense of self.

Whichever way, this creates a scenario that you can't die for the very life of you, and that if there is one thing in all of infinite creation that is innately impossible, it is the ceasing of existence of our consciousness. The latter concept being related to God, but God and exactly what God is, I will cover later in this book.

I digress, it appears that from phenomenological accounts that the more the brain is damaged, the more a person's consciousness will be detached from their physical body. This, at times, seems to leave them more in Heaven than still here with us. I'd like to now share a story with you that will demonstrate the phenomena of communication between mediums and the spirit of persons who are in a coma.

Communication in Comas

Amy

"I was just four months pregnant with my third child when my mother passed away. And incredibly enough, I hadn't realized that I was pregnant until I was 16 weeks along. Working full time, taking care of two toddlers and a very ill mother, I hadn't been paying much attention to my body.

I was in and out of emergency rooms, at all hours of the night, for months, as my mother's illness progressed. I was beyond exhausted and felt worn to the bone. I remember one late night at the ER; I was feeling so awful that I asked the ER attendant to wheel me up a gurney too. "Hey, what's another bed in a hospital room?!" I half-jokingly said to the poor attendant. I'm sure he didn't know what to think of me.

After weeks of not feeling well, I finally called the doctor, who suggested I take a pregnancy test. I practically laughed on the phone. "That's impossible!" I retorted. However, there it was on the little white stick... "Pregnant". I made an appointment to see the doctor, and that's when I found out I was already sixteen weeks along!

I couldn't wait to tell my mother! She was my best friend, and we spoke on the phone at least once a day. As her health began to falter, I decided to move closer just to be near her and help her as much as I could. My mom was ecstatic to have another grandchild and joked with the nurses taking care of her that she was having another baby. They teased her and said that if she kept talking that way she'd end up in the psychiatric ward. Her reply back was that she might rather be there than in the cardiac unit! She had such a wonderful sense of humour.

In early September, when it seemed my mother's health had stabilized, and she was home, I booked a trip to the Caribbean for the family for the end of the month. I desperately needed a break, some rest and the enticement of warm weather was too hard to resist.

On the morning of the last Sunday of September, I received a call that my mother was in an ambulance on her way to the hospital. Evidently, she was having some chest and back pain. I arrived at the hospital as soon as I could and was told that my mother had a minor heart attack and that she would be ok, but she would be kept in the hospital for at least the week.

The doctors were very optimistic about her prognosis and told me that she was the most improved patient on the cardiac floor, so I felt reassured. Our planned family vacation was on Tuesday that week, and I was not sure I should leave with Mom in the hospital, but her doctors told me she was doing quite well, and even she insisted I go. I asked if she was sure and she said, "Don't worry honey, I'm fine! Go, go, my babies need to have a little fun."

On my way out, I spoke to the nurse attending her, and she said, I don't know why the doctors are not telling you that your mother suffered a massive heart attack. If I were you, I wouldn't leave her. Quite shaken by her remarks, I called her vascular doctor, and he, once again, assured me that my mom should be fine.

We left for our vacation, and I called continually to check in on her. On Wednesday, my mom was scheduled to have a routine procedure to help her breathe a bit better. I called her shortly after and she said she was doing terrific and that she had never felt better. I was so happy to hear that!

I told her all about the children's sunny antics – jumping in the warm water waves and building little sand castles on the beach. She was thrilled and made me repeat the things they said during the day, over and over.

The next day, Thursday, I called her several times to check in. She seemed fine. At the end of the night, we headed back to our hotel, and when we arrived, I checked in on her right away. She sounded very tired. I asked if she was feeling ok, and she replied, "I'm beginning not to feel very well, but you all enjoy yourselves! I'll be fine. I'll be fine. Just take care of my babies."

After settling the children in their bed and crib at the hotel, I received a call that my mother had another heart attack, the doctors had resuscitated her, but she had suffered a stroke and was in a coma. The damage was extensive, and it was unlikely she would wake from the coma, and if she did, most likely she could be in a vegetative state. I was heartbroken.

So not to wake the children, I sat in the hotel bathroom and uncontrollably sobbed as quiet as I could. I finally dozed off on the cold tiles. I woke up at 1 am and lay down on the bed and wept silently until I dozed off again. Strangely at 3 am, my cell phone rang. It was my mother's hospital room number; fumbling in the dark room for the phone, I answered as fast as I could, but there was no one on the line, just static. I kept repeating... Hello? Hello? Hello? And nothing... just static.

The entire plane ride home I cried. I felt so overwhelmingly guilty that I was not there for my mother. I tried not to let my children see the tears streaming down my face. They were too young to understand. It was torturous. When I got back and spoke to doctors, they told me her condition had worsened, and there was no way back for my Mom.

The only thing keeping her body going was the medical equipment. They suggested discussing with my Dad ceasing the life support. After speaking with them, I asked who could have called me the night she went into the coma at 3 am. The hospital had no records of a call from the hospital room and I was told that they would not have called from her room.

If a call went out, it would have been from the nurse's station or administration, and my cell number phone wasn't in their records. My family had long since left her room by then so I didn't know what to think.

The discussion with my Dad was the hardest I've ever had in my life, he just wept into my shoulder, and I wept into his. Neither of us had any words. Eventually, we managed to string some sentences together and decided to wait for my sister to arrive before my mom's life support was turned off.

Earlier that day, I had received an email announcement from a local bookstore saying that a young medium from England, who was well known for being the youngest professional in his field, was in town. His particular focus was an evidential approach. I thought about the email and was overcome with an urge to book a reading.

I called the store right away and asked if there were any spaces available in two or three days because I knew by then my Mom's life support would have been switched off. They told me he was fully booked; except for one space at 10 am the next morning. My initial thought was to try to communicate with my Mom after she passed.

However, my overwhelming question was to find out if there was an afterlife. I wanted to know if I was going to lose my mother. If I knew there were an afterlife, then my family and I would know my mother would be ok and going to a better place. I decided to book that 10am slot.

I arrived at the bookstore and sat down in the waiting area. I took a few deep breaths to try and contain my nervousness. I saw Ross walk out of one of the rooms, with an empty glass in his hand and go to the room behind the counter of the store. He seemed very focused. It made me more anxious. He was wearing a white t-shirt and ripped jeans.

I heard a couple of young girls in the store whisper to each other "That's him! That's him!" This made me, even more, nervous. The sales clerk called my name, and for a moment, I hesitated. Garnering all the courage I could, I followed the clerk into a room.

She said Ross would be back in a few moments. He is just getting another glass of water. A minute later, he came into the room, and all my nervousness disappeared. He had such a sweet, kind and compassionate demeanor. I immediately felt comfortable around him. We sat facing each other, and he soon began the reading.

Ross told me there was a gentleman who had come through who was quite dapper. "Do you know what that means?" I laughed and replied, "Yes, it means he is very well dressed." Ross said, "Well, this gentleman is walking around me and sizing me up, looking at my tattoos, looking at me like, so this is the bloke then?" Ross said his name was "Joseph, not Joe, not Joey. He is emphatically telling me, Joseph, over and over again. Very formal."

I immediately recognized him as my mother's youngest brother who had passed away fairly young. Ross then put his hand to his head. He told me that he felt like somehow, something about my uncle's head had been a problem. Sure enough, my uncle had died unexpectedly from a brain aneurysm at 37.

Ross said a woman, with dark hair and who looked like me, was also coming through. "There's a name, Catherine? Is this familiar to you? She wants to tell you that she is taking care of your mom." Catherine was my mother's mother! I started to well up when Ross mentioned that my grandmother was looking after my mother. I could hardly believe it!

Ross said that there were several other people coming through to speak with me, but that there was one woman who was finding it harder to come through strongly. The others were coaxing her forward and trying to help her. I was confused and didn't know who this might be. He said he kept hearing my name again and again. This appeared confusing to him. He said, "It was like she was trying to tell him who she was but using my name."

He said she was very, very beautiful in her day and commanded much attention for her looks. He moved his head to the side and before he could continue, I yelped, "Oh my God, could it be my mom?!"

Both my mother and I had the same first name, and when she was younger, she was considered a stunning woman. Ross told me he would ask the spirits for more information to hopefully clarify things further.

As I waited for Ross to speak again, I remember thinking, how could it be my mother? There is no way the life support would have been stopped yet. Could she have passed while I was here? It was during this thought, Ross spoke up again and said, "This is going to sound odd, but is your mother still here? As in, she's not considered clinically dead?" "Yes!" I exclaimed and then he went on to say, "But there is an extensive issue with the brain?"

I was stymied. "Because of damage to the physical body, specifically the brain, your mother's spirit has already all but completely detached from her body." He continued saying that my relatives had brought her here to try to get her to communicate with you, and to let you know that she is ok.

Ross told me my mother was saying that I shouldn't feel guilty. She said I was harboring a lot of guilt, but things were just meant to be that way. "Does this make sense to you?" Yes, that totally made sense and it was an enormous relief to me! My eyes welled up again, and I fought hard to hold back the tears from pouring out. He told me that my other relatives were saying not to worry about my mother and that she was surrounded by all her loved ones. Ross put up two fingers and said there are two males there.

"These two male relatives said they are taking care of her, not to worry." Again, Ross asked me if this made sense to me. These had to be my mother's brother, Joseph, and another older brother who had just died a few years ago. I did not have many fond memories of them. I said, "Yes." He replied that they were giving him a strong message to tell me that they are not the same people that I knew them as.

During their lifetime, my mother often fought with her brothers, about money, inheritance and other awful things. Hearing that they were more loving was very comforting.

"Your mother is saying she was there. She was there with you recently, and you were in a bathroom and you were thinking about her." This must have been about the other night when I heard of her condition while in my hotel room. Strangely, at one point during the night, as I lay there on the cold floor, I lifted up my arm and hand. I cupped my hand and swore that I could feel another hand holding mine. Comforting as it was, it also freaked me out a bit at the time.

Ross went on to say my grandmother had been watching over me from the other side for some time and said she recently managed to organize sending me a gift. He moved his hands around his neck, "I feel like it's something like a necklace. Does this make sense to you?"

I could not believe he said that. Shortly before the reading, my friend ordered a necklace and for some odd reason, it had been sent to her with my name. She checked the order, and sure enough, it was ordered in her name and her address but delivered to her with my name on it. My name was nowhere on the order, but there it was, a moonstone necklace with a dragonfly on it.

There would be no way Ross could have known about that necklace. I had just received it in the mail a couple of days before. All this confirmed to me why he was so well known for his evidence!

Before we ended the session, Ross asked me if I had any questions. I asked him if he could ask my mother about my baby who was yet to be born. Would everything go ok with the pregnancy; would the baby be healthy? Ross said, "Your mother says, as far as she has been told by other spirits, she and the pregnancy will be fine." Ross then pointed to his hair and said, "Your mother tells me she thinks she will have blonde hair and seems quite pleased that she will look just like her!"

At this time, I did not know my baby's gender, and of course, I did not know what hair colour my baby would have. My mother did have blonde hair though and I did not. So there was no way Ross would have looked at me and guessed based on my features.

Ross continued saying that my mother has met two children on the other side, one that passed from being miscarried and another that was stillborn. They were being looked after by relatives of mine, mostly my grandparents. I remember tears falling from my eyes onto my shirt as Ross said this because I had had a miscarriage three years ago and two years before that my baby was stillborn. Both had been very emotionally hard for me to deal with.

As I wept, Ross said he was seeing daisies. I looked up at Ross and cried out, "Oh my God, that is what I named her, my baby!" Ross proceeded to tell me that the other child was a boy, which was correct. As I tried to compose myself further, Ross said he was getting the name, Connor. I remember smiling through my tissue and said, "Yes that was what I named him."

Ross explained that when you have a baby or child who passes in these ways, they go to the afterlife and grow as they would grow here. He explained that their soul's mental body has all the information in it of how they were going to grow and it just follows this process until they choose to halt it through their mind's control over their mental body.

He explained that my grandparents often bring them to see me. This brought me so much comfort knowing they lived on, were looked after and come and see me with other family, who are in Heaven. I had always wondered if they lived on and if they knew me in any way. I had always carried so many unresolved feelings connected to their deaths that in the space of a minute had been resolved by Ross.

I asked Ross if I could ask one final question. Could he ask my Mom about the phone call from the hospital? He turned his head, as if in conversation, smiled the most brilliant smile, and laughed. "She said she was trying to let you know she was on her way! And comfort you. Unfortunately, though, all you heard was a static sound!

She says she tried her best, many of your relatives on the other side were helping, but the energy wasn't strong enough." There is no way Ross would have known about my experience. In all likelihood, he would have thought this was a direct conversation I had with my Mom on the phone. I was amazed!

I didn't know what to say or how to thank him. This incredible experience had freed me from feeling that I had failed my mother somehow. It helped me to know she was well taken care of and was right there holding my hand during one of the most difficult times of my life.

I left the bookstore to go directly to the hospital. I debated all the way to the hospital if I should tell my Dad now or if it would be too much for him to take and might make his pain worse.

I decided to take him to one side and try to explain my experience to him. He looked confused at first. Then he smiled and said, "I'm so glad she is ok, that she is with her mother. She loved her mother so much." Dad asked me if he could listen to the recording of the reading sometime soon. Later that evening the life support was stopped, and my mother was completely freed from the pain her body had caused her for such a long time.

Five years later, our family still listens to the recording. It still brings us great comfort to know there is an afterlife, and my beloved mother will be watching over us until it's our time to be with her again. I thank her, my uncle and my grandmother every day for showing this to us and being there for the family here on Earth. Our family that now includes a beautiful blonde-haired little girl."

What this story also shows is how some people carry a vast amount of unresolved grief connected to the loss of babies through stillbirth and miscarriages. What it also shows is how those babies who pass in such early stages also go to heaven and are looked after by our ancestors who are over there. Their mental body continues to grow and as they get older they continue to take an active interest in our lives.

I've many examples of spirits relating to the souls of babies lost through miscarriage being present and surviving the process of death and crossing over into heaven as early as twelve weeks. That is not to say it doesn't happen sooner than that. I've heard of cases where it has apparently been earlier.

Further, if you believe in reincarnation then it would be possible that the soul does not enter until after twelve weeks or even later. I will address exactly what the mental body is and the concept of reincarnation in later chapters.

THREE

What Is Heaven and What Is Hell?

. . . .

The properties and bizarreness of time

I suggest that heaven is a dimension at the subatomic quantum level of existence, a dimension where the manifestations of energy, like buildings, are moulded by thought. It's not up in the sky. It's all around us, right now overlapping our physical world.

It is a dimension that we can access fully upon the death of the physical brain. This is a dimension where we don't age, and time, as we know it, doesn't have much meaning. You see time is a measurement of change of that which is around us. For example, time flows differently as in faster or slower depending on the conditions and consistency of matter. This is related to the "curvature of space-time time", which is based on mass and gravity.

Time slows down the closer you get to any massive gathering of physical matter. Satellites orbiting Earth have to correct for the fact that time passes ever so slightly slower on Earth's surface than it does in its orbit. In this case, we are only talking a second over an extensive period of time.

Perhaps the best-known example of this, in the physical universe, is a black hole. Black holes produce an astronomically larger space-time curvature than our planet. The larger the space-time curvature caused by a black hole, the larger effect it has on time around it. So, even time in our physical universe is not as static as we may commonly relate to it being.

The speed an object is travelling in relation to other objects is also a part of the process of time flow and perception of time. This effect is stronger the faster an object is going, to the point of, if I were on the sun and I set off at the speed of light, from your perspective it would be a number of minutes for me to get to your home, but for me no time will have elapsed. There is no way my physical body would be able to move at the speed of light. But there would be no physical matter, as we know it, in a quantum dimension of thought and consciousness. Therefore, there would also be no space-time curvature like we would find in the physical universe and thus, time may not flow in a way that we are used to.

However, a recent experiment Batalhao et al, (2014) has suggested time does still move forward at the quantum level. It may be that time is also a factor at the quantum level, perhaps because at the quantum level, just like our physical dimension, change is always happening and it is change that is our basic measurement of time. If there is change, then time is moving forwards.

For time to move backwards change that has taken place would have to reverse. Something that I don't feel is possible. As we have no physical matter in the quantum world, that is the afterlife, to break down during the course of time, we don't have to worry about our spirit body decaying and dying like our physical body does.

Many phenomenological experiences appear to demonstrate that time in heaven does still move forward and actually moves faster than time in the physical dimension. Further, the higher the frequency is in the level of heaven you reside, the faster time is, again, compared to the physical dimension. This may be due to the frequency of your quantum mental body and heaven being at a faster vibration than our physical world.

The less dense the level of matter is and the higher the vibration of energy is, potentially the faster time might flow in comparison to our physical dimension. So, what may be a day here, could be three days in heaven. So when we send thoughts out to our loved ones, it may be they receive these words minutes or even hours apart from each other.

When spirits come and visit with us here, it has appeared to me, in what they have said, that they lose time. For example, if their visit with us is for an hour, in heaven three hours may have passed. This appears to be why at times when I've communicated with spirits regarding not such important matters they have said things like, I must be going back to get on with some things; I don't want to lose too much time. This, of course, does not stop our loved ones visiting us all the time. Especially at important times, sometimes spending whole days with us or longer.

The heaven we will go to looks a lot like our world but overall better. All the good things, but none of the bad. Those that have resided there have built a world of their own, doing this not by the use of hand or machine but by the use of thought. If you have the capacity to think something in heaven, it will appear. Someone with building experience would be an ideal candidate in heaven to design a building for someone else.

Now this ability doesn't mean we can go around thinking up new people. We don't have the capacity to think on such a scale to create such a complex being. An artist though, could think of a picture, and it would appear to the quality in which he can picture it and design it in their mind. It's not, in any way different, from here except without the need for the physical work.

Not only are there architects of buildings, but also, architects of nature, designing gardens all the way up to whole parks and landscapes. At some level, you might begin to imagine the possibilities of creation without the limit of time or the need for physical work. Whatever may have come into your mind, probably isn't a tenth of the miraculous creations of all kinds one will find when they get to heaven.

I remember when I was first getting my head round this concept, and even though I had no doubt about the afterlife and the existence of heaven, I remember finding it hard to fathom that such another world could exist with all the wonder we have on our planet, and much more. It somehow seemed hard to picture and hard to grasp, but I remember thinking to myself, one day, how silly I was. Look at how much we have created on this planet with the limits of time and physicality!

It is foolish to think, after knowing heaven exists, that such a world would not be very much like ours, just as complex and diverse; if not far more so, and overall much more improved. In this way, we must never underestimate the power of human consciousness observing what we have created here on Earth, and pondering what we will create in the future as a reference point.

Something I'm often asked is if time is different, is there day and night? The answer to that is, yes there is. Just like on Earth, certain areas experience more or less daylight in heaven. Firstly, remember time is still moving forward in the quantum world.

However, day and night, cold and hot, is ultimately controlled by the collective subconscious thoughts of those who reside in that space in heaven. Specifically, their perception of time moving forward and their perception of their surroundings based on their experiences on Earth. It's all to do with perception and what the collective of that heaven is accustomed to.

Do I have to be around people in the afterlife that I don't want to be around?

This often leads to questions like, what if you don't want to be around someone over there? Is there a hell? Do all people go to the same place? This is very complex to answer and needs to be answered in several parts.

The short answer is you don't need to be around anyone you don't want to be around. Just like here, we avoid people by going to areas far away from them. We can do this in the same way over in heaven. For those who have done many things that the average person here would consider to be evil, it is different. Such persons go to another place in the afterlife.

In these spirit worlds, it's all about energy. You will go over to either a heaven or what those who reside in heaven would consider a hell. It depends on your consciousness and, in turn, your energetic quantum vibration.

You could think of it like radio waves. We all have our own exact frequency. As an analogy, one could say our frequency will either fit in with FM or AM. Let's say FM is more positive and AM is more negative. This would mean the average person would go over to FM (heaven) when they pass over. A serial killer would go over to AM (hell). Bear in mind, though, such a place does not relate directly to good or evil and right or wrong.

Such things are conceptions based on our current society and what is evil to one, isn't necessarily to another, what is enjoyable to one, isn't necessarily enjoyable to another. What is hell to one person might be heaven to another and vice versa. It's more about two natural and opposing energies. It is all about how we label things based from our subjective conceptions as more positive and more negative. It really comes back to a state of mind.

A person who from our current society's standards, would be considered evil dies and goes to a place that most people would consider hell – a place of chaos, anger and negative intention that could cause much potential mental harm for the average person. However, such a person who is evil to the general society takes some pleasure and potential enjoyment from the above. They get pleasure out of it. Thus, they wouldn't necessarily dislike the place that most people would consider to be a hell.

I would suggest there are many levels of heaven and many levels of what could be called hell. This is potentially an infinite number. As you evolve as a person over there, your vibration will change and in this way, potential progression up, or depending on outlook, devolution down vibrations, in this subatomic dimension, is also very much a reality. It appears to all be about levels of consciousness, mindset, and through this, and karmic forces, how pure and high a vibration becomes. Look at this as a ladder, painted into three sections: the bottom section is painted black, the middle section is painted grey and the top section is white. Each section relates to a different rung of vibrations of the afterlife. Each rung relates to, more or less, certain types of energetic vibrations.

When the current average human passes over, they fall somewhere in the grey, but to us, it's still very much heavenly compared to Earth. From being there, we can move up onto rungs that would be considered more and more heavenly to us, potentially going well up into the white rungs.

Will I be reunited with my loved ones right away?

Some though may be in the lower grey and find themselves wishing to move either down or up. It's all about different manifestations of energy that people relate more to. Mediums can potentially communicate with people from any rung, but it is easier for them to communicate with persons who are closer to their rung (or their vibration).

The more distance between their vibration and the spirit communicating, the harder it can be to get the proper blend of energy and strong connection needed from a mediumistic communication. As I say most humans are grey, they experience emotions and thoughts connected to the black. However, they also relate and experience emotions and thoughts connected to the white.

Their karma is often not great, but it could be worse, so the grey area, somewhere in the middle, is where they fit, and that's where they will go at first. You don't need to worry about people who have passed over before you moving on to higher rungs than you will go to when you first go to heaven, and because of this worry that you will not be able to see them.

They can move down to lower rungs and stay there with you for a while as you prepare to move up. It's no different than how they can visit us here in the physical dimension. It is also very common for spirits to wait for people to move up rungs, or wait for people on certain rungs so that the time they could spend with their loved ones is not overly affected. Their love and wanting to be around the people they love is always their priority. Moving up rungs is not something that comes easily, and some spirits seem to struggle moving up at all. Concepts related to all this will be discussed and explained further at various stages as the book continues.

Those people who are the very best among us, will upon making their transition to a heaven, potentially already be able to access places in the afterlife, which have a higher than the typical human vibration. It's a bit like not having the money to move into a better neighbourhood of the city or not being able to afford to pay for certain experiences, except the currency in the spirit world isn't money. It's your consciousness and soul that affects your energetic vibration, which allows you to access these levels of heaven and experiences.

This is related to the strength of your spirituality, understanding, empathy, compassion, knowledge, love, and essence of being, or lack thereof. This is why people may seek to resolve karmic debts or create good karma. It allows their essence to increase shedding the negative vibration for a more positive one. If you try to access a place you are not ready for, the intensity of the light energy there will drain you energetically and be blinding to you and repel your quantum mental body that houses your quantum soul.

It's interesting that mystics, dating back thousands of years, related to this concept in the same way. This suggests that your spiritual light becomes stronger, as your energetic vibration becomes faster and moves higher as you advance. We now also know through science that the faster an electron moves in its orbit, as part of an atom, the more light is produced.

Some spirituality and scientifically minded persons have suggested there is a connection here between this spiritual concept and this understanding in science. Overall, what we find in the phenomenological data is that it appears we are always in a place in the afterlife where we are around "like-minds" and souls. That when the average person from Earth crosses over into the heaven they fit into, this heaven looks, on the basic level, very much like Earth, as this is the template the people from Earth who passed over had.

However, this place has been changed and developed by those who reside there. There is also much more diversity with colours and much more to experience in general over there than here. In a way, it's a world of dreams, but one that is so very real.

**Physical is just a word for a frequency of energy.
What can be done here, can be done in heaven and
much more.**

In the spirit worlds, communication is often done through telepathy, no differently to how I have explained how the process happens through a medium, but only much stronger. There is not the same amount of hindrance caused by the physical brain processing and physical bodies attenuation on our spirit's vibration.

This ability to communicate telepathically in heaven gets stronger over time as your vibration grows stronger. Communication can also happen through verbal speech and spirits can touch each other, hear and see each other in all the ways that we can here, and more.

Now, this may seem an odd thought, in that we don't have a physical body, so how can we experience physical touch? Well, let me explain to you, if you don't already know, that through science we know at the subatomic level, we actually never technically touch each other in the way we think. So, if "by touch" we mean physical matter-on-matter contact, then it doesn't matter if you are sat, laying, or standing right now, you are technically not touching whatever it is below you.

What you are doing is hovering above the matter with a tiny atomically sized gap between you and the matter. As discussed in Feynman et al, (2013) when two atoms get very close to each other that aren't going to chemically react or bond together, the atoms have great trouble touching each other because the electrons of the atoms repel each other.

When we reach out and run our finger along someone else's skin, what really happens at the subatomic level, is the electromagnetic field of our electrons reacts to the electromagnetic field of the other person. These fields meet, but they repel each other. The nerves on our skin pick up on the repulsive force and our mind interprets that energy field interaction as the touch sensation we experience.

You then may be wondering how can we hold things? And how do we get cut or injured? We can hold things because no surface is perfectly flat at the micro level, and therefore friction exists. Things can stick together through chemical bonds and latch on to the imperfections in the surface of the object. The reason we can get cut and have other injuries is because the field of one set of atoms can force the atoms of another item away from each other.

In terms of seeing, what we often don't think about is the fact that we don't see with our eyes and, depending on your stance, one would say we see with our brain or a mixture of a brain and mind, if you see the two as separate but connected entities, like I do. Information is carried to your eye within light, your eye then sends the information to the mind, the mind puts the information together based on how it processes this information. It tells us what it looks like out there and how we see the world.

This process also takes around a tenth of a second, so technically we are always one tenth of a second behind reality. We can also see the world differently depending on how we process the information. This is why colour-blind people in their reality see colours differently. All the information that comes into the eye is also upside down so our mind, also turns it the right way up.

For me, this really demonstrates the power of our mind particularly the subconscious part of our mind and its ability to perform such amazing sub-conscious processes. You see, from my perspective the brain is just an organ that facilitates communication between our quantum mind and the physical body and world. When we lose the physical body we don't need the physical brain anymore, our quantum mind is free and has a mental body of its own.

Here again, I have touched on how we have a quantum mental body of energy. This is the quantum mind's projection of who you are. It's like an energetic, mental counterpart to your physical body; eyes, brain, lips, etc. In heaven, when my quantum mental body's hand reaches out and runs my spirit hand down your spirit arm the interaction is processed in the same way that it was processed between the energy interactions described above during our physical lives.

That's all our consciousness has ever known to do. Likewise, in this way, if we clap our hands in heaven we will hear sound; move your mental body's tongue in a way to create speech and a verbal sound frequency will be sent out and will be picked up by your mental body's ears and processed by your consciousness. Its processing centre, the mental brain can understand the same terms of speech you could understand on Earth.

In this way, your whole mental body is a projection of your consciousness. Your mental brain's memory of how you looked and how you experience things. When you scale it back, here in the physical dimension and any di-mension, everything is just information as frequencies of energy interacting with other forms of information as frequencies of energy.

Now you see how what you can do in heaven is everything you did on Earth and more. Things like admiring the perfect countryside and the amaz-ingly beautiful colours. You can, through the power of your mind, have much more control of your experiences, though. For example, how hot or cold you feel. You don't have to eat or drink, but you can experience the sensations and tastes if you want, and many spirits continue to enjoy this. You can revert to any age as a template to how you appear to yourself and others in heaven because your mind remembers how you looked exactly at any point in your life.

It doesn't take a typical spirit very long to learn how to use their mind in this way to change their appearance to a younger self from the information that is all stored within our subconscious mind during our physical life, and which is kept when we pass over along with all other aspects of our mind.

We can also continue to change how we appear, regarding hair colour, tattoos, and all other ways we do on Earth, including a piercing. Just like here, you would need to place the piece of energy and information that makes up the size, shape and design of the jewelry through a gap in the projection of your mental body that you can create with your mind.

This, when you scale it back, is not any different than what is happening to the physical body here. It's just that the vibration here is what we call physical. It's all still energy; everything is energy vibrating at different frequencies, faster or slower.

———

People in heaven can continue relationships they had with people on Earth, and they can also form new relationships of all kinds, get married, laze around or learn new things, travel wherever you want. Every choice is yours!

Visit libraries, listen to music, attend lectures, theatre performances, watch movies and go for a walk in the woods, sit in your garden and read a book, play games and partake in any hobby you enjoyed on earth.

In terms of travel, there are many options, from driving a car to instantaneous teleportation through the power of your mind alone. Yes, you read correctly, when you have advanced to a certain level, you are able to instantaneously travel to any location you have been to, have a picture of, is within your line of sight or where someone you know is currently located or you can link your energy to that of another spirit and take them to a place you have been but they haven't.

When you don't have physical matter, faster than the speed of light travel becomes possible. At the quantum level, information has already been observed travelling from one location to another instantaneously. At the quantum level that is what you are, quantum information. For those still wondering, yes, sexual intercourse is very much on the list for those that are inclined, and yes, it's something that occurs regularly. After all, why would you not want to do that if you could?

We are all humans after all, and as discussed all the human parts of us stay with us when we cross over to heaven. In all the excitement, you, of course, cannot forget those families and friends you have left on earth. When someone in the physical world thinks of you strongly, you will experience their thoughts and you will know what they think and feel. The more strongly they send out the thoughts, the clearer it will be to the spirit receiving them.

Naturally, you will want to help them in any way you can, give them guidance and let them know you are just a thought away. The different ways they try to do this will be addressed a bit later. There is no need to sleep, but some spirits may wish to go into a sleep-like-state for a desired time for relaxation purposes. It is also very difficult to get down and depressed in heaven. Others will feel your problem and immediately try to help you feel better and recover.

You can work, depending on your experience, to help others and your karma, everything from building and designing things to teaching of all kinds. Perhaps help others with mental healing through forms of psychotherapy, etc. It depends on your experience from Earth, the experience you gain in your time over there, and what you want or feel you need to do.

Spirits who have been over in heaven longer are more than happy to help guide others to realizations and experiences that have helped them in their life in heaven.

Through their existence over there, they can change and evolve, become wiser, better people. It's a case of keeping and improving on the good and decreasing the negative.

Sometimes, I'm asked, why is heaven a place where people become better? The answer to this is very easy to sum up. Firstly, you're around people of a similar nature, and there is no hunger, money, disease or illness, no physical pain, no fear of death, no materialism and the ability for people to see life and all things from a bigger perspective.

If this physical world was like this, I believe we can all relate to how much better the world would be and how much better people here would be and become.

These properties of heaven are also more reasons why it's much easier for a person to work through mental illness in heaven than on Earth. This is because much of the problems that were a part of the cause of the mental issue no longer exist, and a person in heaven is in the safe and peaceful place of love.

They can get more in touch with themselves and find a much greater inner peace. What we know from the phenomenological experiences of mediumship is that it doesn't matter what your sexuality is; if you took your own life; if you were baptized or not; if you followed a religion or didn't; if you believed in an afterlife or didn't, providing you have been a half-decent person you will go over to a heaven-like afterlife that is a much better place than our planet is currently.

Does anything upset people in heaven?

The only thing that I ever heard that really continually upsets anyone after they go to heaven is if their loved ones, who remain in the physical world are upset or suffering in some way.

They are not able to be physically hurt in heaven. Over time, you get stronger control over what your mental body experiences are regarding physical sensation. In this way, you can sort of block out certain sensations which you wouldn't want to feel anymore. Your mental body cannot be destroyed by another spirit's. It is your consciousness that creates it. You are the one with ultimate control over yourself and the stronger your energy, the more control you have.

The only way I could see that you could cease to exist would be if the information that is your consciousness became dispersed (untangled). However, I would suggest this is impossible. There is no proof that once subatomic particles are energetically entangled, they ever become fully un-entangled. In fact, I would suggest certain experiments indicate they always remain energetically linked. I have never heard any spirit talk about a soul becoming dispersed, nor have I heard any other medium suggest this.

When I have asked the spirit world if this is possible, I have always been told specifically that they have never experienced or heard of it happening to any being whose consciousness has been formed through information becoming energetically entangled. I will discuss energetic entanglement and more about what it means a bit further on in the book.

With all this being said, I have been asked before, is it possible to give birth or create a form of human life over there through means of sexual reproduction? The answer to this is not straightforward. It's best in this book, for me just to say while it's very rare to hear of such a thing, it is not unheard of in certain cultures that contain mediumistic practice.

However, as stated above, the creation of a life form through such means in heaven is not often spoken of. That could be because everything else is more than enough for most people on Earth to get their head round as it is, without worrying about such things.

FOUR

The Process Explained Further

• • • • • • • • • • • • •

Apart from what has been discussed so far, some people may have an issue with mediumistic readings because they don't understand the processes involved and are confused. This may be exaggerated if an aspect of the recipient's psychological needs isn't adequately addressed by the reading, and that may not be the fault of the medium.

I will now further explain aspects of how a mediumistic link works and functions, to further illuminate the realities of the process.

How is a mediumistic link established?

Firstly, I'm often asked how is a mediumistic link established? Well, quite simply it's not established, it is already there, the medium just tries to make the link stronger. I suggest every single person who has ever lived in this physical universe is energetically connected and linked. This is the general phenomenological-based perspective of mediums and many spiritual persons. Regarding relating this to science, people can relate it to quantum entanglement.

Quantum entanglement is a phenomenon within quantum mechanics that shows that subatomic particles can be energetically linked, and it appears, at least in certain cases whatever you do to one particle instantaneously affects the other. It appears information travels between one particle and the other instantaneously; seemingly travelling through some form of invisible energetic field. This entanglement happens from two particles being once a part of one single particle.

This can be related to the theory that everything in our universe started out from one densely packed particle that has now separated out to form our universe. This belief of how our universe began is quite widely accepted. It might be possible that everything within our physical universe became entangled from being a part of that very first particle. That could mean if we do have a quantum mind and consciousness, our quantum mind it is energetically linked to the minds of all persons who have lived in this physical universe.

This could also explain the energetic connection in which the information is transferred and explains incidents where individuals claim to have experienced an emotion, images or sensation related to a person, even though they are a great distance away. An example of this is a person getting a feeling of a loved one being fearful or in pain.

It could be that the closer we are to a person, the more energetically entangled our quantum souls become. Perhaps, through this energetic entanglement, it relates in some way to our connection and feelings of love for people who have been or continue to be in our lives.

This would add another potential dynamic to the bereavement process. That even when someone is gone, at a subconscious level, we still feel a connection to the spirit of the person who has passed over. That part of our minds through this connection and/or other means, knows they are still living, and thus wishes to remain connected with them and close to them.

Further, what this would indicate is that every human being is psychic and is able to communicate with spirit, to some degree. Although you may not be able or wish to give five-star readings on a consistent basis, as you may not be as naturally in tune with this aspect of yourself, everyone can develop that aspect of himself/herself somewhat.

I very much believe this to be the case, and it is the reason I teach psychic, mediumistic and spirituality development workshops and courses that are open to all who want to try to develop these aspects.

More on how a mediumistic link works

When a medium's telepathic link and energetic connection reaches a certain level with the spirit communicating, the spirit will, in their mind, think about images they want the medium to see. When the spirit pictures these images in their mind, the information is transmitted through to the mind of the medium. It is the same process for feelings and words.

A key part of the process is that for the medium to understand the information, the connection needs to be as strong as possible. If the connection is not very strong, the images won't be as clear, the words and the feelings won't be as strong either. The other part of the process is how the information is being processed by the mind of the medium. If the mind does not make sense of the information, then this information will be sent to the subconscious parts of the medium's mind and never come into their conscious awareness. Thus, they will not be able to pass it on.

As the mind makes some sense of the information, it may come through to the medium in a way that is not literal. It can often come through in a way that their mind most relates to and understands that piece of information. An example could be the medium sees the Golden Gate Bridge in San Francisco, where the spirit is only trying to convey that they lived near a bridge that was painted red.

Another example could be the medium sees the old red Ford their grandfather used to drive, but what the spirit has tried to communicate is they are the recipient's grandfather, and he passed down a red car to their grandson just before they passed away.

You might be thinking, well how on earth does the medium ever know exactly what to say? That is hard to explain. Basically, the medium with practice and time begins to know when he sees certain things in his mind and what they mean based on how his or her mind interprets and relates to things. The medium begins to know how literal or not to take something depending on certain feelings during the reading and importantly how strong and clear the connection with the spirit is at that time.

It is certainly nothing like what is portrayed on television in shows like Ghost Whisperer, for example, where the medium sees the spirit as clear as he sees people on earth and hears the spirit's voice easily and seemingly out loud. If it were this easy, mediumship would be much more established as a real phenomena in the academic world than it is.

Whilst some mediums may claim to see a spirit standing next to their loved one in the audience or next to them while giving a reading, etc., I would say this is very rare, and it certainly doesn't happen to me on a regular basis. In fact, I've never seen a spirit whilst doing a reading for someone. When I have seen a spirit in whole form, it's not been when I've been doing readings, not something I've sought out. It is, in fact, an extremely rare occurrence for anyone to see a spirit figure in full form.

I also don't agree with mediums saying to someone they see their relative next to them in the audience, as it gives the impression the medium is seeing them in full, complete detail. When they clearly are not. If they were, they would have no trouble describing that person in very specific detail, which I have never seen a medium do after making such statements. Also, if it were that clear, the spirit would only need to hold up cards with words on to convey messages to the medium.

Typically, a person will see a spirit, when the energy is very strong for the spirit, for one of potentially many reasons, and the person is in a bit of a limbo state mentally. It is normally out of the corner of their eye or just for a few moments – when their conscious mind is at a stiller place, and the information can come through in such great and clear detail without too much interference.

If I talk in a reading about what was the physical appearance of the spirit or how they choose to appear in heaven, I do so through seeing still, generic images of blue eyes, brown hair, a scar in an eyebrow, a freckle on a nose, etc. Those who have seen my mediumship work will have seen that I sometimes motion to a spirit next to me, and I talk in the direction of them. It is not because I'm seeing them. It's because my connection has grown strong enough with the spirit world that I feel their presence so strongly that I know where they are positioned.

Many times, I talk out loud to them during readings because talking to them has become second nature to me. Just as if I were talking to a physical person, I would look in their direction and speak out loud. At times, I do this with those who have passed over. Even when I'm talking to them in my mind, I will often look to their direction; it's just what one does when communicating to a person.

I telepathically receive information back in feelings, images and words, which brings me back to clairaudience and (hearing) spirit. It's not hearing them, as in hearing them with your physical eardrum. Clairaudience is a telepathic hearing.

It's as if a thought, a word just suddenly came into your mind, but you know it wasn't your original thought. This is not to be confused with hearing them out loud, as they hear each other in heaven when they move their mental body's tongue etc. and produce an energy wave that our mental body's ears pick up on, just as if it were a physical sound to our eardrums here.

Spirits can also pick up on our sound vibrations. When we talk out loud and they are in the same space as us, they can actually hear us. The hearing a spirit's voice out-loud phenomena is much rarer of an experience for mediums and general people. Again, it often happens at an unplanned time, in the same way as I described seeing a spirit in full figure with near perfect detail.

We are limited here by the processing of our physical brain and body, which is the system we automatically use and rely on all the time. It is only, when free from it, this hidden system comes into full functioning and takes centre stage. When that happens, we all become more powerful than any medium on Earth has ever been. Capable of experiencing everything easily and in full detail, just like we normally can here.

This is also not to be confused with direct voice phenomena where the spirit does create their own physical vibration and in such cases, everyone in close enough proximity hears the communication. This phenomenon will be discussed further later within the book. Generally with clairaudience a medium will not be able to distinguish if the communicator has a male or female tone or pick up on an accent.

However, if the connection is very good, the words in my mind may come through in a deeper or higher pitch, with different tones and at times with an accent. This is very rare though and when it happens, it is normally only a single word or a few words that come through like this.

When using clairaudience, distinguishing between the medium's thoughts, and thoughts that originated from the spirit is, again, something the medium gets better with over time, with much practice. Some mediums may claim to hear an external voice all the time. This is unlikely, but not impossible. The mind does project things externally. Auditory hallucinations come from within the mind, but are often perceived as coming from an external source.

I would think that if this does happen with other mediums, it's very rare, as many people would have trouble dealing with this constant external voice and the potential dissociation that comes with it. Based on my experience, clairaudience being projected by the mind to appear external could lead a person to lose grip on reality. What is real and not real, and could lead to actual auditory hallucinations because of its effects on the mind.

With all this it helps to think of mediumistic information, like mental radio waves. These radio waves are transmitted and the stronger the connection and the stronger the transmitter (the disembodied spirit), the clearer the information is perceived by the receiver (the medium) who needs to correctly process the information that is being transmitted.

The better the receiver, the more information is processed accurately. When it comes to clairaudience, if the medium is not familiar with a particular name, for example, it's more difficult for the medium's mind to process it and only a section might be received. Using the name Amrita as an example, the medium may only perceive Am or Rita instead of Amrita together, or the medium's mind may process it as Anita as they have experience with that name, but have never heard of the name Amrita.

Around a handful of times, a person has suggested that I must have found the name on the Internet, as I didn't pronounce it correctly. Each time this has happened, it has been a name I have no experience with, and it's come through to me clairaudiently and had not been processed exactly correct, but obviously close enough that the recipient knew exactly which name I meant. This misunderstanding is most likely because of a lack of understanding of how a mediumistic connection works and how clairaudience works. If I was looking up people's names and I had gone to the trouble to find out this odd name, surely, I would also look up how to pronounce it?

To me, it is important for a medium to have as much all round life experience as possible, so their mind interprets whatever piece of information they are given better and more accurately. Be it an image, feeling or word, this may be why some pieces of information don't come through in a reading. It's not for the spirit's lack of trying, it may be because it either hasn't come through into the consciousness, awareness of the medium, or the medium's mind processed it differently to how the spirit was trying to convey it.

I would say from experience, even in a really good reading, around 15 percent of the information the spirit tries to express never comes through to the medium's conscious mind. I believe it's best for a medium to allow the recipient to ask questions to the spirits toward the end of the reading, given that within that 15 percent, there might be a topic that is important to the recipient. However, in a great reading, it's possible that all the information the spirit tried to convey comes through to the medium without issue!

Other elements that can affect how strong a communication can be is how long the spirit has been on the other side. I always recommend the person wait at least six months before getting a reading after a loved one has passed over. A year, I would say, is even better. This is because it appears the more time that passes here, generally the stronger the spirit gets in heaven. They grow and evolve as energy beings over in the afterlife. This allows them to generally communicate stronger, the longer they have been passed over.

However, there is also the potential of them advancing to a point where their vibration is so beyond that of the medium, the communication can become more challenging again. The closer in vibration the medium and the communicator are, the easier the communication will be.

That being said, every spirit appears to progress at different levels. Outgoing personalities and more spiritual people or mediums, for that matter, often find it easier to communicate stronger and faster. I have known spirits who with help from other spirits are able to communicate relatively well, as little as a few hours after they have passed.

However, a year later the same spirits can communicate stronger again. At first, they will be getting used to life in heaven and beginning to learn how everything works. If before they passed, the spirit already had knowledge of this process, it is quite helpful and generally leads to a faster and easier adaptation to life in heaven.

There also appears to be a correlation between persons who suffered from mental illness and needing a bit more time to communicate well.

What physical and mental problems stay or go when we get to heaven?

Physical related problems disappear when we shed the physical body. Mental issues, however, are caused by imbalance in the mind. Generally, this is something which mediums from all cultures will relate to. These mind issues are caused by stress and anxiety, and could be depressions, types of hallucinations, phobias etc.

Mental issues brought on by substances are something that stays, as it is a mental issue which was brought on by chemicals causing an imbalance between the brain and quantum mind that can lead to an imbalanced quantum mind. Whereas with other illnesses like Alzheimer's, the memory loss is a symptom caused by the problems with the physical brain. The quantum mind is not able to function properly through the brain, and thus the thinking process is disturbed, but the mind itself is not necessarily out of balance. Of course, that can happen as a part of the process.

In this way, someone who passed with Alzheimer's will be able to access his or her memories like normal in the afterlife. If, however, the Alzheimer's caused an imbalance in the mind that led to schizophrenia, then that could stay for some time after the death of the physical body and would need to be worked through. If you lost sensation in your right arm that would return when you get to the afterlife, as that is an issue with the physical body.

As another example, Parkinson's is another disease that is instantly gone. The key is to understanding the perceived difference between the mind and the brain. For example, a phobia is something within the mind, connected to information stored within it. Depression is something within the mind, connected to information related to perception, emotions and feelings, but loss of visual field caused by a stroke has to do with the brain.

The information is coming to the brain but due to the damage to the brain the connection between it and the quantum mind is hindered and thus the quantum brain does not get the chance to process the information and give you sight. When the quantum mental body leaves the physical body upon physical death, your quantum body is no longer hindered by the physical body. The body that it was being forced to work through can, again, process the information without hindrance and give you sight once more. If you were to completely lose a limb, your quantum limb, of course, is not damaged.

To help get a feel for this, imagine you were born in a robotic suit. This robotic suit is connected to your body in a way that you can feel the robotic arms being touched as if it were your arm. The robotic suit, over time, grows and you grow with it. You see through the robotic suit's visor an image based on how your mind is interpreting the signals being sent from the robotic suit to your brain.

If the robotic suit got hit on the right arm and the censors broke and were not able to transfer the information to you, you would no longer feel sensations in that robot arm. It would feel as if you had no right arm anymore. If the part of the robotic suit that transfers the visual information from the external world to your brain was severely damaged then you would no longer be able to see.

Through all this, you get very depressed and you wouldn't want to go on. This carries on for a while, but when that robot finally shuts down, you can then release yourself from the robot and step outside of it. You do this and become aware of sensation in your biological arm again; as it is no longer connected to the robotic system it is free to sense on its own. You see again because you can use your biological eyes to receive the information, and your brain to process it.

Not only do you see again, but you realize that the robotic suit only picked up on duller shades of colours and that they are actually more vivid: you see shades of colours that you had never seen before. You begin to see and sense so many things that your robotic suit hadn't picked up on. It's a whole new set of experiences, a whole greater existence, a whole new body but one that feels like home. Unfortunately, however, you notice still feeling depressed because this is within your deeper real self.

However, as so much of your depression was related to being stuck in this suit in that state, this soon begins to lift, and eventually it is gone altogether. This is exactly what it is like between your quantum mental body and the biological physical body. Your physical body is the robotic suit and your quantum mental body in the deeper reality of you: the body within the body, the consciousness and mind at the heart of the system.

So yes, the mind-related issues remain with spirits for a time. This does affect their energetic vibration and vitality. However, as I have mentioned, in heaven, there is plenty of help for them to overcome these issues through forms of psychotherapy and support from their loved ones, who are also in heaven. Such things are not a big problem. It is much easier for persons who suffer from mental issues to be helped over there than it is here.

It is true to say that generally spirits, who have been over there longer, are stronger. This is actually very important, as often it is our older relatives on the other side who are around as well. Not just the closest people to us who have passed over. Maybe it is your great-great-great grandfather, who you never met, who is very aware of you from heaven and has always taken an active interest in your life and has tried to watch over and help you from the other side. Often, it appears we all have, at the very least, one person like this who watched us being born and has been interested in our lives since and has a great love for us.

Sometimes, these individuals become very important helpers to us from the other side, specifically, if we acknowledge them and ask for their help. When grandparents or other relatives who we didn't know come through in readings and describe to the recipient, for example that they have been watching you since you were born, it is often quite surprising to people, and sometimes not so easy to immediately understand.

What we must remember is whilst we may not know them, they know us very well, and they can see us, hear what we say, hear our thoughts and feel our feelings. It is very easy for them to form a natural connection to us and as a child of theirs, have a natural desire to do so. They may have even been a right crabby person here, who most people didn't like. However, with time in heaven, they have changed the negative aspects of themselves.

It is also worth mentioning that to other cultures that have used forms of mediumship, cultures that are often referred to as "practising shamanistic-based practices", this is not strange to them at all. In many of these cultures, there is a significant emphasis on the connection between our older relatives and our distant ancestors. In such cultures, it is very common for older spirits to communicate with, and aid persons through spiritual channels.

Their presence is often very much welcome as they are often the stronger, more evolved and more powerful spirit energies that can work with people here to help heal them and guide them. It is really only in our Western culture where such little emphasis is given to the older spirits, and their wish to communicate. I would suggest this is because, in our culture, we are generally only interested in our most immediate loved ones and family figures, where in other cultures this is different.

It is often in readings that older spirits will come with the person we are looking to communicate with; someone who has passed much more recently and help them in their endeavour to communicate with us by adding their energy to the communication and boosting the link between the medium and the more recently passed spirit.

In truth, I have never known a newly passed spirit be able to communicate without the aid of older spirits. Often the older spirit or spirits work to help momentarily strengthen the vibration of the more recently passed spirit or help to control and stabilize it. Having a stable vibration is very relevant to the communication because, without it, the communication won't be very strong. It will be more fragmented and not as clear. This is because the medium's link with the spirit won't be as stable and the medium's mind would constantly be trying to process things on slightly different frequencies. The information being passed along would be more fractured.

Being able to connect with a medium and keep a stable vibration through the process is, again, something a spirit appears to get better at over time. Sometimes when a spirit is going through what I often call a transitional phase in the afterlife, a phase of a big expansion of consciousness, learning and growth, their vibration is less stable, it fluctuates and during this time, even a strong spirit has issue communicating.

Sometimes, the medium may not even be able to get a strong and consistent sense of the presence of that spirit. This is the biggest reason why a person can go and see a medium and a spirit, who has passed a decent length of time, and the medium is not able to communicate with that spirit at that time. This is something I rarely hear being talked about. Ideally, the client should notify the medium if they strongly wish to hear from a specific spirit and then the medium will be able to inquire with people in heaven about when is potentially a good time to book the reading and avoid any transitional phases the spirit, who is the desired communicator, may go through.

This again, is often not commonly practised and is one of the techniques that I have tried to implement as much as possible. It has helped with the consistency in my work. Other reasons a spirit may not be able to communicate at a given time or find it difficult are, the vibration and or experience of the medium does not match well with the spirit; the medium is low on energy or for some reason the spirit chose not to communicate at that time. The last one is very rare but it does happen, and there is always a good reason.

What I'd like to do now is share a story with you, from Sarah and Paul, that demonstrates how a relative we never knew can be very connected to us from the other side, the spirit that has been watching over us as much as anyone else.

FIVE

Saved By Our Grandfather

• • • • • • • • • • • • •

Sarah

"I can still remember the morning of the reading very well. It was raining out, pouring actually. I remember feeling nervous. It was exactly two years to the day since our father passed away from lung cancer. My mother had left my father seventeen years ago and left us along with him. I was only four at the time and have no clear memory of her. My brother was six and remembers her much better. Apparently, she was never nice to my father. That's what he always told us, anyway.

My brother would always say they would just argue all night long. She would end up smashing stuff and walk out into the night. That is what she did the last night she was home, apparently. And she never came back. She wrote to us for a year, but the letters were short, and the frequency of them didn't last.

To me, it had always been my brother, our father and me. "Dads" as I used to call him and still do. He was very manly, always pretended everything was fine, a man who didn't take any nonsense, very old-fashioned in many ways. He wasn't ever the best at conveying his emotions, but oh, how I had missed his hugs! My brother was always so sensitive, and he took our father's passing just as hard as I did.

When I suggested to my brother about going to a reading with me, he was intrigued but also apprehensive. It took me several weeks to convince him to go with me. I knew he had a lot of emotion he wasn't expressing. I knew he was afraid of the reading not going well, or if the reading did go well that our father was displeased with him in some way. I knew he needed this, though. He was really struggling, and his grief was getting the better of him."

Paul

"It was sodden that day, downright miserable weather, windy, cold, even a bit of hail. I decided to wrap up as warm as possible, so I went to look in my drawer for a scarf, and that's when I remembered there are two scarves, one that I normally wear and a matching one I had given our father about two years before he passed away. He only wore it once, and when we cleared out his house,

61

I found it. It had been in this drawer ever since. I had cut the label of my scarf and my father's still had it attached. I'm not exactly sure why, but I decided I would wear his that day.

It's odd when I look back on it. I had never had a reading before. I'd not really ever believed in an afterlife. If someone had stopped me on the street, there and then, and asked me do you believe in an afterlife? I would have said, No, I just don't see how it's possible. Just like our father used to say... when you've died, you're food for the worms. He really knew how to cut a lovely spin on things, if you liked being depressed, that is.

He had a good heart deep down though, and he was always there for my sister, and me. Whatever we needed, he would find a way to get it or make it happen. Very much the tough love kind of man, old fashioned, stoic, some could say. If he ever did show you affection, you knew he really meant it. You would get the odd hugs, my sister got more than me, but that's probably because she was a girl and I was a boy, and that's how it worked with our father. I knew he loved me, though; I did feel loved, he was always proud of us."

Sarah

"I remember trying so hard to keep my emotions together and not cry, and I only just managed it. When my brother arrived and walked in, I could tell he was suffering from a strong hangover. He'd been out drinking the night before. Since our father died, it was all he did. He'd slumped in a hole that I was afraid he could never get back out of. He had become an alcoholic just like our mother was before she left.

Don't get me wrong, our father also liked his drink, and he was no saint, but he was not an alcoholic. He liked his cigarettes much more than his drink. Sadly, I don't think my brother hardly had a sober moment since our father had passed. There was a lot he never got to say to him. A lot that just wasn't said all round. I thought about how our father was always very proud of how well he had done in sports, when he was younger, and the fact that my brother had gone out and started his own business, and that he had won several weightlifting competitions and became a "real man" as Dads, would say.

My brother hadn't done much of anything the last two years, though. His business had all but gone under, and physically, well, let's not even go there, but, needless to say, he was not going to be winning any weightlifting competitions, nor did he look that well in the face.

We got in the car and, in around twenty minutes, we were there. I think all of our nerves were building with each mile that had passed.

We sat down in the chairs in Ross' room and then it really dawned on me, oh my God, we're actually here having a reading. I had read so much about Ross, and my expectations were very high, but I tried to downplay things in my mind and convince myself that if Ross couldn't get any information from our relatives, then that would be fine."

Paul

"Ross had gone to get a glass of water, and I looked over at my sister who seemed a little anxious. I remember thinking to myself; I don't think this is possible. It can't be something that happens. He is just going to make generic statements, not the specific information like what my sister had heard he says to people.

At that moment, Ross re-entered the room and sat back down in front of us. He went through with us how the information would be coming to him and how aspects of the reading would work and asked if we had any questions. We didn't, and he replied, "Fab, let's start the reading then."

He looked to his right and began to make sounds as if he were acknowledging someone talking to him, things like, "uh huh, mmhmm, yep," and so on. He then said he can feel the presence of two males from the other side, and one of them seemed to be communicating the name, Arnold. He asked if we know of a person on the other side who had this name?

I turned to look at my sister, again, who at the same time turned to look at me. We both looked at each other and at the same time murmured, "Yes" and we both glanced back at Ross, who said, "Well, he tells me this was his name, and that he has been passed over a fair time. Over thirty years." He asked if we knew who this male could be, we replied, "Yes, it could be our grandfather."

Ross said that he felt Arnold was a generation older than the other male, and said, "Could this make sense?" Sarah replied, "Arnold was our grandfather's name, our father's father, our father has passed as well, so it could be him."

Ross asked if we knew much about our grandfather, and I replied not really, but our father did talk about him sometimes. So, we had heard stories about him and his life. Ross talked about our grandfather living on a farm and how he was a very strict man, some would say harsh. This was very true from what we had heard. Ross then described to us how he had changed as a person through his time in heaven and had become mellower and much more calm and that he had taken an interest in our lives from the moment we were born."

Sarah

"As Ross talked about our grandfather being around watching over us from heaven, and visiting with us to keep in touch with our lives, he quickly went on to describe my personality to a tee. He talked about how when I was younger I was afraid of everything. This was very true; when I was a child I was afraid of so many things, the dark, elevators, car washes, loud noises, dogs, mice, spiders, deep water, and so on.

I am remarkably different than my brother who appeared to be afraid of none of these, or anything at all. Ross said to me, your grandfather, Arnold is showing him a clown, and asked if I was particularly afraid of clowns as a child. Well, I wasn't afraid of clowns. I was petrified and out of all the fears, I had, this was the one I still had to this day. I can't be within 10 feet of a clown without freaking out. Why I don't know, it's been that way since I can remember.

I was astonished how accurate and relevant this information was, but before I could really get my head around it further, Ross asked if I had recently spoken to a friend about looking for a new job, and sure enough, I had. Ross then went on to ask if I recently had a problem with a lamp on a bedside table. Two days previous, the bulb had blown in the lamp on my bedside table.

Ross then proceeded to say that he was feeling a sensation that would indicate our father had passed with a condition that would have affected the lungs and respiratory system. At this point, I couldn't believe what was happening, and it hit me, this is real, and this is really happening. Then he addressed my brother and his personality; his description was spot-on. I think he described him better than he could have described himself.

He followed by asking if Paul recently had a discussion with someone about them falling down some stairs. Paul was about to say no, when it clicked that he was on the phone with a customer yesterday, and the customer mentioned he had fallen down stairs and broken his leg. My brother was awestruck. He had explicitly talked and joked about this several times during the phone conversation. Ross explained that our grandfather was sharing all this information because he wanted to show us he had been with us during our lives and around us recently.

Ross then said, "On that note, I need to explain that your father isn't quite ready to communicate well through a medium, so your grandfather wanted to step in and let you know he is ok and show you he has been watching over you and knows you very well. This was something he would not have been able to say when he was here, but as I said, he evolved in his time in heaven and became much more in touch and balanced with his emotions."

Paul

"Ross then said he had some messages to pass through from our father, and he said he was getting the name, Kenneth, from Arnold and did we understand that name? "This is our father's name," we replied, in unison. "Your grandfather tells me your father wants you to know, Paul, that he loves you and that he also wishes to bring up the name, Darrel." I felt the biggest chill move up my spine I have ever felt, and my eyes welled up.

Following that, Ross took a while where he appeared to be conversing with our grandfather, and eventually said, "It is an odd feeling and set of images, but it appears that your father wants you to know that he knows about Darrel, and he wants you to know he still loves you. That you are more of a man than he even knew." I could no longer hold back the tears, they fell on to my jeans. I nodded to acknowledge that I knew what Ross meant.

What I didn't say to Ross at the time was that Darrel was my first boyfriend. I never told my father I was gay. This was the reason that my grief was even worse. I felt like I had never been completely honest with him before he passed away, and whenever I did think of the possibility of an afterlife, I always wondered if he would have resented the fact I was gay or the fact I had kept it from him, or both. When he was here, he was never accepting of homosexuality, but here he was telling me he now knew, and still loves me.

Ross went on to say our father wishes I was not beating myself up so much emotionally since his passing, but he understands, and it is time now to get back on track. It was these two things, the love and acceptance from our father, and his words on getting back on track that gave me the strength to get over my alcoholism."

Sarah

"As I looked over at my brother crying, I grabbed his hand and thought I can't believe it. That was exactly what he needed to know. The emotion he had been bottling up was being released right there in front of me.

Ross then turned to me and said our grandfather was telling him that your father was visiting me earlier today, and you were thinking about his hugs. He wants to let you know he misses your hugs just as much as you miss his. That was it for me, I started crying as well, but most importantly, we were both crying tears of joy, not tears of sadness.

Ross then asked me if I had been having any lower abdominal pain, and I told him I had been having it for a while, but I thought it was pain due to constipation. Ross said our grandfather believed it to be more complicated than that, and I should have it checked into by a doctor, as he feels there is a treatment that will hopefully be able to make it go away.

After going to the doctor and receiving medical tests I discovered I had bowel cancer. Because I got on to it when I did, it was dealt with before it could get worse or spread to other areas of my body.

The last thing Ross said was, "Your grandfather is giving enough energy to allow your father to bring one thing through directly to me: he appears to be showing me a book, and ducks; it may be a reference to the ugly duckling story?" Well, our father used to read us that story when we were children. When we got older, he would make up more stories about what the ugly ducklings got up to. He used to call us his ugly ducklings when we were children.

From this, I feel he was telling us we were still his children. I know if it were not for my grandfather telling me to get my abdomen checked out, I wouldn't have until it was too late. So, I now send my thoughts out to my grandfather and father every day and thank our grandfather for saving us from our grief, my brother from alcoholism and me from an early passing."

—

Whilst it is common for the medium only to talk about one spirit, maybe two during a communication, I have found that if the medium's mind is open enough, he or she will realize there is nearly always, at least, two spirits present that relate to the recipient; if not three or four or more. There may be times when a medium may link with one spirit and then become unmindful of the energy of the other spirits that are present: spirits who also may wish to bring through messages.

In my experience, it is very common for the medium, first to sense the energy of a spirit, who is not supposed to be the main communicator or, at least, is not the person the recipient is most looking to hear from. They might be the recipient's grandfather or great-grandfather who they didn't meet on Earth, but as demonstrated in Sarah and Paul's story, they will often know much about us, and feel very close to us here.

These persons, who have been in the spirit world longer, tend to be stronger spirits and are often there to help the communication by first establishing a good link with the medium and give energy to the communication in order to help a person who has not been passed over as long.

I have often found that there are, at least, three if not four spirits present, who are connected in some way to the recipient and logically this would make sense. If we visit loved ones here, it's much more common for us to do so with our partner, or sibling or parent and sometimes even with friends. Just as we tend to do things in twos, threes and fours here, this doesn't change in heaven.

In my experience, having several spirits can be vital to a successful communication because with the energy of the different spirits, the right blend of energy and power of energy can be created. However, sometimes, the spirits' energies don't blend as well together, or one lot of energy can overpower the other, for example, three communicators might be very masculine and outgoing, and there is one who is very feminine and reserved.

It can, at times, be hard for the medium to flick between different types of energies and communicators but if the energy is strong enough, then it's not a problem. Each reading can have a better or worse blend of energy and power of energy. This all depends on the medium's energy, the energy of recipient, the energy of any other persons in the same room, and of course, the energy of the spirits present in the room.

If a spirit's energy naturally blends better with the medium's, then the medium will find it easier to communicate with spirit. However, with experienced mediums, if the energy is strong enough, and the medium can relate enough to the spirit and what the spirit is bringing through, a poor blend can be worked through. However, if the vibration difference is too great a good reading will not be produced and good communication can be impossible.

Spirit guides

Spirits connected to the medium, who help the medium with their work, are commonly referred to as guides or helpers and are in the background, so to speak, working to make the blend and power of energy as strong as possible. They also help guide the medium in developing his/her psychic abilities by giving advice and working with the medium's energy to make him/her as strong a channel as possible.

Contrary to common thought, these spirits are often, at first, ancestors of the medium. They might attract more advanced, and older spirits as the medium becomes stronger or shows substantial promise and, most importantly, the right sort of intentions and being. This process is the same for all people. You will have a set number of ancestor helpers looking out for you, but in time and as your life evolves, you can attract more advanced, older spirits.

For instance, if you are a painter you might attract a spirit to come and help you who themselves was a painter. The reasons spirits, who are originally more detached from us, choose to do this is because they wish to help us out of love and respect. It also helps them further express their own creativity and helps them karmically. The more people we help through what we do, the higher our chance of attracting a more evolved guide/helper.

How mediums develop their psychic abilities

Whilst different cultures have many different practices to develop mediumship, I will discuss the typical process for spiritualist mediums, and relate to other techniques I have used that would be not so spiritualist.

It all starts with meditation, learning to connect with the spirit world and focus the mind through a number of meditation techniques or techniques related to shifting one's mental awareness to other places separate from the physical body and internal thoughts, that causes, what can be thought of as a meditative state.

You then begin to practise readings often using aids to help the process. Examples are reading a person with the guidance of the spirit world using things like flowers, fruits, vegetables, cards, tea leaves, sand, etc. As an exercise, you ask the spirit world to direct your attention to parts of the item to which you and they can draw inspiration. Thus, the item acts as a physical clairvoyant image in which to draw inspiration and helps to make up for the person's lack of a strong connection with spirit at the time of development.

It can seem like you're being very random at first, and you can be unsure where the information is coming from, and if it is spirit communicating or just things from within your mind somehow. It seems and feels less grounded, you have to open up, let go, and in a sense free your mind from the confines it has been used to. I often refer to this stage as the "hippy stage". As the person begins to get more and more accurate, and the connection and feelings become stronger, this is replaced with a stronger, more tangible set of feelings and experiences of communication. This can lead to a point where the medium has a clear and strong awareness and feeling of the presence of the spirit next to them and can converse with the spirit much easier.

I have also practised more extensive techniques such as four-day non-stop meditation and prayer sessions in complete darkness. When I say non-stop, I mean no break at all and that includes sleeping, eating or drinking; so that means no food, water or sleep for four days as a part of that process. I have meditated in sweat lodges and practised praying whilst holding scorching hot rocks to further train and focus my mind. I have used hypnosis techniques to train and focus my mind. I have sat for hours making prayer/intention ties. I have also worn and mediated with crystals to allow their energetic vibration to affect my own.

Remember everything has its own energetic vibration. Whatever comes in contact with ours, affects it especially if done over a lengthy time period. From my experience, certain crystals and stones can change our vibration to enhance it for mediumistic communication.

Such approaches have been used with various stones, plants and other items in different shamanistic cultures. There is also a particular plant that I go through stages of eating, which works in a similar way as the crystals. Before anyone jumps to conclusions, I will say the plant is not a psychedelic or a drug of any sort. It's something that could be found in anyone's garden. I don't smoke, drink alcohol or do any drugs. In fact I just drink water 99 percent of the time and even avoid taking over-the-counter pain killers.

I need to and want to keep my vibration as pure as possible and my mind as clear as possible at all times. Therefore, I stay away from anything of this sort.

⁓

To help my mind better understand names, town and city names and road names, I would read lists of first names and surnames starting with English, and then expand that list to all countries, reading it over and over. I would play recordings of me saying the names over and over while I slept. Likewise, I would read "A to Z" books of road names of cities over and over, to get the names in my mind, so when the spirit tries to communicate one of the names, I can recognize it, and it comes through to me as strongly as possible, and doesn't get lost within my subconscious.

In one of the papers I was tasked to write for my MSc, I related to an increase in psychic functioning when I changed my diet to vegetarian and then again when changing my diet to vegan. I have heard many mediums say their spirit guides and helpers have said to them that a vegetarian, and even better a vegan diet, will increase their psychic ability. Regarding why this may be the case is again connected to energy and vibration. There is a suggestion that animal products contain on various levels residual energy of the animal, and when you consume that product the energy is absorbed into your energetic matrix.

The theory is that because many animals are farmed in very poor conditions they experience constant, physical and emotional stress and fear, all of which are spiritually attributed to being the slower and most dense forms of emotional vibrations. When you absorb that flesh, the residual energy is absorbed into your own energy and this lowers your vibration.

As a medium, you, of course, want the highest and purest vibration possible to give you the best chance of being able to connect with spirits more strongly, and especially spirits from higher levels of the afterlife. This process could be seen as part of a natural karmic process. It is important to note that spirits in the afterlife, of course, do not consume negative forms of energy from eating meat and thus their vibration is not decreased.

The consumption of animals or plants or other things to absorb the energy is something done in many shamanistic cultures. In many cultures that believe in karmic forces, if you eat the meat of an animal, you also become a part of its karmic circle. Some cultures have practised this in a different way for good karmic purposes; they raise an animal full of love and care and then after it passes of natural causes, they consume the animal through which they believe they can absorb good energy instead of bad.

Further, it can be thought that through quantum entanglement, our interactions with anything may affect our energetic vibration. When you pass over, it is this vibration, regarding how pure and strong it is, that allows you to access higher or lower levels of heaven. This perhaps is a slightly less ethereal way of explaining the karmic process.

Through the process described, some mediums can get in touch and close to spirit, with clear and consistent two-way communication between them and the spirit worlds. Others remain more inconsistent, one-way channels. In many shamanistic cultures, it is more like the medium mentally lives in the spirit world. It can be very difficult for such persons to live ordinary lives. For myself, I have a decent control over how open I am at any given time, which is something I make sure of through the way I approach meditation and mediumship practice. I have seen how being open all the time can lead to too much disassociation, to hallucinations and loss of a grasp of what is real and what isn't.

I have also seen such effects happen to persons attempting to use psychedelics to promote psychic experiences and potentially strengthen their psychic senses, and it would appear that those who are innately more psychic are more prone to such adverse effects through using psychedelic substances.

SIX

The Endless Miracle of Life

....

Spirits talking about the future and psychic predictions

Mediums are not all-knowing and all-powerful; this is one reason we don't have an unlimited supply of lotto numbers. For most mediums, getting a single door number correct is extremely challenging, let alone six or more correct numbers. It's not impossible for the very top calibre medium, but for myself, my motivations are not money.

I've never taken the time to try and get the lotto numbers psychically from the infinite, Great Spirit or God, whichever you wish to call it, or asked spirits on the other side for such information. It would not be an easy thing to do, and would require a good amount of time and effort, and aside from not feeling very motivated to do this, I have so much else to do in my work and also, life outside my work.

There are other more important things I simply need to be doing instead. Right now, I wouldn't even have the time to stop and put energy into such an endeavour. I also try to let my actions be guided based on my link to the infinite consciousness. So far, I've not been guided to take several months off to get the lotto numbers.

For spirits to give me the numbers, there would also have to be a good reason that wasn't materialistic and there would likely need to be no other way for me to get the money for that purpose.

Spirits might also need to believe that only good would be done with all of the money if it were given in that manner. It might well be that other talented mediums on Earth today, who are capable of such feats of mediumship, feel a similar way and find themselves in a similar position.

Writing about the Lotto then is to emphasize that mediumship is *not* about fortune telling. The spirits do talk about the future sometimes, and they will talk about it when asked, but they too are not all-knowing, and may not know exactly how an event will turn out or when someone may meet the love of their life. The spirits have to get the information in the same way that a psychic would, by sensing it from the universal infinite consciousness, Great Spirit, God, again, whatever you may wish to call it.

Psychic predictions from a psychic are not something that is necessarily set in stone. You may have heard of psychic predictions also called "psychic forecasts". This is because they are more like a forecast than anything else. These are not too different than a weather forecast, where a person can take into account various pieces of information and relate this to the weather and estimate this is how things will likely come together.

It is the same with psychic forecasts. If asked to do one, I connect to the infinite; that is something that is not difficult to do, as the infinite is every vibration including my own, so I use my vibration as a way to make the connection. I don't use the normal link-up process that I do for doing mediumistic readings, I simply sit there and turn my mind first inwards and to my vibration and from there out towards the universe, and then specifically the energy related to the topic and sense things and see things based on that energy. From there, I would make a prediction on how things are likely to pan out. However, I may have missed something or not taken something into account enough.

Sometimes, just like the weather, certain information or combinations of information, lead to a clearer picture. It can be 50 percent chance of rain or 100 percent chance of rain. It can be 50 percent chance you will meet your next love interest next month or a 100 percent chance. The better the psychic, the better chance they have of getting things bang on.

This process as a whole, connecting to the infinite and getting information from it, is actually not too hard to learn to do. It is easier than learning how to connect with spirit and easier than developing mediumistic ability. The spirit people are, of course, better at doing this than psychics. They are not hindered, in any way, by the physical body and because of this, are of a higher vibration and the higher you go, the easier it is to connect with the infinite in this way. However, again they can only work with what they can work with. Sometimes spirit will say, something like, at this point it's not clear enough yet for them to confidently comment on the matter, and may point to a possible later time.

That being said, it is important to note, that sometimes a psychic can connect to the infinite and understand much from it, and it can be very clear and sometimes, the spirit communicating can know a lot, and it too can be very clear. Just as prophets of old and shamans could seemingly, at times, predict very specific happenings, this is still very possible today.

For instance, a lady once asked me about her missing husband. He had been gone for many months, and nobody knew if he was ok or what was happening. I asked the spirit world, and they indicated to me that he would return home in two days' time, the date of which was Wednesday. Naturally, I had to be very careful with this. I didn't want to tell this woman who is full of grief, that her husband would return home next Wednesday, and he doesn't. So, I explained my feelings on the matter and told her I can't be 100 percent sure, etc. Thursday, I received an email from her saying her husband returned home Wednesday evening.

Many times, I have connected to the infinite regarding something with myself and received a clear and very concrete answer. Likewise, I have at times, asked spirits for information relating to future events, and it has been given. When the spirit world does give information relating to future events, they must also be careful what they say; they don't wish to cause negative effects. For example, I was doing a demonstration, and I went to a lady in the audience and the communication was coming through very clear from the spirits communicating to her. She was able to understand everything I said during the reading, except for a date and a name that I thought was connected to a place of importance. A big part of the message related to this lady's father's health and that message was those in heaven were looking out for him.

Many months later, I received a message from this lady via email. In this email, she thanked me for the reading and said she now knew the significance of the two pieces of information she was given at the time. She explained that sometime after the reading her father's condition had gotten worse, and he had to go into care. The family subsequently selected a nursing home for him to live in and receive the care he needed. The lady who was writing this email to me was not involved in the selection process, nor had she told her family about the information in the reading that she couldn't make sense of at the time. The name of the nursing home matched the name I mentioned in her reading. Further, her father eventually passed away, several months later, on the date I mentioned in the reading.

This shows the spirits communicating knew this information but did not wish to divulge the full significance because it could potentially be disturbing to the family at that time. However, putting it over as they did brought the family much comfort, as the lady mentioned to me in the email that this proved to them that the spirits, who communicated, really were looking out for him, and would have been there to welcome him to heaven.

Something I'm often asked, related to this is, do I ever hold back or censor information? The answer is, I don't normally even need to think about having to because the spirit communicating knows what to say, how to say it and when to say it. Sometimes, I need to be mindful that they may have accidentally passed information to me that they didn't mean to. As I have discussed, once that link is strong, whatever goes through their mind at any level, potentially comes through to me.

In such cases, I will discuss the information with the spirits communicating and work out if they want to pass the information on as it came through to me and if so, how potentially to best word things so that there is no negative impact on the person receiving the reading. This can mean a little bit of appropriate censorship as not to cause offence to the recipient, or if it is a public demonstration any audience members.

Sometimes, the way we think things can be more blunt than how we say them. This is no different in the afterlife. Again, it can also involve wording something in a way that, at the time, the person receiving the information doesn't fully understand or comprehend, but when it happens they will know that is exactly what I was talking about.

This is a delicate thing to do, and requires a sensitive and understanding person and ideally someone with a good knowledge of certain psychological processes and factors and a good amount of experience with giving readings.

Destiny and free will

Whenever this topic is discussed, it always leads to the questions, do we have free will or don't we? And if we don't have free will, do we have a destiny? This can sometimes be very important to bereaved persons whose loved ones passed away from an accident, or in cases where a loved one was killed by another person or took their own life. Some people even want an answer to this question when their loved one passed from natural causes.

From my perspective, the answer is we do have free will, and we also have a destiny. Things will always end up how they will end up, but we also have free will. To explain my thoughts further, I must first explain my take on the creation of this universe, which can be referred to as the physical dimension and the creation of all other dimensions. Whilst this perspective is more philosophical, than scientific, many of my points are connected to certain scientific understandings.

The creation of the physical universe and more

The general perspective from mainstream areas of science is that the universe is made from smaller and smaller things. When we say that very small things make up the universe, many people's minds refer immediately to subatomic particles, but a question arises, well, what are they made of? One could say smaller particles, but then what are those made of? Even smaller particles again? But, what are those made of?

A modern theory known as "String Theory" suggests the answer might perhaps be vibrating strings of energy, but then the question is what are the strings made of or where did they come from?

Yes, answers have been proposed, but then the question is where did that next thing come from? So, this goes on with science seeking to find the next smaller item that stacks up to form the universe and how these may relate to the world and link together to each other, etc. And it goes round and round, forever stuck in the thought of something can't be made of nothing. Whatever the smallest particle is that we find, it has to be made of something smaller. It seems in mainstream scientific thinking there is likely no way something can come from nothing.

We can relate this all the way back to the energy that created our universe. The Big Bang Theory suggests an unfathomable amount of energy exploded and expanded out to create our physical universe. But what created the energy that created our universe? So, round and round we go, again. That is unless nothing is actually everything. You may say, Ross, how can nothing be everything?

Let me start by saying I feel that we have to completely redefine several words in the English language. To explain, let me discuss what there would theoretically be at a point before the Big Bang if there was no energy, in the form of the frequency of matter and no energy had changed form in any way and there was just a void. What we would have is a point that was outside space-time, and from standard thought an eternal endless nothingness.

We typically look at a void as being something that is completely empty: the ultimate extreme of nothing. However, I suggest we are entirely incorrect to do so. It is actually a void where all creation is possible. It's not a nothingness. It's an infinite potential, and an infinite everythingness.

A void would be the only true thing outside space-time as we know it, and modern thinking would suggest, if you are completely outside space-time there is no beginning, and there is no end, just an infinite now; an infinite, all encompassing moment. So what does that leave? Possibility, infinite possibility.

So this great big nothing, which is a void, actually, in my thoughts, would contain an infinite number of every type of particles in potential form. I'm also not alone on this thought. Many scientifically minded individuals think exactly the same. Science also now knows nothing does not exist, and there is no such thing as a complete vacuum in our physical universe, that space is an illusion, as space always contains something, it always contains a substance, a manifestation of energy, a possibility.

That possibility I propose is actually what pure energy is. This pure energy, being pure possibility is by nature, infinite information. From my perspective and many others, consciousness is information stored in energy, so this pure possibility, this pure energy, is also an infinite consciousness. Therefore, this universe and all other dimensions are one large infinite ever-changing possibility, which are infinite manifestations of energy and consciousness.

What is God?

This takes us away from something being made of nothing because with the theory that I am suggesting, nothing has become something. In fact, it has become everything. What we see as nothingness is actually everythingness and the key to everything.

A void state is an infinite power of creation, which we can come closest to wording as pure energy and information/consciousness or what some refer to as God or The Great Spirit, etc. I propose nothing doesn't exist and what we mistakenly see as nothing, actually holds the key potential for the existence of everything.

We exist because nothing holds all properties to life, as we know it, and beyond. The nothing we have created is a lie, born from the limited perspective of humankind. A world that the typical human mind has become trapped by, one that has led them to believe a state that doesn't exist. This is modern Humankind, who struggles to try to comprehend the infinite in any form.

Now, what I have just explained to you is not something new, the way I have worded it, may well be considered new and fresh or modern, but nearly all cultures that believed in an afterlife believe what I have just said. They just have different ways of wording it, which are more ethereal.

The way I see a void is the very same core properties cultures attributed to God – God is outside space-time and thus has no beginning and no end, just like a void. The void is pure possibility and energy, and we know from a branch of physics called "Thermodynamics", that energy cannot be created or destroyed. It can only change forms. God cannot be created or destroyed. Everything is made of that possibility/pure energy; God is everything and everywhere.

In any religion that has a supreme deity, the deity has these properties. To me, ancient prophets tried to explain exactly what I just did but to very simple people who had a very limited understanding of the universe and its workings.

Today, there is just enough general understanding to explain this in the way I have, and a lot of individuals can understand it. This God is, of course, not a man with a beard sitting on a cloud. It's an infinite flux of energy and information that we are a part of, just as it has been said in many old religions that God is within all of us and we are a part of God.

The God on a cloud is something created due to the limited perspective of humankind. In whatever way one might try to comprehend God, God is greater than we could ever fully comprehend. We can't comprehend the infinite, as we are just one infinitesimally small part of it.

I have often said, humans trying to totally comprehend and grasp the infinite, are like humans trying to go to the moon with a horse and cart. With our limited means, we are trying to grasp something far beyond us.

In this perspective, it is important to remember there was never a nothing. Nothing does not exist. There is just pure possibility, pure potential that humans now call energy. Our physical universe is just one of the manifestations of possibility and the heavens we go to when we pass, are others. We are now within the manifestation of the void, the pure possibility infinitely changing, which is why I suggest, even at the quantum level, time, as we perceive it, still moves forward because change is forever happening.

Information is interacting with other forms of information that produce that constant change, and it is that change that we call time. We are a part of that change, and we are within the void, within God, and a part of the void and a part of God. The void that houses an infinite amount of dimensions and each dimension naturally has different properties from the next.

The collective consciousness formed by the infinite information within the void, within God, remains at the base level outside of time and space, as does a part of all our consciousness. Specifically, a part of our subconscious that is all linked together to each other, potentially through quantum entanglement. This collective consciousness of the human race forms part of the overall collective infinite consciousness.

This part of the concept is in some ways similar to the thoughts of Jung, (1936) with his collective unconscious theory that suggested there is a collective subconscious mind shared among beings of the same species on a universal scale. Really, at the most basic level everything is happening in one eternal now. We just are an infinitesimally small speck of the infinite.

We can't perceive infinite change with our minds, so we are stuck with this limited perception measuring our existence and time by how fast change appears to happen to us, and around us. When in reality, all the changes that will happen to us, are happening in one eternal moment, one eternal now.

This is something you could say only the infinite flux of consciousness that is God could perceive and comprehend in totality.

More on destiny and psychic prediction

This infinite consciousness that is outside time and space is what a psychic connects to, and spirits connect to, in order to sense information regarding the future. The future that is determined by our free will. The choices we make every second of every day.

If a psychic or spirit does see the future clearly, what he or she sees will come to pass. This is because the psychic or spirit is seeing an event that is destined to happen based on the choices we will make leading up to the events that will happen at that time.

At that point of change, it occurs to us within our perception as an event in our future. For all intents and purposes it is our future, it is a point of change that in our space-time, our change-time, has not yet occurred. However, often it is not so clear and the further into the future something is, generally the less clear the vision or feelings will be, and, hence, it remains a lot like a forecast based on what the medium or spirit can see and sense.

For example, let's say Mr. Psychic keeps getting clear visions of his wife dying in a certain way, so he makes some conscious decisions to avoid her passing based on what he sees. What could happen is that the decisions he makes to try to avoid it will end up causing her passing.

He was always going to see what he saw and based on decisions he and others had already made the events he saw would happen. He had the free will to decide what he was going to do, but it was always going to end up the way he saw it would, no matter what, as he saw how his decisions and others would pan out.

In this way, nothing is by chance. It is all a number of decisions that lead to an outcome. Accidents technically don't happen. It's all an outcome based on decisions made.

So a plane crash is destined to happen, and the persons who pass over from the plane crash were destined to pass over from the crash, but it was destined this way because of the free will decisions people made to be on the plane and decisions in conjunction to any natural phenomena that led to the plane crashing, ie., a lightning bolt hitting the plane.

It's important to note that when a medium relates to spirits guiding us, spirits only try to make us have certain thoughts, see things, or experience things that will make our decisions clearer and better. They do not affect our free will. They can be a part of a process to get us to make a right decision, to guide us to do good things, but they have no power to change what will happen.

They either get involved and are part of the process that leads to a happening or they don't get involved and are not. They are just a part of the free will decision-making process that will lead to the future that psychics and spirits may sometimes get information on.

This process is not to be confused with déjà vu; that relates to certain processes of the brain being out of sync which cause you to specifically feel familiar with the event you are in, as discussed by Brown, (2004). Although, some mystics have connected the déjà vu phenomena to the subconscious mind's connection to the infinite. What I can say is when I have had experiences of seeing events before they happen, I have literally seen the event clearly in my mind, and then later find myself in it. It is a very odd experience indeed.

The theory of God, the creation of the universe and our existence that is discussed in this chapter, however it is worded, I feel, explains everything we already know and don't know. This is a theory that makes everything make sense. For instance, I'm not saying our modern conception of relativity or reality, is wrong. I'm saying it's just one piece of the infinite puzzle we have. It is an observation of something in a particular dimension that is a particular frequency range of the whole at a particular point in change, or space-time as we often call it.

The infinite and God, overall, is something that most of science will likely always find hard to grasp as it struggles with the concept of energy not being able to be created or destroyed. How can something have always been? And how can it not be destroyed? How can something possibly have such properties?

To reiterate the answer I have proposed, is that energy that makes up everything in our universe and beyond is, at the basic level, pure possibility/potential. Think about it, you can't create possibility/potential, it is always there, and you can't destroy possibility. For example, even if I were to burn a wooden box, what I'm doing is changing the manifestation of the possibility/potential that is the wooden box. What is formed from the burning of the box, are other forms of possibility/potential. In destroying a possibility/potential I have only really changed it to others. Heat energy, for instance, is one that emerges, and that heat energy will change again into other manifestations of possibility/potential.

Possibility and words related to it, like potential, are the only words we have in the English language that could be said to have the same properties as energy and the properties of God. I suggest they are all one in the same. Similarly, we should be calling energy and all things as a manifestation of infinite possibility/potential, and recognizing that this is the base substance of existence.

The issue is that we will never be able to measure infinity with our minds, only with our hearts, often with the aid of meditation and you have to go outside the bubble of the perception we have created to comprehend that nothing does not exist; only pure possibility and that is the endless miracle of life.

Thermodynamics demonstrates energy cannot be created or destroyed. It can only change forms. In my opinion, this also has a strong relation to the Orch-OR theory and the possibility of an eternal quantum soul. As it means that the energy that forms the quantum consciousness, proposed in Orch-OR, can never be destroyed. Therefore, when the body dies, and it can no longer function through the energetic matrix and biological system of the body, it is released, no different than the heat energy from the burnt box I mentioned.

So, that energy would do what energy has to do, continue to exist and continue to evolve and change. Providing that the information in the energy remains intact and not dispersed it would be an eternally existing individual consciousness always experiencing the endless miracle of possibility/potential – an eternal quantum soul in the endless miracle of life.

SEVEN

Deeper Still

. . . .

The difference between a ghost and a spirit

Moving on, what has surprised me is that many people do not know the difference between a ghost and a spirit. Spiritualists and those who investigate what is considered "paranormal phenomena" generally have an understanding that both ghosts and spirits exist, but they are quite different entities.

A spirit is an energy that contains the fully conscious soul of a person. You are a spirit, here and now, and when your physical body dies your spirit is what moves on into the afterlife. A medium communicates with the spirit of the person who has passed over. A ghost is like a residual energetic impression that is left behind in the energetic matrix of physical matter.

It is often related to being caused by strong emotions expressed by a person in that space or potentially by a person repeating the same action over and over again in that space. This is commonly referred to as the "Stone Tape Theory" on ghosts. This was first put forward in the West by Lethbridge, (1961). In this way, there is a bit of a ghost of us everywhere we have been.

Mediums can connect psychically to this energy. I could walk into a building and connect to the energy within that building and tell you things that happened in the building from the past. I would be picking up on the energetic imprint that is left behind. Some imprints, for the reasons just mentioned, are stronger than others.

Hollywood has been keen to relate to ghosts as a spirit of a person who has not moved over to heaven or some sort of afterlife away from Earth. This is simply not true. A spirit, who has not moved over to heaven and stays around Earth and this physical dimension, would be classified as just exactly that. A medium can't form a two-way communication with a ghost, ask it questions, and get replies, etc., as it does not have a human level of consciousness. It is like a picture or a film of something that was once there, one that a medium can also pick up feelings from as well.

A medium can, of course, communicate with a spirit, ask it questions and receive answers back, etc. Other cultures have different names for different energetic entities, which can translate to mean various things in English. Often the language is so different and the closest word in English may be ghost, but it doesn't mean what the other people mean as exactly what we think of a ghost as being. From my perspective, the way I have described is the best way to define, separate and categorize these two very different entities.

Why do some people who meditate, and religions that practise meditation regularly, not communicate with spirits or possibly not believe in a heaven?

Another question I'm regularly asked is, why do some cultures and religious followers who also practise meditation on a regular basis not believe in heaven? Well, firstly it's important to highlight that meditation can be practised secularly, with no spiritual or religious connection.

As for religions who practise meditation regularly, but do not believe in an afterlife, or do not experience the presence of spirit around them, I would suggest it is related to the mind not being open to it, and their thought processes in their practices only focusing on one aspect of existence or several aspects that do not include heaven and discarnate human spirits.

Through this, they blot out the other frequencies of energy and life and are not aware of them. For instance, with certain schools of Buddhism, they are interested in getting to the state that they believe is beyond the illusions of the mind to a place of no self, where the ego is no longer there, and there is just a simple awareness. For example, if the frequencies of life were one to a hundred, they are tuning into frequency one, the most basic aspect of our spirit and consciousness. Frequencies two to a hundred contain all the aspects of our personality and self that also survive physical death.

In such philosophies, there is often a lack of description on what exactly happens to the energy of souls between lives, and some, like Tibetan Buddhists, even reference a stage in-between lives known as the "Bardo", where a spirit will have certain experiences before they reincarnate.

Ultimately, they don't seem to have a conclusive perspective on how long the Bardo lasts, and everything that may occur during it. I would be intrigued to know if the Dalai Lama would, in any way, be open to the Bardo involving a heavenly experience, or if it is possible to contact spirits who are going through the Bardo.

In some ways, Tibetan Buddhism, other schools of Buddhism and my thoughts and experiences related to many aspects of existence, are quite similar and potentially would need very little crossover to fit completely.

For instance, in Tibetan Buddhism when the time comes for the Dalai Lama to pass away, he follows a practice that allows him to choose not to go through the Bardo and to reincarnate immediately. Lamas then consult the seer of Tibet, who spiritually receives information related to the location of the reincarnated soul of the Dalai Lama.

In the past, Lamas would sit by a specific lake and receive visions that would guide them to the Dalai Lama. This sounds very much like psychic practice to me. The soul is then found, and he is taken to the monastery to begin his studies to enable him to actualize his soul's potential again. His personality is also suggested to be the same each time around, which infers to me he is bringing back with him his personality contained within his quantum soul.

Conversely, it is also important to note that mediums will practise meditations that these other religions do not, meditations that are specifically designed to help you connect to spirit. These meditations are not like the ones that help you get to other aspects of reality, like a state of pure egoless, awareness, etc.

Reincarnation

As for reincarnation, it is by far the most argued topic in spiritualism with many persons wanting to believe one reality or another, often without any real logical thinking. It certainly doesn't help that many cultures and religions have such different takes on the potential process.

As for my personal thoughts and understanding, let me first mention a point that isn't often raised which is that any person who believes in trance mediumship or possession should also believe reincarnation is, at the very least, possible. Because technically, such things are a form of reincarnation but are never really related to being such. However, the fact is standard possession is a discarnate spirit, reincarnated in a physical body for a limited space of time.

If that is possible, it is a strong indication that a spirit could also do this to a physical form that doesn't also currently house a spirit and then remain in the body or be stuck in that body until the death of that physical form. Of course, that doesn't mean a disembodied spirit would want to do it or that it occurs at all.

Personally, I have never consciously recollected any previous lives, but there are some who apparently have. The majority of stories I've read about or heard of where a person seems to have remembered a past life, the phenomena itself occurred during childhood. Often, these children forget the information as they get older, but some seem to retain it.

Some researchers like Ian Stevenson have gone to great lengths to research if the information these people relate about their past life is, in any way, true and has seemingly found results that could indicate the phenomena occurs. Stevenson, (1980) published an interesting book based on some of his research entitled *Twenty cases suggestive of reincarnation*. Stevenson, (1987) published a further book of interest entitled *Children who remember past lives*.

When it comes to academic studies, there are not many that support reincarnation. I have used hypnosis techniques to induce people into potential past life regressions and found the same results as most academic studies that have taken place. The reincarnation experience always follows the belief system and expectation of the person. As does any reincarnation attempt to regress people to remember a potential life in the afterlife between incarnations.

Also, when academic researchers look into if the information conveyed during the regression has any bearing on real events that took place and a real person's life, they often are found not to have any truth. This has also been the case when I have regressed people and researched the information conveyed.

That doesn't mean though that it doesn't ever happen. It could also mean the memories are lost, or the subjects were not able to go deep enough to access the memories. It could be the regression process used is not adequate to take the client deep enough to access past life memories. Further, I feel that the participants in the studies I've read could have been better selected to potentially produce more fruitful results.

I suppose within spirituality, reincarnation could be considered one of the most controversial topics. It is certainly the one that often stirs up the most debate. The main problem, even with stories of reincarnation that appear to be genuine, is that you would never be able to know for sure if the person was recalling their own memories or had psychically received information about another person's life. Perhaps persons are receiving that information through their connection to the infinite, and they are confusing this information as their own memories. I could see this happening very easily to a child.

With mediumship, there are a number of phenomena that suggest the mediums are very likely getting information from an individual consciousness, such as unassisted and spontaneous ADCs (after death communications) that happen to regular people, the out-of-body experience (OBE), physical mediumship phenomena and the medium's subjective suggestion that the process of connecting to and receiving information from the infinite and connecting with an individual spirit is a very different experience.

There is none of this extra phenomena or information to help offer more validation or understanding to potential past life recall. Indeed, I could connect to the infinite and acquire information about any person's life, past, present or future. Therefore, it could be happening with these people.

Overall, I've also never heard a theory of reincarnation that appears to make total sense with our perception of life from our experiences here, and often there are many holes in the theories when they are connected with other understandings we have of the afterlife and the survival of individual consciousness through various forms of mediumship or other cultures and religions, Spiritualism included.

For example, some may say you have to come back here to learn lessons you can't in the afterlife or people have no challenges over there, so they come back to be challenged and grow. Well, firstly if you can do everything there that you can here, that negates that thought right away. Without taking into account, if the afterlife is infinite, which by nature, it must be, there should be an infinite amount of things to do, learn, experience and challenges to face, should you wish to face them, that don't involve Earth or the physical dimension.

When you look at this world and how it is so full of pain and suffering, why anyone would choose certain forms of it and certain lives just doesn't make any sense to most. Whilst an argument can be made that we must go through pain and suffering to understand it, most would feel they go through enough pain to learn the lesson without having to experience certain worse awful things that happen in this world.

Most would not see sense in why some people also have such short lives. I also know the spirits say that when we get to heaven, we no longer have to do anything we don't ultimately want to do.

Further, it appears well demonstrated by science as discussed in Watson, (1930) that we are the people that we are because we are a product of the programming of our environment, our interactions with the world and potentially certain things that have been passed down through the evolution of the body and physical brain.

Even certain people who take extreme pleasure from inflicting pain are made to be that way, and it often starts with desensitization to violence in their childhood. We are not born evil or born a saint. We are born nearly a clean slate that is moulded by our life to come. Can we find deeper spirituality in our self? Of course, but that appears to happen through our experiences of life, spiritual or otherwise. The more we pursue spiritual growth, the more we will get it. Some people's experiences lead them towards what we see as the light and some to the dark.

From my phenomenological experience, certain spirits I've communicated with seemingly have related to either themselves or the client having a past life. But it might be I, or the recipient has misinterpreted the information. There is no way definitively to prove it was that person's life. Ultimately, if I were to say to you, I believe in any form of reincarnation, it would be a thought that is a hundred times less grounded than my thoughts on mediumship and consciousness surviving the process of physical death. For that reason, I'm not going to say I believe in it, or I don't.

Do animals go to Heaven?

Discussing the realities of mediumship communication and what mediums sense, often leads into something I get asked very often, and it certainly does appear to be something that many people think of and worry about. That is, do animals go to heaven?

There has been much less scientific study to highlight the potential for this, but what I can tell you is, yes they do. I can't recall any medium, from any culture I have interacted with or read about suggesting that animals do not go to heaven. This appears to go for all forms of life including birds, fish, and reptiles. I have done many readings where animals of all kinds have been brought to the room with the help of human communicators during the reading process; everything from dogs and cats to ducks, donkeys, lizards, goldfish, rabbits, buffalos, parrots, horses; the lot.

I often then get asked, well, do they still eat each other? The answer to that is an emphatic no. Animals kill for food not pleasure; without a physical body, they do not become hungry and thus have no desire to eat food. It never comes into their consciousness to kill or harm another animal for that purpose anymore.

Further, if they would try to cause physical harm by say clawing another animal, the energetic body of that animal would just instantly revert to its untouched, undamaged state.

Overall, it appears that animal consciousness survives the process of physical death and continues to live on in a form of a mental body in heaven. Again, when relating this in any form to science, I'd refer to Orch-OR theory, in that providing microtubules are key to quantum consciousness. If any life form has microtubules and can support a certain level of consciousness and quantum vibrations, then it is likely they will have a quantum soul at least equivalent to their earthly capabilities, which has all the potential to survive the death of the physical body, just as with humans.

A dog's consciousness may not be as evolved as ours. However, it still has all it needs to continue as a dog in the afterlife. It appears these animals can reside in the same vibration in heaven, as the average person goes to when they pass. This means when we get over to heaven, we will be reunited with animals we have loved here. In the meantime, our loved ones and ancestors who have passed before us look after these animals. Of course, since they don't need to be fed anymore, the job is easier!

I would like to share with you now Jessica's story, which demonstrates that most assuredly, animals do go to heaven.

Jessica

"As I'm writing this it has been a year to the day since I went to Ross for a reading. When I went to see him, I thought what I was looking for was quite unusual but after the reading and talking to Ross about it, I now know that it is more prevalent than I would have thought.

I had never been close to any person who has passed. My mother's grandparents are still on Earth, as are my mother and father. The only people I have ever met that passed away are my father's parents, my paternal grandparents. They died in a car accident when I was three, so I don't have any strong memories of them.

However, my best friend in the world was my dog, Peter. He was a golden Labrador who I loved with all my heart. I got him when we relocated from South Africa, I was ten at the time, I'm now 25. It was a very difficult time for me, but Peter was there through everything and provided me with companionship and friendship. He was such a gentle dog. He never barked at anyone ever. You could have stood on his tail, and he would just look at you with his big brown eyes as if to simply say, why are you on my tail?

One day, around eight months before I went to see Ross, I went outside to call him in, but on that day, Peter never came to my call. He always came to my call. He would run from wherever he was at full pace. I immediately knew something was wrong. My heart sank. It felt like it had been weighed down by an anchor and physically hurt. I started by going to all the usual spots he liked to hang out, and he was not there. I started to shout his name out louder and louder, but again he did not appear.

I ran as fast as I could to look out in the road fearing that he had wandered on to it and been hit by a car, but again there was no sign of him. I searched up and down the cul-de-sac, looked in the front gardens of the houses; he wasn't there. I went back to our house and searched everywhere in and around our home, and again he was nowhere to be found. I sat on our front doorstep calling him for another twenty minutes. It felt like twenty hours.

I got up and decided to knock on the doors of the other houses in the cul-de-sac, and ask to see if, for some reason, he was inside. I knocked on every door. Nine answered, and all said he was not there. I went back again to our house and by this time, I thought whatever had happened must be bad.

Hours turned to days. Every time our house phone would ring, I would run to get it but two more days had gone by, and we hadn't heard a thing. The fourth day, I was at home by myself and the phone rang. I rushed to answer and on the phone a male's voice said, "Hello, I'm wondering if your dog is missing?" I frantically said, "Yes, yes that is right! My Peter, a golden Labrador!" My heart was racing, my emotions on edge, then I heard his tone of voice change sombre, as he said, "I'm sorry, miss. I own a farm and today I found your dog buried on my land."

Tears began streaming down my cheeks as I found it hard to acknowledge what I had heard. He asked where I lived. I just about managed to mumble the words out. He then asked if I would like to collect him. I replied with an emotionally muffled, "Umm hmm, please, thank you." He told me his address; as I wrote it down on the piece of paper two teardrops fell onto the paper, a bigger one and a smaller one. The farmer instructed that I could come anytime that day to collect Peter.

I wanted to go right away, but I waited for my mother to come home. She was due to be home in a matter of minutes. When she got in, I met her at the door and told her the news, as I cried in her arms. I had by this point, found where the farm was located, some twenty minutes drive from our house. We got into my mother's car and headed for the farm.

On the way, I remember thinking, how he could have gotten so far away? And why would someone bury him on someone else's land? Had someone taken him and harmed him? As I looked at the piece of paper that had the address on it, I looked at the tearstains and thought how they symbolically represented Peter and me.

We arrived at the farm, and the farmer was out in the front of the farmhouse. We said we are here for the dog. He replied, "Yeah, I thought it must be you." It's all so very vivid in my mind still. He explained that he found him in a corner of his land. He noticed the earth had been dug up, and he inspected it to find our dog buried. He took us round to the side of a barn and wrapped up in a blanket was the body of Peter. The farmer explained he was buried in the blanket. He offered to pick him up and take him to our car. The farmer put Peter's body in the back of our car, and we left.

Late that afternoon the veterinarian came over and informed us upon inspecting Peter's body that his leg had been broken, and it appeared his neck had been broken by a forcible impact. Being hit by a car could have caused that, but he couldn't say for sure. This information offered little help to my grief. Later that evening, we buried him, still in the blanket, in a spot under a tree where he often liked to sit.

———

When I contacted Ross, I told him I wanted a mediumistic reading but not what for. I decided I wanted to travel to see him in person even though he was in another country from where I was living at the time. My friend had originally told me about Ross, she had lost her brother to cancer, and she was originally told by a friend of hers, who had a Skype reading with Ross, that he must be one of the best mental mediums on earth today, if not the best.

A year ago, my friend travelled from the country she was living in at the time to see Ross in person for a reading because she felt she would prefer an in-person reading, and I felt the same. My friend told me all about her experience, and I was blown away by the information Ross gave her. So, I couldn't wait to arrive at Ross' door and get the answers and closure I was seeking.

When I finally arrived, he was very welcoming, as were his friends. As I sat in the room waiting for him to come in and begin the reading, I felt nervous but also, there was lightness in my heart that hadn't been there since Peter disappeared. I think it was the hope that I would receive answers to Peter's passing and that he may still be living on in heaven and he didn't cease to exist altogether. As I sat there, those thoughts lifted my heart. Ross soon entered the room, and the reading began. He started by saying there were three males and a female there with us in the room, that one of the males and one of the females had both passed suddenly. I replied by saying I know who they could be. It was clear this must be my paternal grandparents. I told Ross I knew who these people were, but they passed when I was very young.

Ross said that my grandparents were still very much in love in the afterlife, and they had been around me, visiting me since they had passed over. Also, that they were really interested in giving me some advice about my future but that I had come with a question that needed to be answered first.

Ross asked if I knew what they were referring to and I said, "Yes, I know exactly what they mean. Could you ask my grandparents if they know what happened to Peter?" Ross said, "I will converse with them and see what they have to say."

I couldn't hold back the tears any longer. They came pouring out of me, as the grief came to the surface. Ross took, what seemed a while to reply, but perhaps only a minute and then said to me, that he was seeing a dog. I smiled, and nodded, I said, "Yes, Peter is a dog."

There was no way Ross would have known Peter was a dog. Naturally, one would think when asked about a Peter that they were asking about a person rather than a dog. This convinced me that Ross really can speak to spirits. He continued to say that Peter got hit by a car and the person who hit him took him away from the area.

He asked me if the body was found, and I said, "Yes it was." Ross replied, saying based on the images it must have been buried at some point before it was found, "Did I know about this?" I replied saying, "Yes, I did." He said he believes Peter was hit by a car and the driver decided to remove him from the road and then bury him in what looks to be a field, with farmland around. Again, I acknowledged to Ross this was correct.

Ross continued and asked if I knew and remembered the name of the farm? I said I did. He then told me the name of the farm, the burrow the farm is in, and the postal code of the farm, yes, and the whole address. You may be asking how I remembered the postcode? Well, I kept the piece of paper I wrote the farm's address on. It was in my handbag and had stayed in a pocket in the handbag since that day.

Occasionally, I would go into that pocket for something else and look at it and see the tear stains on it. Before I left the hotel, I had been looking at it and running my thumb over the tear stains. I was truly amazed; Ross could not have known the location where Peter's body was found.

He told me that my grandparents were looking after Peter for me and that Peter was happy on the other side and had formed friendships with other dogs of the family that had passed over before I was born.

Ross said that he didn't know many dog breeds, but he had been shown a Golden Labrador. My heart fluttered as he said this. Of course, this was my dog! This was my Peter! I remember looking at him as he continued to communicate with the spirits, and a puzzled looked came on his face, and he laughed. He then said, this may sound a bit odd, but I'm also being shown a jackal. I laughed out loud and confirmed to Ross that my paternal grandparents used to own a jackal.

They adopted him as a very small pup. It was a funny story because when people would visit their house they would get all sorts of funny reactions when people saw a jackal. Ross said he also saw a parrot, and I confirmed to him that the same grandparents also had a parrot.

Ross told me that my grandparents had brought Peter here today, and he could now feel Peter's energy next to him quite clearly. Ross said, "He has such a gentle energy. He must have been a very gentle dog." I confirmed that was the case.

I noticed the longer the reading went on, the more I was smiling. Ross told me that Peter visited me often and that my grandparents would bring him along to see me. This made me cry again, but they were happy tears, and I was smiling through them.

Ross mentioned he was getting the name, Winifred. This is my paternal grandmother's name. He said there was also the name, Johann. This is my paternal grandfather's name. I don't think I could have gotten anymore amazed than what I was before he mentioned these names, but this too was incredible.

My grandparents relayed a lot to me about the future and gave me some really sound advice that I have followed, and it has really helped me moving forward into my future.

Just before the reading finished, Ross said he had asked the other two males for their names and they had told him, Dawie and Hendrik. Unfortunately, I told Ross I didn't know who they might be. He asked them for more information on who they are, and he said they are older than my grandparents, perhaps a couple of generations more. They told Ross that they were watching over me from when I was a baby and had both become spirit helpers to me; basically spirits who try to help me in life whenever they can. They are often trying to guide me through my subconscious thoughts, Ross explained. They had come to tell me this, and also according to Ross, they were quite strong spirits and were there to help strengthen Peter's energy so Ross could sense him clearly at a point during the reading.

Ross finished by saying that he thinks they are both from my father's side of the family, as well as both being from the same generation. He said that both my grandparents wished me to pass on their love to my father and that they wanted him to know they love him very much and are always around him. Additionally, "that even though he doesn't believe in an afterlife, he talks to them sometimes, and they listen. Recently, he was thinking about a painting... mention this to him."

Ross carried on and said he was getting a name through, but it wasn't coming through clearly but it sounds like Andre, although he thinks it's not quite that. Andre is a part of the name maybe. I let Ross know that my father's name is Zandre. Again, I was amazed.

I asked Ross one last question before the reading finished, and that was if my grandfather could answer if a person needs to believe in a religion, be baptized or confess all sins in order to go to a heavenly afterlife? I asked this because my father had told me that his father would say if a person didn't believe in Jesus, they wouldn't go to heaven and if they weren't baptized, they wouldn't go to heaven.

Ross asked my grandfather and said that my grandfather had told him, whilst he used to feel this was the case, he found out that everyone naturally lives on after the death of the physical body and baptism has no effect on what stage of heaven you are allowed to enter.

It is only a ritual that can spread some good intention to the person, and also that the act of confession did not mean, all of a sudden all the wrong you had done never happened. It just suggested the person wanted to let go of the burden of their wrongdoing and at some level wished to change things.

Further, that whilst it is better than nothing, you could confess all you want, but it won't change where you naturally fit in the afterlife. It is ultimately about what is in your heart and soul. I was glad to hear this, as it was something I was always a little worried about, given I did not follow a specific religion, I had not been baptized, and I had done multiple things in my life that I regretted.

Ross explained to me that it is all about where your vibration fits and "higher-evolved spirits will forgive all your wrongdoings as they have control over their ego, access to forms of unconditional love and that they realize it is our experiences that have so much effect on who we are as a person.

Ultimately, it is suffering that causes wrongdoing, and it is a cycle of suffering that continues to create wrongdoing on Earth today. Most importantly, all humans have a chance of getting to such a place of understanding and forgiveness."

When I returned home, I shared the recording with my family. Both my father and mother were astounded by what Ross brought through. My father was always very skeptical about this sort of thing, but even he said that Ross must have been communicating with his mother and father. He had been thinking this week about a painting he found in the attic that belonged to his mother and that he couldn't get rid of it, even though it looks old and isn't really something he likes because it reminds him of her and she liked it so much.

I did some family tree research a few months after the reading and found out that Dawie and Hendrik are my great-great grandfather and great-great-uncle. How amazing to know our ancestors watch over us like this!

Our family has been totally changed by the reading. We now all talk to our loved ones in heaven on a more regular basis. My grief over Peter's passing has been healed, and now I know he is with me often and is happy.

Ross also taught me a meditation to help me to potentially feel the presence of Peter and my grandparents around me. He told me it wasn't guaranteed to work, but if I kept practising, it just may. When I sit down and meditate in this way, I ask if they can come and visit me and then I feel a tingling and some sort of presence next to me.

Sometimes, I put my hands out, and I can feel something in my palms as if my grandparents' hands or Peter's paws are in them. This world is a better place because Ross is in it. I'm sure he will go on to do bigger and bigger things to change this world. He truly is an Earth Angel.

EIGHT

Nothing Gets By Spirits

• • • • • • • • • • • • •

Other ways spirits let us know they are around us

Those we have loved who have passed over are desperate to let us know they are still very much alive in the heaven. They wish to talk to us, to explain they understand and hear our troubles, give us some advice and prove they are still very much alive.

In reality, they find it extremely difficult to let us know they are near. Far too many of us have no conscious realization that the afterlife even exists and often people are too distracted by living our physical life to be aware of spirit. Of course, those of us who have further developed this mediumistic awareness are often aware of spirits visiting us. Unfortunately, we are in a small minority.

In desperation to contact us our loved ones, who have passed over try and attract our attention, in some way, by affecting the physical world around us, in the hope, we will take notice. It is not easy for spirit to manipulate physical matter. The faster energetic vibration of the spirit world and the very lower vibration of the physical world are completely incompatible.

The spirit learns to lower their vibration and merge their energy, as much as possible with the matter to influence it with their mind in whatever way they are wishing. Once they learn the skill, then they can do several things. It is most commonly seen that they often affect electrical devices. This is often attributed to the spirit potentially manipulating the electromagnetic field of the object. Typical occurrences are turning lights on or off or getting a light to flicker or affecting a radio and television by turning them on or off or causing static.

Often, the very best way spirit can get the attention of the person is to move an object whilst the person is watching it.

An example from a client of mine

"I remember looking at my daughter's ball. It was over in the corner of the room. She had been playing with it that morning before she passed, which was only three days prior. As I sat down looking at it, to my astonishment, the ball rolled

its way over to me across the living room floor. The floor is completely even, and there was no way it could have moved on its own. I burst into tears and thanked Karina for showing me that she is still alive and was there with me at that time."

There are also many more not so common ways spirits try to let us know they are around and attempt to communicate with us. Some people have professed to receive phone calls from their loved ones who have passed over.

Parapsychologist C.E. Cooper, (2012) wrote an interesting book called *Telephone Calls from the Dead* regarding this phenomenon. If the cases are true, again, this can be a slice of Heaven Therapy, but certainly the phenomenon appears to be exceptionally rare.

Dreams are often also seen as a common way those in heaven can communicate with us. This is the way in all cultures I've come across who have spirit communication, and it is only in our modern culture where such a large number of people do not consciously believe in spirit communication through this means.

Academically, there have been many experiments on dreams and dream theory, especially regarding what dreams are and why we have them. To date, we are far from having a unanimous verdict on dreaming. What many suggest is that while we dream, our conscious mind drifts back, the subconscious mind comes more to the forefront and therefore, our experiences in dreams stem from information in our subconscious.

I agree with this, but suggest that as there is very little interference from our conscious mind that typically gets in the way of spirit communicating with us, spirits are able to project their thoughts into our minds much easier in dreams and because of this, it is quite common for them to try to communicate information while we dream. That being said, they still have to momentarily block out all the clutter from our subconscious, and that is a very difficult task.

Very often the information the spirit tries to convey appears to be distorted. This, dream communication itself, can at times be a slice of Heaven Therapy. It is, of course, far too inconsistent to be a real ongoing answer to bereavement and afterlife communication. This process of connecting to the afterlife does remain popular in many shamanistic cultures; for example, spirits communicating in dreams remains a very important part of Native American spirituality.

Do they watch us during more personal and intimate moments?

Something I'm commonly asked related to spirits visiting with us and their continual presence in our lives is do they watch us during certain personal and intimate moments like, when we are in the shower, having sex, etc.

Well, the answer to this is, no, they respect our privacy in the same way they would have when we were here, and just as my grandmother wouldn't want to watch me in the shower when she was here or watch me having sex, that doesn't change. They are not oblivious to us doing such things, just like we aren't oblivious to each other doing them. Nothing really gets by those in the afterlife who care about us and each good reading demonstrates this and confirms we don't have secrets from them.

Can mediums communicate with spirits when they don't speak the same language?

With this in mind, I would like to share with you another story that I feel demonstrates the points I have made in this chapter, and also demonstrates that communication between mediums and spirits who do not know the same language is very possible. This is also why spirits who don't know the same language in heaven are able to communicate with each other with ease.

Nana

"My name is Naruemon, but everyone calls me Nana. I'm originally from Thailand. Growing up in a culture that follows a particular branch of Buddhism that believes in a heaven and a hell, most people believe in the afterlife. This was particularly true for my family. I seemed to have a stronger sixth sense than other people.

Growing up, I often had dreams that would later come true. For example, I once dreamt about my granddad who had passed away over twenty years ago. I asked him why he had come to see me, and he replied, "I came to get your Nan." A few days after that, my Nan passed away suddenly; it was a huge shock to the family.

When I moved to the UK in 2005, I had never heard of a medium. To be honest, when my husband, Gary, told me about what they do, I was a bit skeptical! I did believe in spirits and the afterlife, but to believe that someone can talk to people in the afterlife? Well, it sounded like a joke to me at first. I thought what a shame that someone must earn their living by fooling other people. I wasn't keen on the concept at all.

Two years later, my beloved mum, who was not only my mother but also my friend, sadly passed away. I was so immeasurably devastated. Before she passed away, for a number of reasons, my relationship with her had faded. We were not as close as we once were. This brought me great sadness because we were once so very close.

When I heard she had passed away, I still had many questions that I wanted to ask her, questions about my life, life choices, our relationship and me.

With these questions burning away in my soul, I went deep into depression without having the answers. I was even tempted to harm myself so many times, but looking at my children's faces stopped me. One day, my husband said to me, "Why don't you go to see some mediums?" I replied to him that I don't believe in them, plus my mum cannot speak English; how would they understand each other?!My husband showed me some TV programmes on mediums, and slowly I began to feel a bit more open to it. However, I was far from convinced.

Overall, I was still not too keen to book a reading with just any medium. I wanted to see a famous one, who also had a great reputation. Time went by, and I just gave up, but one day, Gary came across Ross' book Earth Angel *while he was Googling spiritual books. He bought it on Kindle and couldn't put it down. He became very excited about how good Ross sounded. We visited Ross' Facebook page and Gary booked a reading for me.*

I kept putting it off for a year, and Ross was very good to me and kept his patience, even though I cancelled three times before I finally went to see him.

Waiting to see him I was nervous. My first impression, on seeing him, was he looks like an angel. He was even wearing white and had a big white smile He explained how the reading was going to work and that he would record the reading for me to keep as well.

He started by closing his eyes for a few seconds and then said he feels a female energy quite strong, and it feels like a mother figure to me. At that point, I thought hmmm, I posted on Facebook that my mother died, so this cannot prove that he is real yet. Then he said she is quite a big lady, had a very strong personality and did not hold back with giving her opinions on anything... I started to think well, this is not on Facebook and the person he described did sound exactly like my mother! But, I remembered I also have a godmother who passed, who also had a big body and I called her mum as well.

I asked Ross which one was with us in the room? He carried on and said he had been shown a river and a tree and asked if I understand what that meant? I said it was likely my biological mum. When she was young, she lived near a river and was always walking along it. Then, I thought my mother and godmother are related and lived in the same location. So, I still couldn't put my finger on which one it might be.

Ross continued, saying the lady with him kept showing him the tree and that she climbed up and sat in the tree. That was it! I burst out laughing, as this was certainly my biological mum. My mother had told me when I was a young child that when she was a kid, she was walking along the river one day, and she really needed to poop; it wasn't going to wait until she got home, so to avoid anyone seeing her she climbed a tree by the river to sit on it, and then she pooped from the tree down onto the ground!

I couldn't think of any way that Ross could have known that this was the story in our family about my mum, as it is only a few family members who know about this story. Of course, you don't normally think of girls climbing trees, so it was very surprising to hear that out of all the things Ross could have come out with at the start of the reading, he mentioned the lady with him showing him a tree on a river and climbing up to specifically sit in it. This was the inside story our family had about my mother. There was no way this could have been a shot in the dark or a coincidence.

My heart was inflated knowing that my mum was here communicating via Ross. As the reading continued, at one point, Ross pulled his sleeves up and started to laugh saying that my mum was shocked and not too happy to see so many tattoos. This was another validation to me. My mum was always really against tattoos of any kind. She didn't like them at all, and whilst she is probably now more accepting in heaven than when she was here she would have probably started to tell Ross off.

As Ross continued, he explained he was having a bit of trouble with telepathically getting some of the Thai names. I can understand this as many are quite unique and difficult to pronounce for English people. He eventually said the name Pim. At first, I couldn't connect that with anything, and then I realized it was my sister's new name. She had just changed her name to Pimrapat, Pim for short. Ross talked about her and all the things he said made perfect sense.

Ross then went quiet again, closed his eyes and began nodding his head and said repeatedly "Pam?!" "Pam?!" At that point, I almost fell off the chair. I didn't tell Ross anything about Pam, yet. As it is also an English name Ross thought it might be someone connected to my husband's side. He paused and said, "Whoever Pam is, your mum is not a fan."

Ross continued, saying that if she were still on Earth, she would have some choice words to tell Pam. She would tell her how she feels about her and certain actions, and nothing would have happened like this if my mum was still here. She was not happy, at all, with what Pam has been doing.

Tears came into my eyes, as I wish my mum were still here sorting this problem out, just as she had done with all the other problems our family had faced. However, I was very glad she could see what had been going on with Pam and the family. Pam's actions had been extreme and I was so comforted knowing my mother was offering us her support and had seen how Pam's actions had affected the family.

Ross went on to discuss many very personal things regarding my life; decisions I have made and my relationship with my mother, that have really helped me to move forward with my life and feel better again. What had hurt me was I always felt I was number one to my mother. However, I felt that this changed when I got married, moved to another country away from her and had more than one child, all of these against her wishes.

At one point, she even said that I'm not the same person, and I had gone stupid since I got married. This uneasy feeling between us had never been sorted out before she died. Before the reading, I was heartbroken thinking that my mum hates me.

However, Ross addressed all these areas in my life. He told me that my mother had told him that she now supports my decision to have more than one child and that she was watching over my children. Before she passed away, she had been so adamant with me not to have more than one child, so when Ross mentioned this, I was so surprised and so happy that she supported this.

Ross went on to say that my mother told him she had found it difficult to deal with the fact she had to let go of me somewhat and let me get on with my life. She still thought of me as her little girl and the one who was always so sensitive and always there for her. She wanted me to herself, even though she knew that was selfish and things couldn't be that way. It was hard for her to be at peace with it all and her ego at times got the better of her, but now she is at peace with it and feels sorry she didn't offer me more support with all these things when she was on Earth.

It was also interesting that Ross said amongst my mother's communication that he telepathically heard the word "nam". Nam in Thai is water. I was surprised when Ross brought this word up, but he explained the connection for that moment must have been at a strength where my mother's thought process came through more directly.

Thus, when my mother was thinking and showing Ross about living by and walking along by the water, the Thai word for water came to Ross. Further, when reflecting back on the reading, I can now understand why Ross said several times during the reading that my mother kept emphasizing the water and the river, which had so much significance. My mother's nickname, from when she was born, was the name of that very river. Though it didn't occur to me at the time.

Many things in Ross' reading proved to me that he is the real deal. I was skeptical about mediums. I am still skeptical of people who call themselves mediums, but I believe in Ross, one hundred percent with all my heart, mind and soul."

Nana's story demonstrates that communication between mediums and spirits who speak a different language to the medium is very possible. This is because our minds translate the information coming through in relation to our own experiences. Often, in such communications, the information is conveyed more through images, symbols and feelings than exact words.

Of course, foreign names are still very possible. I have been given countless foreign names where I had no knowledge of that name previously, including some African and Asian names that sound very odd to an English mind and sound very different to how they are spelled to a person who has no familiarity with the particular language. The stronger the connection, the clearer the name will come through to the medium. However, there is nothing stopping people in the afterlife from learning other languages they were not familiar with when they were here. I have come across this on many occasions.

One of the lovely things about this reading was the information that related to Nana's mother's story about pooping by the river and in the tree. It is not uncommon for such personal family stories to be brought up in a reading, no matter how obscure they are. These stories, of course, often have a humorous element to them, and it brings a nice bit of laughter to a reading.

I can think of many examples of this from my work. For instance, I can remember an African gentleman who had a reading and his grandmother was communicating, and she brought up playing hide and seek with this man when he was a child. The man confirmed he remembered this, and what I then saw was a set of images that represented the recipient as a child hiding in a basket full of clothes. When I relayed this to the recipient, he burst out laughing and said yes, when he was very young he was playing hide and seek with his grandmother, back in their country of origin.

One day, he was hiding in a basket of clothes, and someone had come to the door with some news of a family member needing help with something on their land. The recipient's sister, who was several years older, was due home in a few minutes, so his grandmother left to help this person, believing the sister would watch over the recipient until she returned home shortly.

It had been a very busy day, and his grandmother went off to help this person. She kept getting distracted by family and subsequently, forgot they were playing hide and seek. He stayed in the basket for two hours before he got out and realized his grandmother was no longer there, and there was no sign of anyone else.

His grandmother returned around five minutes later and asked him where his sister was and if she took good care of him. He reminded her that they were playing hide and seek and his sister must have gotten home, thought no one was home then left again while he remained in the basket for the last two hours thinking how this must be the best hiding place he had ever found. The story had been brought up often in the family since then.

⁓

It also doesn't need to be that the spirit communicating was personally involved in the story. For example, several years ago I was doing a set of readings for a production company who had organized some participants. I was given no information about them leading up to the day, only a basic facial picture for me to meditate on and pray with, to, hopefully, make the connection as strong as possible on the day.

Whilst I was in the process of reading one of the males, a communicator showed me the recipient as a young boy falling over on ice, and conveyed to me that there was a joke in the family about this. When I said this to the recipient, he burst out laughing and told me how he is a hockey player and when he first went ice-skating he was far from a natural.

In fact, he fell over within two seconds of being on the ice, and almost every time he went to visit his family they would bring this up and tease him about how could a professional hockey player be so bad when trying to ice skate for the first time? And that if he became a hockey player, it showed anything was possible! As no one, including the family would have ever believed he would become a hockey player because he was so bad at ice-skating the first time, compared to others who took to it with much more ease.

It was the biggest inside-joke in the family, he said. These types of stories come up often and provide definitive proof for the recipient. I have many stories of that specifically being the case. Ohhhh, so many stories and how I wish there was time to share them all with you!

To wrap up, what Nana's story demonstrated, as have the others, is nothing gets by those who care about us in the afterlife. Big things and small things, older things or things, hours or less, old. It is very common that spirits will bring up things to me that the recipient was discussing or did earlier that morning or even on the way to the reading and even things they thought when arriving at the location leading right up to when I start the reading.

Why do some spirits seem more capable of moving objects, etc.? And why do some people never have any paranormal experiences while others claim to have many?

I'm often asked why do some spirits seem more capable of moving objects, etc.? And why do some people never have any paranormal experiences while others claim to have many? I have found that it is more common for such activity to happen not long after a person passes away.

After a while, this activity seems to decrease and often comes to a stop. I suggest that it is the raw emotions of the bereaved individuals that help the spirits produce this activity. The raw energy is very much of a lower vibration. It's not very ethereal. It's not calm, it's not consistent, but raw, and vibrant. Emotions, connected to anger and sadness, fall into this. These emotions appear connected to powerful life energy.

In certain cultures, they take energy from the above, ethereal energy and from below, which is more raw earth and life energy. They then bring this to a balance within themselves. It appears the spirits can use the more raw, earth and life energy created when a person is often going through these troubling types of events to cause the phenomena.

People are often putting out an abundance of this emotional energy during such times, much more so than a person would usually be doing. In a similar way, people have connected physical mediumship phenomena and poltergeist activity to the energy given out by children. Children often have an abundance of earthy life energy and experience very raw feelings, very strong feelings, very easily. Physical mediumship and poltergeist activity will be discussed in more detail later in the book.

You see the spirit world is also always using our energy in any form of mediumship. They don't have enough power on their own to cause the phenomena. They need us to be part of the process. This may be why mediums can find it easier to do public demonstrations to larger audiences, rather than private readings. In a public demonstration, the spirit world can use both the energy of all the persons in the room, as well as the energy of all the spirits there wishing to communicate with the audience members. Whereas, in a private reading, it is just the energy of two persons and the spirits present connected to them.

For persons who never experience any contact with spirit, it appears to be most often because their energy is always too closed off. They don't produce enough of the right energy for the phenomena to happen and the spirits connected to them are just never able get things right on their end. It isn't easy for them, by any means, and if the conditions aren't right all around, there will be no results.

No matter if we have these physical related experiences with spirit or not, those who love us in heaven always know a great deal about what is going on in our lives, and you can see that from the stories in this book. They know all the things we tell them if we talk to them and send out thoughts to them strongly.

They also know things by connecting to our thoughts, the things they hear us say and see us do, while they are visiting with us. This is how they know when to attend a reading with you to communicate through a medium, or visit the medium at the right time, in the case of a distance reading via a method like phone, Skype, etc.

NINE

Why It Works

• • • • • • • • • • • • • •

Perhaps the most important questions after going through everything the book has discussed so far, and indeed, one of the most important questions overall, is why do mediumistic readings in certain cases appear to heal grief caused by bereavement? Why is it in some cases, as found in the examples of this book, and countless other accounts from persons who have received readings, people experience huge reductions in grief connected to their bereavements?

When it comes to the academic study of mediumistic readings, most academic studies have focused on the accuracy of mediums' statements under controlled conditions. It is only in very recent years that research has been undertaken which focuses on the potential therapeutic benefit of mediumistic readings and is irrespective of any presumed "reality" to the source of the readings. The phenomena itself must first be connected to ADCs, (After-Death Communications) which I mentioned near the start of the book.

The phenomena of ADC appears to have been associated with many types of research of a "first person spontaneous experience of communication" with what is normally referred to as the deceased. Of course being dead is not what we have associated with it; if you are dead, you are actually in many ways more alive than you are here and death is just a transition to this.

This notion of ADCs being labelled as only spontaneous experiences appears to date back to the first papers published on ADCs that labels them as a spiritual experience that happens when a person is contacted specifically directly and spontaneously by a deceased relative or friend. Even recent academic papers on ADC have failed to recognize any non-spontaneous and channelled ADCs, involving mediumship, and defined ADCs in a similar way to those before, seeing these events as spontaneously occurring encounters with the deceased.

An example of such an encounter from a client of mine:

"As I walked down the hallway, I unmistakably smelt one of my mother's perfumes. It was there for a few seconds and then it was gone. She wore two per-

fumes, and the one I smelled was the one I disliked. I was confused, because I thought if it was my mind seeking some comfort causing me to imagine things, surely I would have imagined the perfume my mother wore that I was very fond of, and not the one I disliked. It was due to this that I felt that it really was my mother trying to let me know she was around me still and I took comfort from the experience."

Research of these types of ADCs has shown a number of outcomes can happen from an ADC; those most relevant to the subject in this book are:

- After an ADC, mourners report immediate relief, comfort, hope, love, emotional stabilization, encouragement, forgiveness, and the joy of continuing relationship.
- the mourner may reframe the relationship with the deceased as a result of ADC.
- ADCs can assist the mourner in completing unfinished business with deceased.
- The mourner may reframe relationship with self, as a result of an ADC.
- The mourner may reframe relationship with God or the Divine.

As it has been discussed, these encounters are normally seen as short, sudden and almost fleeting. This type of experience, of course, differs greatly from an ADC experienced through a medium. Mediumistic ADC experiences are commonly planned out with the recipient knowing the exact date and time that the experience will start. They are often between thirty to sixty minutes in length and are seen to be reinforced by the medium's lack of knowledge about the deceased person before the reading.

In my experience, it is this type of external corroboration through the medium's work that aids the grounding of the experience as being real for the recipient – primarily because the phenomena did not take place in the recipient's mind. The mechanics of the process and the experiences themselves are very different to a spontaneous ADC. Therefore, it cannot be assumed that the psychological forces at work, or that the outcomes are the same.

Data from a study by Beischel, Mosher & Boccuzzi, (2014-15) on mediumistic readings and bereavement from the Windbridge Institute suggested that mediumistic reading experiences led the mourner to reevaluate their relationship with the deceased, and indicated that the thought of a continual bond with the deceased greatly aided in lessening the feelings of grief for the bereaved.

This is similar to other ADCs. Psychologists Everden, Cooper & Mitchell, (2013) interviewed persons, who in the hope of alleviating their feelings of grief, had been to a reading with a medium. They found similar themes regarding a person having a successful reading and suggested that the feeling of a continual bond between the mourner and deceased person being established was key to the recipient's healing.

Their research suggested that if the psychological needs of the recipient were met, then recipients were able to move forward in life and form adaptive coping mechanisms. Moreover, it was in the belief that their loved one is still alive and not displaced from them, that further healing was fostered. The researchers connected this healing to the emotion of hope, which appeared within the mourner when these needs were met.

At the centre of the modern psychodynamic view of bereavement and bereavement healing is something called "attachment theory". Attachment theory seeks to illuminate the meaning and mechanics of attachment. In the past, unfortunately, views were held that continued attachments to the deceased were unhealthy and pathological. This can be seen clearly in psychologist Bowlby's work between 1969-1980. However, by the mid-1980s, it was becoming clear that this model of thinking was inaccurate and replaced with a "continuing bonds" perspective, where the resolution of grief involves an enduring bond that the bereaved maintains with the deceased.

Field, Gao & Paderna, (2005) suggested that continuing bonds with the deceased may represent a transition from a physical-based bodily attachment to a spiritual attachment. The data suggested early on in the bereavement, there is a sense that the deceased is missing, and then later after contact is made between the bereaved and the deceased, it appears the deceased is recovered as a spiritual being.

Worden, (2008) a psychologist, known for his work on attachment, grief and bereavement suggested a four-part process of mourning:

1. To accept the reality of the loss.
2. To work through the pain of the grief.
3. To adjust to an environment in which the deceased is missing.
4. To find an enduring connection with the deceased while embarking on a new life.

Notice that the fourth and final task relates to the concept of continual bonding. Worden supports the notion that the mourner does not eventually withdraw from the deceased. Instead, the mourner seeks to hold onto the deceased in some form. Further that the mourner often actively seeks a continued relationship with the deceased. However, as with all areas of science not everyone agrees on the effectiveness of continual bonds. What types of continual bonds are most effective? For whom are they helpful and for whom perhaps not? I will discuss this further now.

Understandably, it's been noted in some cases of anxious attachments it can potentially be more therapeutic and healing for the mourner to relinquish attachments to the deceased and withdraw on an emotional level. There are quite a number of academic studies that demonstrate this. An example of this could be where a parent was physically abusive to their child. If the parent passed away, the child might be better off detaching from the parent rather than forming an ongoing connection.

In a similar vein, a study in which Worden was one of the researchers discovered that in some cases children, who felt the presence of their deceased parent, found the experience more emotionally disturbing than comforting. However, from my experience, the majority of the time this is certainly not the case. Many children desperately seek a lasting connection with deceased loved ones and are very comforted when they find a transpersonal connection with their deceased loved ones.

Academics, as well as many mediums, note that for most people the acceptance of a transpersonal existence often appears to lead to an "emotional opening" or awakening. Wilber, Engler and Brown, (1986) suggested consequences of this may not always lead to a spontaneous awareness of a reality, which is free from issues.

Why some people dismiss mediumship and are not ready for a reading

Concerning that, I would suggest, based on my experience that some people may have experienced much emotional trauma in their life and, both consciously and subconsciously, have tried to detach from, forget or bury these experiences and connecting emotions deep within their mind causing emotional closeting.

At the very least, these individuals appear to me to be aware of this at a subconscious level, and It appears to me that, at the subconscious level they are also aware that an acceptance of a transpersonal existence could, as mentioned above, lead to an emotional awakening. In their case, this could open up the trauma and emotion that has been buried under the surface.

It appears at some level their psyche feels that this may be too much for them to confront and deal with in their current life, and could lead to psychological disturbance and mental instability. Thus, a dismissive and, at times, an apprehensive anti-transpersonal feeling is produced as a psychological defensive mechanism.

This could present in other complex ways. To give you a few examples of this, perhaps an individual does not want their deceased relatives to have gained knowledge of bad actions they committed in their life; or be aware of a traumatic experience they went through in their life that they have always kept a secret. This could be a secret they feel they are still not ready to share with anyone.

What I have seen in my years of practising mediumship is that the potential to withdraw emotionally is most common in, but not exclusive, to males. I would estimate the persons who attend mediumistic readings, are about 85% female and 15% male. Emotional closeting appears to be much stronger in males, and I would suggest this is most likely the major reason for the smaller amount of male interest in mediumistic readings compared to female.

Most often, it seems that females appear much more comfortable when dealing with their emotions on this perceived level. This emotional closeting was found strongly with Paul in the chapter entitled "Saved By Our Grandfather". Paul closeted away all kinds of emotions connected to his life and his sexuality. Hiding these from his father made the emotional grief of his father's passing worse, as these were unresolved and not well expressed.

Some males carry locked up emotion and grief their entire life, and it can start at any age and any point. In this next story, you will see how Alex had more emotional grief closeted away in connection to his grandmother's passing, than his mum, Lynne, who sat with him during the reading and who has kindly written their story on their behalf. It is not uncommon or a bad thing for a female to provide extra emotional support the first time a male has a reading.

I can say from experience, that this emotional support is very often needed, as I have had more men cry in readings than women. That may surprise some, but it's very true. It does make sense though, because as I have discussed, it appears that men have more emotion locked away than females. When these emotions are addressed, and when their mind begins to accept the transpersonal existence of the soul as a reality, the emotion often comes flooding out of them, in the form of tears.

Of course, this emotional closeting does happen in women, as well, but it generally appears not so strong in women. In general, most women are more in touch with their emotions and seem to be able to express and vent emotions much easier, which appears to make a consistent difference.

Thankfully in Alex's case, there wasn't enough emotional closeting to stop him from wanting to have a reading and explore the possibility of reconnecting with his grandmother.

Lynne and Alex

"My first exposure to mediumship came when I was a very young teenager, and my mum and dad were reading books on mediumship. They were utterly fascinated by these books, and I can recall them talking about the content together and to other family members. As a keen reader, I asked to borrow them – and so my journey began.

I attended our local spiritualist church in Grays, Essex, England with my mum and dad a couple of times and whilst nothing relevant came through, I still found it fascinating – because essentially it was something that just couldn't be explained. Clearly, however, some of the information that came through for other people was just mind-blowing.

My Dad died quite suddenly when I was 20. The years following his passing, I visited several mediums and psychics. I think I just needed some kind of validation that he was still around, like the books I had read. In those years, I had received readings from a number of mediums, both by way of public demonstrations and private readings. In all cases, I had been given my dad's personality, a few keywords, but to be fair, a lot of it was open to cynicism and coincidence I guess.

I do recall that on my 21st birthday, I was celebrating with my brother and his wife, my sister and her husband, my niece and nephew, my mum's twin sister and a couple of very close friends, for a meal local to where I grew up (I had moved to Kent by that time). When we arrived, our waiter came and took our drink orders whilst we all looked at the menu. The waiter returned, handing out the drinks and then had one left on his tray. Looking at us all, with our drinks duly received he said, "Who ordered the Glenfiddich?"

Honestly, the table fell silent and gasps flew around. You see, Glenfiddich was my Dad's absolute favourite tipple. He loved a little whisky but Glenfiddich – that was for very special occasions, if he had the money – or if someone had bought a bottle for his birthday. Of course, no one had ordered a Glenfiddich. The rest of us couldn't stand whisky!

My mum, who was sitting opposite me, said, "Well I never! You see Lynne, he would never miss your 21st!" My brother decided to take the Glenfiddich and raise a toast to my Dad. Funny enough, my brother now loves whisky too!

Roll forward ten years and I was back living at home with my mum in Essex. I was a newly single mum with a 6-week-old baby boy, Alex. My mum having been there at his birth, adored Alex and had such a special bond with him. I remember him being born and my mum just looked at him, cozy and swaddled in her loving arms and said, "It's like looking at your Dad, Lynne."

One day, there I was frantically rushing around the kitchen, washing up baby bottles and preparing the next lot for sterilization whilst my mum was feeding Alex with a bottle on her lap in the living room. I could hear her talking to me but couldn't for the life of me work out what she was saying. "What? Mum, I can't understand a word of what you're saying!"

I was frustrated because I was shattered; I was on a timescale of washing, sterilizing, preparing next feeds before having to do it all over again. I went into the living room, full of exasperation, and mum spoke to me again. It was complete and utter gibberish, but there she was, with six-week-old Alex in her arms, bottle still firmly in his mouth, lolloping over to her left side and face drooping.

I knew immediately she had had a stroke. Chaos ensued, although I am one to remain reasonably calm under situations like that – I have to be in control, you see. The main chaos was that I was trying to hear the emergency dispatch person over the awful din of Alex screaming because I had taken his feed away and put him back in his "Moses" basket while I dealt with the situation at hand. Life as I knew it changed after that day, but mum stayed alive for a further ten years. Having had a major, debilitating stroke, though, I wouldn't say she actually "lived".

During those last ten years of mum's life, I met and married a Welshman, called David who took on Alex as his own and I had another daughter called Rhiannon and we moved to North London. I managed to visit Mum every week though, taking the kids with me, doing chores, keeping her paperwork in order, etc. She loved those visits but particularly loved seeing Alex and he adored his Nan.

Mum had started collecting miniature clocks that were placed in beautiful jewelled ornaments, and he so loved looking at them. She also collected miniature Big Ben clocks, post-boxes with little clocks in, teapots, airplanes, ladybirds – about 40-50 clocks in total and Alex loved looking at them, as well.

In February 2009, a major stroke took mum's life. I remember so clearly hav-

ing to tell Alex and watching his ten-year-old face dissolve in gasping sobs and tears in front of me. With all the tidying up of affairs, each grandchild took a clock of their choice and the rest went to Alex. These were small gifts at a very sad time for a young boy.

Some people say as one life is taken, another is granted – and so it was that two months after mum died, I found myself pregnant with a third child. That was surprising at the time, but she would be a girl so I could give her my mum's name – older-fashioned names were becoming popular again, thankfully!

I saw a couple of mediums over the course of the next few years, really desperate to get a message from my mum. I got messages from my Dad but each time I was given the message of a purple flower or "Iris". That was my mum's name – Iris. I always guessed that it was a little too soon for mum to come through or just that my dad was such a dynamic character and mum was far more timid, that it was just the natural order of reaching out from them. I have always told Alex about readings I've received, and he asked if he could come one day. He'd like to find out more and wanted to know that his nanny was still around. I said he had to wait until he was sixteen.

After attending a demonstration by a different celebrity medium, with some friends, a lady was talking to my friend and recommended Ross and his book Earth Angel. This friend had seen Ross in Bournemouth and said he was simply incredible and his use of names and detail was bewildering.

I bought his book on Kindle and before I had finished reading it, I reached out to book a reading. If I was going to introduce my Alex to a medium, it had to be Ross. A young, edgy lad, covered in tattoos – someone closer to his age than mine and from what I'd read, this guy could be dynamite.

—

So, it came to the day of our reading with Ross. I drove from North London to Southampton and one of my friends came too with her 16-year-old son. We nattered all the way down, as friends do, talking about the types of things that Ross might say and explaining a little about the process to our boys. They were both very nervous because they didn't know what to expect; probably a little skeptical too. We spoke about putting thoughts out to the universe or just "please tell me this one particular thing" so that they might get enough evidence.

We arrived a little early, and Alex and I decided to have the first joint reading. We were shown into a room while Ross meditated and linked in. Having read his book, I understood a little of what he was trying to do. Alex sat huffing and puffing in a 16-year-old way, "why is it taking so long?" Ross came in and talked us through the process that he would go through and that there would be a time to ask questions. He then started the reading.

Ross started with "First of all, I seem to be aware of one female, two males. None of them are further forward in my mind and awareness right now, so I'll probably just pick one, and we'll go from there." Both Alex and I looked at each other and admitted afterwards that we both put out thoughts of... "the lady, the lady, the lady, the lady!" Ross spoke again saying, "Ok, I've been polite and I've started with the lady first." Yessssss.

Alex and I sat bolt upright in our chairs. Come on, come on, come on Mum, you can do it! Ross explained that some of the first images he was being shown seemed to relate to this lady visiting with lots of different family members at their homes. It figures really – you see, mum was all about her family. She just loved to be around them. Ross then told us, "She's bringing a reference that relates to a name that is connected to a flower of some sort." Here we go. "Yes!" I exclaimed, "Absolutely fantastic – that's her name."

I was ecstatic. It appeared that Ross was actually linking in with my mum. Not my dad, the dominant figure – my mum!! I could see Alex jerk his head towards me and his eyes grow wide. When having a reading with Ross, there are lengthy periods of silence while he's trying to communicate with the other side. I was having a little chuckle to myself as he sat there in silence and then would nod his head and say things like, "yes, yes, ok" and "try that" – not talking to us, but someone we could not see!

Ross then went on to tell us a little bit about her character, she was family orientated, he was finding it very hard to get any information about her though – what made her special, what would she be remembered for? He reported that he had the feeling she was quite humble as she was brushing him aside, doesn't see herself as anything other than ordinary and someone who found happiness in the simple things in life. My mum in a nutshell! None of this meant very much to Alex though.

However, the flower and the name did. But at 16, he just wanted detail – he wanted to know his Nan was around, and then Ross looked directly at Alex and said: "Alex, this lady is particularly happy to have the opportunity to talk to you today, as she's spent a lot of time watching over you from the other side, and she really wants to talk to you about that today."

My big, 6ft 1" strapping 16-year-old boy covered his face with his hands and absolutely sobbed. I could see and feel all of the tension of the moment, the love he had for my mum, his Nan, come pouring out of him. "This is SO weird!" he cried. Ross smiled and said, "It's funny you say that because she's *telling me she finds it weird too, because she really relates to you when you were a lot smaller than you are now! You were so tiny, now you're so big!"*

Ross told Alex that the lady is with him a lot and she really draws close to him because he talks to her and about her quite a lot. Alex cried – again. Ross told Alex that the lady remembers him being such a sensitive lad and that there was no one like him in the family group – but in a good way. He was different/special. The whole time, Alex was full of tears and in his sixteen year-old, uncommunicative way, spouting, "This is just so weird!"

And then Ross got into full flow.

"This may well relate back to the flower reference, and I don't know a lot about flowers if I'm honest. I think they're Irises, though? And is there a Den or a Dennis on the other side?" Oh, my word. That is my Dad's name! So there we had "name proof". Iris is my mum, and Den/Dennis is my dad. Ross said someone had been talking about getting a car or a first car. We nodded. Alex was nearly seventeen and obsessing about learning to drive, what car he would get and so on.

Ross then said that mum was referencing a programme both Alex and I watch on TV. One very particular TV show. Well, Alex is sixteen. We don't watch TV together. He's either out partying with his friend, playing on Xbox or doing anything other than sitting with his family in the sitting room. Ross wouldn't let it go. "Has there been a TV show you both specifically watched together? I'm getting the feeling you both watch this together, and she wants you to know that she has been with you then."

Hang on! There is that one TV show! Alex looked at me at the same time as it dawned on me and said, "It's got to be 'You, Me and the Apocalypse', mum!" Alex's friend's little sister was in this particular programme, and we both snuggled down to watch it, together, each week. We actually recorded it just so we could find time to watch it at a mutually convenient time, together. The last episode was just a few days before our reading with Ross and had such a great ending. I had goose bumps throughout much of the episode.

Then more names. "I'm being given the name David as well. Can you take that?" Err yes, that would be my husband! It was then Alex's turn again. Ross said he was being shown an image of a wardrobe and some drawers, images that related to a bedroom. He explained that he felt he was being taken to Alex's bedroom. Ross said it would usually be that something had changed in the bedroom and that was why he was being shown the image.

Whether anything had changed or not – he was being told he had to look for something in Alex's bedroom. Alex and I gasped and looked at each other

*wide-eyed. We knew exactly what this could be. If Ross got this, utter, abso-
lute proof would have been given to us of life after death. Ross was silent for
a while, nodding his head and finally saying, "Ok, ok." He turned to Alex and
I. "I'm getting a reference to something like a clock or clocks – tick tock, tick
tock, time – something like that? Does this mean anything to you?"*

*Both Alex and I cried out, Oh my God! In Alex's bedroom, on two shelves
above his chest of drawers, he has laid out impeccably, all of my mum's miniature clocks. Alex was shaking his head. "I don't believe this; it's just so weird!"
I had a feeling "weird" was Alex's new word of the moment. In the car, on the
way to the reading we discussed that if Ross were to mention the clocks there
would be no doubt in our minds that there is an afterlife.*

*However, Mum wasn't done. She had other people to reference. Ross said,
"The name Ian is of relevance. Where does he fit into all this?" Ha! – Well, that
is my older brother.*

*And then Alex again. "Alex, this is going to sound odd, but have you had a
problem with your toe?" Absolutely staggering. Alex had had an infected big
toe for around three months and kept forgetting to take the antibiotics. I had
been constantly nagging and telling him his toe would fall off if he didn't take
the antibiotics! It was only recently back to normal.*

*Then mum had another name. Ross said "Dawn. I got that name earlier on
but I forgot it, sorry. She has just said it again. Has she been around a boat
for some reason? Iris just wants her to know that she's there." My sister, Dawn,
has in the past few years spent pretty much every week or weekend on a canal
boat, her and her husband moor on the Norfolk Broads.*

*So, now mum had come through and given her name, Iris, my dad's name
Den, my brother's name, my sister's name, then Ross moved on to the grand-
children. "I can't quite get the tail end of half a name here. I think its Olivia or
Lydia or could be something close to that." I laughed. My brother's daughter is
called Lydia. My youngest daughter, who came along after mum died, is called
Olivia, but then Ross clarified.*

*"This Lydia, a teenager, is she a very good looking girl?" I said yes she was
considered to be very good looking. "I feel we are definitely with her." He
continued, "She's been around Lydia a bit recently and, Lydia is talking about
changing something with hair. Does she have blonde hair at the moment? I
think it's something to do with Lydia's hair being changed. She was actually
vocalizing this to a family member – not just thinking about it. Iris wants
them to know that she was there and was around them." I promised to speak
to Lydia and pass this on.*

Ross then asked about a ladder. Apparently someone had been talking about a ladder when mum had been visiting them. He then referenced something changing in a kitchen and it related to the ladder. I wasn't quite sure. It was a bit random really. Then another name. "I'm getting a reference to a surname. Mills or Miller. Can you take that?" Holy Moly. Sure could – that was my mum's maiden name.

As one of ten kids and with most of them now on the other side, Miller was fairly significant! Mum's energy waned, and Ross explained that the two males in the background of the reading were giving her energy. We were delighted. My mum had come through. She had given us her name, my dad's name, my sister's name, my brother's name, my niece's name, her maiden name, my husband's name – and some incredible information about toes, clocks and boats that Ross could not have found out about!

When our reading finished, Alex and I sat in the waiting area while our friends had their joint reading. I sent texts to my sister and sister-in-law telling them what had happened and that they had been mentioned. I promised to type up the transcript from the CD and send it to them. My mind was buzzing on the drive home, and I couldn't wait to listen to the CD, type it up and send to my family, which I did as soon as I got home.

I then received an excited call from my sister-in-law and her daughter, Lydia. "Lydia and I were only talking a couple of days ago about her wanting to change her hair colour from blonde to red. How would he know that? Also, we are having our shed knocked down, a utility room built and knocked through into the kitchen. The workman had to leave early yesterday without finishing the job because he'd forgotten his ladder. We've just been talking about it today."

When I went to bed later that night, I was smiling. No, actually, I was beaming. I was so, so very happy and looked up at my ceiling, and said, "Thank you mum. Thank you for proving to me that you are still around." Because you see, she is.

She may have left me physically, but I now know, beyond any doubt whatsoever, that there is a life after death. I don't know how it works but I know it is real, as does Alex. The reading allowed him to let go of bottled up emotions connected to his Nan's passing and has been such a great comfort to us both."

TEN

MSc...Towards Healing Symptoms Of Grief

• • • • • • • • • • • • •

You may be thinking, ok Ross, I can see where you are coming from with the previous research, the people's stories resonate with me and I can see they have received healing and their lives have been changed for better from the mediumistic reading process... but are there deeper mechanics to this process and how might they relate to my mind and a potential pathway of healing for me? What do they tell us about the minds of every person and humankind's continual life on Earth?

I will answer these for you by walking you through the study I did on the potential of mediumistic readings to heal symptoms of grief caused by bereavement for my MSc, and the theories that arose from the data, and my reflections.

To understand the processes of bereavement healing in an area where little previous research has been undertaken, I felt it required a methodology where the ultimate aim is the generation of novel theory. To be at all robust or valid, I felt this new theory must be rooted in the people who have experienced healing through this approach.

At the start of the study three participants were recruited by me, (the researcher), through a post on my professional Facebook page. The initial number of participants later expanded, which is detailed as you continue reading. After collecting the data, I became aware of several emerging themes, which I detail below. So, I decided to expand the study further in order to get more clarification on these themes and the data as a whole, including the bereavement process in general.

Later during the study, I made the decision to recruit three more participants. I chose two individuals who had experience with both mediumship readings and counselling. One, Jane, was also a client of mine and worked professionally as a counsellor. The other person, Sam, was a working acquaintance, who works professionally as medium and counsellor, specializing in bereavement counselling.

The third individual, John, had experience with receiving mediumistic readings, and through his career as a doctor of medicine, is experienced with medical approaches to bereavement healing in the form of medication, counselling and psychiatry. I also knew him as a client. I believed their expertise would be relevant to help clarify the emerging data and could also be of use in the discussion of the concepts generated within the study.

As the study continued, a clear theme of continual attachment arose from the data. To gain a greater understanding of the dynamics to process in the data, I decided to recruit two more participants whose religious beliefs and practices related more to non-attachment. Thereafter, I recruited two Western Buddhist participants, Ben and Mary, whose contact information was passed on to me through networking circles. I felt their experience of non-attachment could also shed some light on the data I was seeing.

After I had submitted the paper, I decided to add to the study results by recruiting and interviewing two new Buddhist participants, David, Jill and a working psychiatrist, Chris. I did not know the two new Buddhists before the study, and Chris, the psychiatrist was again, known to me as a client.

Many times in academic research, it may be frowned upon to use clients, even though many of the classical figures of psychology like Freud, Jung and many others often used their own clients in experiments. Many of their understandings and theories were, at the very least, based on their observations of their clients, at first. Whilst it is true, it is not the strictest methodology to follow. Even now, it is certainly not uncommon in the research world, especially at a Master's degree level.

For me, the potential benefits of using my clients in the study outweighed the concerns. In no way was I, as the researcher, looking to gain vindication of the accuracy of readings I performed for the participants. What was important to me in having my clients participate was that I would be able to vouch that the participants had been through a deep bereavement and did receive a proper mediumistic reading at an appropriate standard, and that they would have been satisfied with their experience.

Further, because of my rapport with these participants, I felt I would be able to explore the issues on a deeper level with them, as I have already discussed at length the very sensitive, emotional and private matters that related directly to the focus of this study. If valuable results are found in such client-based studies, the next standard academic step is to see if the results are duplicated when involving participants with no connection to the researcher.

Strong innate needs

My study illuminated particular forms of emotions and feelings that arose from bereavement. These were connected to strong innate needs within the psyche which appeared after the participants experienced a bereavement. The first quotes below related to the individuals seeking forms of emotional closure connected to the deceased.

This manifested in different ways. For non-Buddhist participants one form was a need for an emotional closure of the safety of the deceased and was expressed in ways similar to this example:

> "I want to know he still exists and that he is now ok. I mean, now ok but I don't mean that in comparison to when he was with us. I just mean that he is ok."

In some individuals, there were more complex areas of emotional closure that needed to be addressed. With one participant, it was the need for her father to say he was sorry for things that happened in life.

> "She (Medium) brought through someone who was undoubtedly my granddad, and she said there's a man behind him, but he hasn't the strength to come through on his own, and I thought the only person it can be is my dad, and all he's got the strength to say is thank you, and I'm sorry, and just that, that was enough. Everything was put to rest and I was a much calmer person after that."

For another participant, it was an understanding of why her son took his life and the resolution of his last action, which was that he left a message blaming her for his actions.

> "The first reading, I was very emotional. I felt really emotional. My son had left and had blamed me in a letter. I wanted to know and I was hoping that something would come that suggested he didn't mean the things he said."

It was further apparent that the minds of all participants actively searched for a continual connection and bond with the deceased.

Differences and similarities –
continual connections

Whilst the non-Buddhist individuals consciously recognized ways they sought a continual connection with the deceased, none of the Buddhist individuals appeared to consciously recognize a search for ways of continual connection with their deceased loved ones. However, it was clear to see that they found ways to do this without directly realizing it.

Sometimes, this was exhibited as a feeling, a mental or physical-related connection or a combination of these. Examples were visiting the deceased's grave or the place where bodily remains were kept, or scattered with and without gifts, displaying photos of the deceased, relating to the deceased as if their opinion still matters, and relating to the deceased as if they are still around them in some form or another. A good example of the latter was:

"I feel him in the warmth of the sun, hear him in the whistle of the breeze, and see him in the earth and the sky."

This quote was remarkably similar to quotes of two other Buddhist participants who related in this way to the deceased still being around them.

Two of the most interesting examples of that feature was that one of the non-Buddhist participants got a tattoo that related to the deceased, and one had by choice slept in the car previously owned by the deceased several times; actions that related more to attachment than detachment.

The non-Buddhist participants also took the same actions of visiting the deceased's grave or the place bodily remains were kept or scattered with and without gifts, displaying photos of the deceased, relating to the deceased as if their opinion still matters and relating to the deceased as if they are still around them in some form or another, etc. This seeking of a continual connection led them to having the reading.

This was expressed in similar ways to these examples:

"I was looking for reassurance that he is still around."
"I wanted to know if my loved ones who had passed over were still around me."

It was apparent with all persons, including the Buddhists, that the need of emotional closure was tied directly to the deceased, either in regards to the deceased's safety or their thoughts, feelings, opinions and relationship to them.

As such, it is likely that the need for emotional closure couldn't be completely resolved without the belief of active input on the subject from the deceased themselves. From my perspective, it was clear to see with all Buddhist participants that there were various levels of need for emotional closure. Examples below:

> "I was already starting to deal with the fact that there were certain things between us that I might like to have resolved."

> "I was really beginning to have feelings that it was not possible to resolve these things and get certain answers before he passed and understood more about me, perhaps before he passed. So, there was a sense of loss, a loss of opportunity."

> "My relationship with my mother wasn't great. I wish it had been better."

> "After he died, I just wanted him to know that I wanted the best for him wherever he may go with his body lying there. I had obviously a very emotional time due to this, and I went off food a bit, obviously."

> "There were so many things left unsaid between us and things that were never resolved."

It was demonstrated that strong emotions that arise in the bereavement process are connected to certain innate needs within the psyche. These needs led persons to seek forms of emotional closure and continual connection and bond with the deceased. This was the case, even if the person had no refined belief in an afterlife and even if the individual did not believe in any form of afterlife. Their mind still found ways to make continual connections.

This to me strongly suggests there is an innate need in our psyche to make a persistent connection and bond with the deceased. A need for our psyche to find the deceased after death and create a new narrative from that point, even in cases where the person consciously believes that the individual, as they knew them, ceases to exist or is unsure of their state of existence. These emotions and needs in the participants, who at the time had no philosophical concept against the possibility of an afterlife where the soul remains intact, led the individual to pursue having a reading with a medium as a means to establish a continual potential connection and find forms of emotional closure. At times, these were complex and very specific in nature; and commonly to the point, the only likely way to resolve the emotional issue would be to discuss the matter with the deceased.

Importance of a successful reading

Additionally, the study highlighted factors that had come through from the data, which directly affected if the mediumistic readings were successful and healing, or unsuccessful and potentially more psychologically harmful. The Buddhist participants were not asked questions directed towards healing factors of a mediumistic reading, as they had not received one. The first examples related to the importance of the accuracy of information being conveyed.

> "The information I've had has been quite specific about family members and what I'm looking for in these kinds of things is about the names and personalities and who's who, but also about a percentage of hits."

> "The accuracy is very important. I would put it number one at the top there."

The next examples related to the apparent importance of the type of information conveyed during a reading. In the example below, it was clear that for the reading to be a success for this participant, she needed to hear her son tell her it wasn't her fault he took his life.

> "The first reading, I was very emotional. I felt really emotional. My son had left and had blamed me in a letter. I wanted to know, I was hoping that something would come that suggested he didn't mean the things he said."

Putting the above together within the study these elements clearly related to the importance of both the accuracy and the type of information conveyed in order to meet the psychological needs of the person going into the reading.

The example that follows demonstrates this well. The participant needed the accuracy of the reading to be at a certain level to believe it was her deceased son who was communicating the information that it wasn't her fault he took his own life, that together fulfilled the participant's psychological need.

> "I needed the accuracy to believe he was really communicating and to take on board the message that it wasn't my fault. Without it, I would not have believed that message was real and then I would not have been healed by it."

Several participants acknowledged that if their psychological needs were not met, and specifically if things were said, that was not indicative of their needs, then it would have made their feelings of grief much worse.

> "I was nervous and at the same time, not apprehensive; scared, maybe in case he didn't come through because that would have been worse than anything else."

> "If he didn't come through, it would have finished me off. I had planned in my mind that if he didn't come through and if the reading failed in some way, I would kill myself. Likewise, if he came through and, in some way, blamed me."

Psychological needs met

Not surprisingly, the study demonstrated that if the psychological needs were met, multiple healing benefits emerged from a mediumistic reading and this then related to a sense or feeling towards something or an understanding of something.

In the interest of the study, I also chose to explore if the Buddhist participants felt that they would find any benefits from receiving a mediumistic reading or some other form of spontaneously induced reading or paranormal experience. They were asked to speak hypothetically on questions relating to the themes that were established from the earlier participants.

Whilst I was aware that speaking hypothetically on the scenario was not concrete information and hard-grounded data, I felt that it would still have some worth to the study. Thereby, potentially helping to further the understanding of the psychological forces and needs, along with the healing factors that arose from the study.

Continual bonds

The important theme was that healing was obtained through the belief in a continual relationship and bond with the deceased. Examples:

> "I knew from that point on, the bond I had with my father was still there and that there was a continual relationship and connection that we shared. I can't describe to you how healing this was."

> "I think I feel closer to them all. I think, I've got, obviously at my age, a number that I have loved and have gone. I think it's drawn me closer to them. I feel that they are probably all quite aware of me, and some very much so, and watching over me. That connection is still there, and that's lovely."

Also, that healing was obtained through a belief in a form of transpersonal protection and aid.

> "The understanding my father was around me, watching over me protecting and aiding me was further greatly helpful to my healing."

> "For me, it's really comforting to know that he is watching over her, protecting her."

Additionally, healing was obtained through the resolution of unresolved emotions. It appeared that through the reading process, previously unresolved emotions were worked through and then resolved.

This was expressed in similar ways below:

> "Hearing Terry tell me it wasn't my fault that he took his own life, that there were so many things on an emotional level he was struggling with, and it was like a knee-jerk reaction, was so very very healing. It was like for the first time since his passing I could breathe again."

The study also highlighted that the simple assurance of the deceased's wellbeing seemed to have a strong healing impact. This was expressed in similar ways to the following:

"I felt very comfortable because it was so simple he was continuing with his life, and he wasn't just you know... and the light hadn't just gone out."

"I felt comforted knowing my father was ok, that he didn't cease to exist and also that he was no longer in pain. It was so helpful, so healing."

The study also demonstrated a gained conscious belief in a conscious transpersonal reunion, was seen to be healing. Examples:

"I know that when I die, I'm going to be with my son, and I find that so comforting and healing."

"I have no fear of death. I know when my time comes I'm going to meet up with my loved ones on the other side and that in itself brings strength and healing."

The last point found, and perhaps the most interesting, is when the psychological needs of the reading were met in the participants who had what they considered a successful mediumistic reading.

The process established what I could only describe as, a transpersonal sense that the deceased was still around them and connected to them in a transpersonal way. Again, this was found to be comforting and healing.

This was expressed in similar ways below:

"I personally left with a huge bounce, because it made me feel like he was around still."

"I now have a stronger feeling my relatives continue to be connected to me and around me and that I find quite comforting."

"I had such a strong feeling after having that first reading that my relatives are still around me. I can't exactly explain that sense very well with words. I felt connected to them again. I suppose it's beyond words that it, in itself, is what you could call transpersonal."

What was also discovered in the data is that the Buddhist participants appeared to have experienced little, if any, actual healing of the innate needs that were highlighted in the study; the needs that appeared present in all participants. They did not acknowledge any experiences and practices that directly helped these innate needs, and their bereavement experience, all around, seemed to have a much larger element of coping, as opposed to healing.

This was signified by the use of the word "cope", appearing several times in each Buddhist interview, when relating to bereavement feelings past and present.

Granted, I'm confident, if asked, at least several of the non-Buddhist individuals would still relate to some sense of coping. However, it appeared the healing benefits from the mediumistic readings had decreased the elements that require any coping, to the point it was no longer something of enough substance to be brought forward organically.

From my experience in the field, after such healing benefits have taken place, it is normally only the lack of physical connection and interaction that the bereaved individual feels they must continually cope with. It appears as highlighted above, that the reading re-establishes an emotional and mental connection, whilst potentially facilitating a level of transpersonal connection that is not commonly consciously experienced by the bereaved individual before the reading.

This transpersonal sense appears to be the defining factor in fulfilling the innate needs of continual connection and emotional closure with the deceased. At times, leaving the bereaved individual feeling overall closer to the deceased than before the bereavement. Facilitating long term healing as described in a similar fashion to the quote below:

> "I just feel closer to Terry now. It's bizarre to say it but from losing him, I realize how much I'm like him, as I actually am. As a parent, I wasn't quite as aware how similar we were until I lost him, and the reading has made me feel so close to him again, closer than I ever was to him. I just feel incredibly close to my son. It's just a beautiful feeling, and I talk to him. I don't think it's daft. It is something I continually find comforting and healing."

With the Buddhist participants, it was also interesting to find that the participants, Mary and Ben, who appeared to practise less detachment from emotion, hypothetically speaking, both suggested that they feel they would benefit from all these possibilities. This was described in similar ways to the following:

> "It might be an opportunity to look at things. Like the previous time with my father, when opportunity slipped to re-establish something between us, when something went wrong. Find out what we both did mean at the time. We would be able to repair that if you like, so a compassionate act, so I'm not limited in any way to something coming from beyond the death of my body."

> "Can they help you? There may be some natural laws that could help, or I can use my own mind to start off that kind of process that would enable these things to come in. Yes, it would give me comfort. I'm sure it would, yes."

Emotional closeting

It was equally interesting to find that Buddhist participants, David and Jill, who appeared to practise more detachment from emotions, suggested that they would find no benefit with these concepts. They showed a lack of desire to even hypothetically discuss the topic, which appeared to be expressed in an almost semi-defensive manner.

Also, at this time, David and Jill seemed to show visual signs of some level of emotional unrest. It appeared to me as a mixture of defensiveness, being emotional, yet trying to stay as calm as possible on the surface. It was interesting that during the discussions of emotional feelings connected to bereavements they had experienced, and hypothetical bereavements in the future, these two participants overall seemed uneasy.

It appeared that emotions connected to the innate needs of the psyche were still present with all Buddhist participants, but were hidden under the surface and the ways in which their psyche was trying to find a continual connection and emotional closure was seemingly not enough to really heal the innate needs discussed.

Strangely for Buddhists David and Jill, there were clearly parts of their psyche that could make use of a mediumistic reading, just as there were for Buddhist participants Mary and Ben. Yet David and Jill wouldn't even explore the topic, whereas, Mary and Ben were happy to. In regards to this, I reviewed the data looking for an answer and found evidence to support the concept of what I have termed "emotional closeting" causing anti-transpersonal feelings.

To define for you what emotional closeting is, I suggested earlier that an emotional trauma a person consciously experienced in their life, which they have tried to semi-forget, detach from, can be "closeted up" in their minds. With David and Jill, they both appeared to be aware of this closeted emotion, albeit at a subconscious level. Based on my experience, at least, in some people, if not all, too much emotional closeting can lead to producing an anti-transpersonal feeling in their psyche.

This may be due to being aware at a subconscious level that an acceptance of a transpersonal existence could lead to an emotional opening. In their case, this could potentially open up much trauma and emotion they had closeted. A part of the psyche appears to feel that this may be too much for them to confront and deal with in their current psychological position. Further, allowing these feelings could lead to psychological disturbance and mental instability.

Thus, a dismissive and, at times, an apprehensive anti-transpersonal feeling is produced as a psychological defensive mechanism.

Emotional openings

At first, I found evidence to confirm mediumistic readings causing an emotional opening in several participants. This was described in ways similar to the examples below:

> "I became a lot more emotional which my family can't cope with. They don't do emotion."

> "I also became much more emotional and open. I felt like I had woken up."

> "I feel I've become a bit more open and emotional since having the readings."

One participant related to going through an experience of expression of emotions that were subconsciously closed away:

> "What surprised me from the loss of my daughter, soon after she died, within the week, friends and I were talking about this partic-

ular issue and the bereavement, and one of the men burst out into uncontrollable tears, and I found myself doing the same, which really surprised me at the time. We are talking a long time ago now, the early nineties because I'm not the crying sort of person. Yet, I clearly had emotional stuff going on inside me."

Another participant, over time, and through his emotional connection to his wife, and expression of emotion with his wife, became more open to the concept of mediumistic readings.

"I suppose it was talking about mediumship and death, emotions in general with my wife over time, who had gone to many readings during her life that moved me to be more open to the topic of mediumship and mediumistic readings. This was over many years. Eventually, I was open to it and decided to investigate and see for myself."

Interestingly, Sam, who worked both as a medium and bereavement counsellor, appeared also to connect a lack of openness to receiving a mediumistic reading with a lack of emotional openness in some individuals. This was suggested to be most frequent in males, due to higher amounts of emotional closeting.

"The males, who as I've described and who really say it's a whole load of rubbish, without ever investigating, I don't think they deal with emotions very well at all. I think they bottle up their emotions, and this holds them back. It's the females that are much more aware of their emotions, open and expressive with them and that's why they are the ones who come for readings most often, and are more open. Often, their grief in a bereavement can ultimately be easier to deal with."

As I reviewed the data further, it appeared when comparing the data of the other participants and most notably the data of Buddhist participants Ben and Mary, with that of Buddhist participants David and Jill, that it was Buddhist participants David and Jill who appeared to have the highest amount of emotional closeting within the group. This appeared to me to be related to their greater practice of detachment from emotions, and stance of having to "get on with life", a phrase used by both participants.

Buddhist participants Ben and Mary's belief system allowed for a greater, and in their case, somewhat transpersonal sense of continual connection to their deceased relatives. They were quite similar, if not fundamentally in the same positions, as the other non- Buddhist participants before their reading experiences when they had no refined belief system against an afterlife and had not practised such a degree of emotional detachment as seen with Buddhist participants, Dave and Jill.

Buddhist participants, Ben and Mary, as a whole, were notably much more open to the concept, and this was further exemplified by their wishing to discuss mediumship and mediumistic-based philosophy with me after the interview had finished. Additionally, going as far as purchasing my autobiography based on my transpersonal experiences connected to an afterlife through altered states of awareness and mediumistic readings.

Buddhist participant Mary ended up having a reading with myself and found the same healing benefits as the non-Buddhists participants did, stating after the reading:

> "It's amazing how much better I feel. I feel reconnected to my father and I now know that he has been watching me and knows how I felt about him. I can now let go of the things I didn't get to say to him before he passed. I wish I had done this years ago. It's perhaps a bit odd to say but I feel spirituality closer to my father now than I ever felt when he was on Earth."

I'm not going to suggest that Buddhism and Buddhist practice cannot adequately deal with bereavement. It is important to note my participants were brought up in the Western culture, a culture quite different to the East, and my participants had lifestyles that Buddhist monks in the East would not have, just like there are many branches of Christianity, and they have different ideas and practices. This is the same for Buddhism. It may very well be the case that Buddhist practices have a means to heal the innate needs that arise within bereavement in the East, or in any culture, but it certainly did not appear in my study.

Finding the deceased

What I found most interesting was four participants used the words "find" or "found" to directly describe the process of reconnecting with the deceased. The reason this is interesting is, as to date, the concepts of continual bonding through mediumistic readings and the concept of continual bonding as a whole in attachment theory, have not been well related to this deeper encompassing need to find the deceased.

Moreover, it appeared, at times, as if a part of the mind, in some way, potentially believes the deceased is missing, as opposed to ceasing to exist and further, wishes to be reconnected with the deceased. As exampled in:

> "This lady is telling me she is always with you, and she is right by your side during the day," and she said, "You talk to her don't you?" And I said, "Yes all the time," and she said, "Yes, she hears you," and all of a sudden there you are, because I always think of her as being right there. It was a real turning point, and I thought, "Gotcha, I know where you are, I've found you."

I will discuss this "missing theory" in greater detail in the next chapter, along with other findings from my study. Together with my personal experience, this leaves me knowing that for total healing to take place, what is key is that the innate needs that appear to arise in all people must be adequately addressed.

To do that it seems a strong transpersonal connection must be established, as there appears to be an innate need for our psyche to find and reconnect with deceased individuals.

In certain cases, it appears complex emotional closure can only be found by active input by the deceased and that would need to involve an ADC.

ELEVEN

Heaven Therapy For All

• • • • • • • • • • • • •

When it comes to why all people may need Heaven Therapy, firstly it's important to say that research like that of Currier, Niemeyer & Berman, (2008) has suggested that traditional forms of counselling have little, to no effect at all, in relieving symptoms of grief caused by bereavement.

During the interview process, several participants discussed information relating to other means of bereavement healing and compared them to mediumistic approaches. The data offered much substantiation and continued to highlight why mediumistic readings are useful. Additionally, it also showed how other approaches may be helpful in the bereavement process, and if other methods can potentially be used in a combined approach with mediumistic readings.

Counselling benefits

What was discovered in some participants was that counselling helped them to deal with the practical changes in their life, at the time of the bereavement and shortly afterward. Additionally, counselling helped them understand the emotions they were going through. However, it appears counselling failed to heal adequately the innate psychological needs that arose in these persons' psyche. Examples:

"I get to sort of express how I feel. I know I'm going to see Laura on Thursday, and I get to express how I feel; just coping mechanisms. She's the kind of counsellor that helps with mechanisms and she's the kind of counsellor that doesn't actually tell me anything, but somehow I arrive at the conclusions. It helps me become a stronger person."

"The mediumship reading is the emotional connection to Terry and it's more about Terry and me and knowing my son's ok and about the healing of my heartbreak over my child dying and knowing I can communicate with him. Whereas, with my counsellor it's practical, more to do with myself. It's about me and not so much about Terry and me. It helps me to get my crap together."

Below is a quote from a participant who works as a counsellor and who has received mediumistic readings:

"My counsellor did reiterate that what you're seeing at this stage is etc, so it maybe helps somebody see that it's normal and that everybody goes through five particular stages. It might take three months. It might take three years. So, maybe if the counsellor is practical, I suppose it can show some sort of light at the end of the tunnel without being condescending. You know you won't always be like this, but I don't think counselling really helped me when I went through bereavement. Perhaps it helped me stay practical and grounded, but that's about it."

Sam, who works as a medium and bereavement counsellor, suggests this:

"Counselling is often about helping the patient to bring themselves to an understanding of how they feel. This can bring some alleviation of the symptoms of grief, but it's not a real answer to the problems in bereavement. It helps people keep on track with their lives. It helps people express emotion that may be blocked up. It helps with the practical things."

Complementing counselling with mediumistic readings and vice versa

Sam goes on to further state that:

"I'm not sure counselling can ever completely alleviate the symptoms of grief. It can help, but it's never going to be the final answer, particularly those in a huge grief. I don't think they can carry that without it having a negative effect for the rest of their lives although the counselling is helping on a certain level.

The weakness is that the real psychological issues causing the grief are never resolved. I would say it's impossible to resolve them without some spiritual source. Mediumship being the most effective I've come across. This is because the needs of the mind are not addressed by standard approaches. By nature, these needs appear to be transpersonal. Even if they don't believe in an afterlife on a conscious level, a part of their mind has appeared to me to still want a connection for whatever reason. Part of their mind still needs to have emotional comfort and closure. As the person is deceased then, by nature, there is no way for them to resolve these feelings without a transpersonal source and transpersonal belief and sense.

From that point onwards, the bereaved has a need to find the deceased again. It is as if that person is lost, and through the mediumistic reading, the person finds the deceased again in their mind through that transpersonal connection."

Both of the participants who work as counsellors were asked if a merged approach to bereavement healing between mediumship and counselling could be useful and their replies were:

"The two can complement each other well. A mediumistic reading gives you affirmation that the person who has passed is ok. Is learning lessons. Is with family. Is right by your side. Whereas, counselling is more about you, how you are coping with the physical loss of that person. How you are coping with the everyday practical things."

And…

"Yes, I definitely feel the two can be used well together. They are different entities but used correctly can complement each other. One deals with the problem directly, the other offers a means to express and keeps the person functioning better on the practical aspects of life."

These quotations and the data gathered from the study help to illustrate that counselling doesn't appear to directly support the innate needs that arise in the psyche. However, it does give people a place to express what they are going through and can help with the practical elements of their life. Further, that mediumistic readings can be used with counselling in a combined approach to effectively address and assist the bereaved individual in all elements of their life: mental, emotional and practical.

Counselling approach is not for everyone

This combined approach however, may not be suitable for everyone as highlighted through further quotes from participants:

> "Counsellor? I just don't care for them, and that's probably grossly unfair, but I don't."

I asked the participant to clarify why she felt this way, and she replied:

> "I once went to see a counsellor just because I had some phobias. I hoped there was a way I could crack these, so I went to see this counsellor, for several weeks and spent more money than I should have done. One week, I told her about an incident in my childhood, which was totally irrelevant to the phobias. I mentioned that had nothing to do with it, a bit of a sad event really.
>
> I mentioned this because she was asking about my childhood, and then after that, every week all she wanted to talk about was this incident that happened when I was a child, and I don't know why. Then, of course, if we're talking about after my son died. My son did see counsellors quite a lot because he'd suffered from depression for ten years. I kind of felt that didn't do him a lot of good, so I suppose if I had one ounce of faith in them before, I certainly don't now, so no, no, I'm not remotely interested in them."

Quote from John, the MD participant:

> "I would not seek any form of traditional psychotherapy or psychiatric relief for it, because I've read what the college of psychiatry says on the matter. What is taught to medical students and doctors pre-graduate or postgraduate is, a sequence of events are expected to occur in bereavement, in regards to a timescale process of which there are phases of varying length, and so I'm well aware of where any doctor, counsellor or psychiatrist is coming from who deals with this.
>
> They are computing phases of bereavement and where you are and what, if anything, to do about each stage. So, I would have an expectation of what's coming. I'm an analytic kind of person, and

my mind is already thinking what am I going through at this point? This is my process that isn't everybody's approach."

It is important for me to say some counsellors, of course, do more than what is said here. As with mediums some counsellors are better in various areas than others.

Medical approaches to healing depression caused by bereavement

Additionally, John went on to say that he believed mediumistic readings were very important to healing depression symptoms related to bereavement. He suggested that a medical approach was inadequate at dealing with bereavement symptoms in the long term.

An example he gave to support his opinion is, if a person comes to a General Practitioner depressed because of a bereavement, they are asked to fill out a questionnaire, and if they meet certain criteria from the questionnaire, mild anti-depressants are prescribed. However, because of their addictive nature, antidepressants are only an adequate course of treatment for patients for the first six weeks; after that they become addictive.

> "We know if a patient becomes intolerant to it in six weeks, then we know they will become addicted to it in roughly that time scale."

He commented that GPs, in general, will shy away from bereavement issues because, in his opinion, they realize the medical profession is not adept or fully trained enough to deal with these types of situations. GPs will most often direct their patients to counselling for severe symptoms of bereavement grief. His belief is that it serves more to help with physical symptoms and practical changes in the person and that psychiatry is an option. However, it's only a mixture of counselling, other forms of psychotherapy and medication. To him, these strategies don't offer a solution to the issues within the psyche. I asked if based on his experience, he feels the medical profession, as a whole, provides a long-term answer to bereavement healing:

> "Oh, absolutely, I don't think we engage with it. I think the best you will get from many GPs is going to see Cruse, the bereave-

ment counsellors, specifically because we recognize we are not very good at it. That route, I would say doesn't offer a long-term answer because it addresses the practical sides of their life and the physical changes that have taken place and gives them a chance to express some of their emotions and try to work through them. It helps keep them together, but it doesn't offer a long-term solution. Psychiatry is the same, but this is a mixture of various forms of psychotherapy, along with different types of medication."

Additionally, if he were to experience a severe bereavement in the future, he suggested:

"If I became overly depressed, I'd probably be aware of that and probably go for pills, and the reason why is that they are effective. I know they are effective, as effective as standard talking therapies. Just as talking therapies are portrayed as effective as the pills and that's fine. They both work about the same. The difference is the pills work much quicker. You can get the pills and within two weeks, they're working. Unfortunately, with talking therapies, under the NHS, at the very least you've probably got to wait eight or nine weeks to get an appointment, and that's a long time."

When asked if, at any point, they would potentially seek out a form of transpersonal therapy such as a mediumistic reading he replied:

"With what I know now, and what I have experienced in the last few years, yes, I would, without a doubt."

A combination approach – traditional and transpersonal

Interestingly, the thoughts of Chris who works as a psychiatrist correlated with the GP's thoughts. Chris stated that he would rely on pills for depression and would be open to receiving different forms of psychotherapy, but ultimately would not choose to do so because he feels the approach is overall inadequate at healing all grief within bereavement, stating:

"For those who would be open to pills at the beginning of the bereavement, if they felt that the grief was strong enough to warrant them, and later having a mediumistic reading, perhaps some counselling. If they feel they need to express their feelings more and physical matters in their life are troubling them, this to me would be the best route to get through bereavement.

The key is that mediumship can really help heal the complex issues of bereavement in a way the other approaches simply can't. There are definitely needs I have seen in all persons who experience bereavement that can't be addressed by medication and standard psychotherapies. What these needs are is difficult to say, perhaps you could call them spiritual needs but, it's some part of the mind that appears to want more, perhaps even needs more than just getting on with things and trying to cope or detach. A part of the mind wants to feel continually connected.

Medication or counselling can't implement this. Mediumship, I would say has the potential to achieve this feeling because validating information is given. The person then knows that the deceased is still around them and still lives on in some form of afterlife. I have seen that it is as if the person, the bereaved, reconnects with the deceased, as if in a way that person was lost and now they have been found.

Yes, I think that is what it's about. A need, within the person to validate that their loved one lives on; a need to find that person wherever they may be. After the reading that connection is there again, the deceased has been reconnected to the person, and the spiritual aspect of the connection continues, and it is then the deeper wants of the mind find some actual lasting resolution."

It would appear from the data, that approaches used, outside of a transpersonal approach, might arise from the mind attempting to heal the innate needs. For example, displaying photographs and other such actions that have been mentioned, that are from my perspective and interpretation, actions connected to the deeper symptom of the bereaved seeking to stay connected to the deceased and find them again.

Traditional forms of bereavement healing practices and aids like counselling and medication appear suited to help the person cope with emotions they are going through or understand the emotions they are experiencing. However, it was apparent with my participants that on their own, these approaches could not adequately address and work through the innate needs within their psyche. There is a strong indication that such approaches on their own would be inadequate at addressing the deeper innate needs discussed in the majority of people, if not in all persons.

However, the traditional approaches show some potential in being used effectively in tangent with mediumistic readings for those open to and psychologically ready to experience such an approach.

MSc study summary

Overall, mediumistic readings show great potential to help symptoms of grief within a bereavement, offering a way to address the deep innate needs that arise. Offering to those open to the process a potential long-term answer. They are particularly attractive to and useful for persons with no strong religious or philosophical belief against the possibility of an afterlife where the soul remains intact. Moreover, as seen with the healing benefits, the mediumistic process as a whole can be very useful to work through unresolved emotional issues connected to the deceased that require resolution in the psyche of the bereaved individual.

Inevitably, as mentioned prior, the inclusion of clients of the researcher as participants will give rise to concerns about participants responding, in essence, to please the researcher. Some persons will indeed take an issue to this. However, as mentioned earlier in the literature review, I felt that the conditions for this study would potentially produce a richer quality of data, allow for a deeper exploration of bereavement and provide more refined and new information regarding the concepts that arose in those few previous studies.

Next steps for greater academic acceptance

Reviewing the data from those studies, and my own, I would suggest this study did delve deeper and produced greater findings, overall, than those previous. I would credit this to the approach taken in participant recruitment and further, my use of purposeful sampling to expand and explore the emerging data. I also believe that the participants answered honestly and openly without influence swaying their thoughts. The fact they put themselves forward in the first place suggested to me they already felt the way they described during their interviews and were not in any way trying to please me.

That being said, the next academic step would be for the study to be repeated using participants with no connection to the researcher to find if the same or similar results are found. I'm sure if this were to happen the results would be very similar. I feel such a study would likely produce less richness in data due to the possibility that participants may be less open to discussing matters related to the study and depending on the recruitment process there may be no way to assure the person has received a decent standard of reading.

However, I suggest the strongest themes would again emerge. The reason I suggest this is because the results very much fit with my experiences and that of other mediums and everyday people who have experienced readings. I'm not suggesting I knew all that would come out of the study. In fact, several things surprised me at the time. On reflection, it all makes sense to my experience as a medium and what I have seen in other people through my work as a medium and also with family and friends. The next page features a diagram depicting the potential model of bereavement and bereavement healing that arose from the study and my experience.

Ambiguity loss

Furthermore, let us look at the concept that a part of our mind wishes to seek continual bonds with the deceased, at the very least with those persons who we have had good relationships with. Certainly, modern views in attachment theory suggest this may indeed be the case. During my study, it had occurred to me that it is as if all persons were treating the deceased in a way that can be defined as an "ambiguity loss". The term I believe was first used by psychologist, Pauline Boss in the 1970s and is seen as a loss that occurs without closure or understanding.

An ambiguity loss is commonly used to describe grief caused by the disappearance of a family member. This could be a loved one being in a state of cognitive decline, or at times due to the termination of a pregnancy. These losses are categorized by elements that are unresolved, such as is the person alive or not? Does the person remember me or not? Or was the person alive or not at any given time?

Boss, (1977) suggests the grieving process for an ambiguous loss differs from traditional mourning because the person is unable to gain closure due to unresolved grief. Further, that trauma, and ambiguous loss often co-exist together, and if the trauma of the loss, or a trauma from the past, is not dealt with, then it can trigger unresolved emotions, which a person becomes hesitant to address. Again, this could potentially be related to my study, Buddhist participants three and four, and emotional closeting. Boss, (2012) suggested ambiguous loss happens when the physical or mental survival of the loved one is unknown.

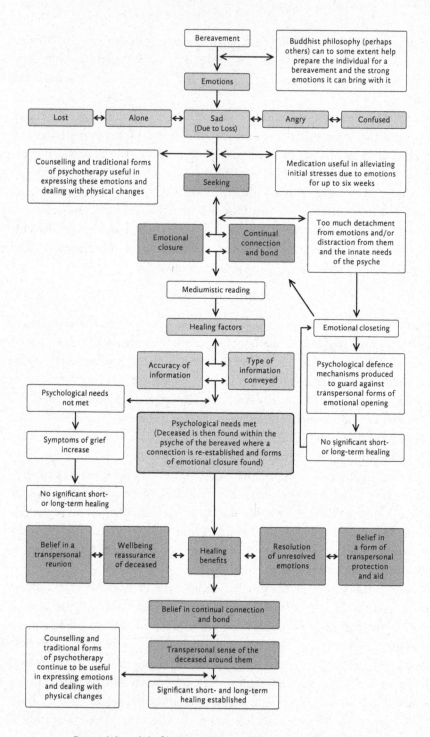

Potential model of bereavement and bereavement healing

Examples are an individual in army service, who is missing in action or an individual, who is in a very difficult mental state due to dementia, which causes "frozen grief". Frozen grief is a result of the ambiguity of death because of the physical or psychological disappearance and, therefore, one's grief is frozen since they do not get a chance to let grief run a regular course.

It would appear, given what I have discussed, and the results of my study that this ambiguous loss that is causing frozen grief goes further beyond these examples of physical and mental disappearances of loved ones, to also include normal death circumstances.

As it appeared for the individuals in my study, the deceased was treated very much in an ambiguous way, very much as if their state of existence was in question and more as if the deceased was missing instead of ceasing to exist. Further, with the non-Buddhist participants, after the reading enacted the transpersonal sense of the deceased, it was as if the person was found again as a transpersonal entity. This earlier example demonstrates this well:

> "This lady is telling me she is always with you, and she is right by your side during the day," and she said, "You talk to her don't you?" And I said, "Yes all the time," and she said, "Yes, she hears you," and all of a sudden there you are because I always think of her as being right there. It was a real turning point, and I thought, "Gotcha, I know where you are, I've found you."

This appeared to lead the non-Buddhist participants to consciously search for a means to 'find' the deceased, and from the above, it seems as if the average circumstances of the passing of a loved one are an ambiguous loss within the psyche. This adds to, and to some extent challenges the modern mainstream thinking of bereavement. This suggests that bereavement grief has additional dynamics that have not been recognized by science to date. From this, I suggest research needs to be undertaken to continue to explore these concepts and to further validate that bereavement and bereavement grief should be recognized as having these additional and potentially critical dynamics.

A spiritual attachment

It's interesting, Field, Gao, & Paderna, (2005) suggested that in their research they found that continuing bonds with the deceased may represent a transition from a physical-based bodily attachment to a spiritual attachment. I would suggest this *is exactly* the transition that is found in my study, where the reading enacts a conscious change of perception.

This can be seen where the bereaved individual moves from states of ambiguity to a grounded understanding, which appears to give rise to the transpersonal sense of the deceased surviving in some form, continuing to be around them and connected with them. This leads to a transpersonal attachment with the deceased, which appears to address the deeper need in the psyche to find the deceased and connect with them again, that appears to foster long-term healing.

The question that arises though is why does a part of our mind desire this? Even in cases where the bereaved individual does not believe in an afterlife, their mind still seeks ways to form continual connections with the deceased. Certain questions do arise from the above, questions like, why do we stay attached to the deceased at all? Why do we seek forms of continual bonds and why do we not completely detach from the deceased? Why does our psyche seek to "find" the deceased after death, treating them as if they are still out there somewhere?

Particularly, why do those who do not consciously believe in an afterlife not completely detach from the deceased? Why does their psyche still seek to 'find' the deceased in the same basic way as people who are consciously open to a form of an afterlife? These questions are integral to answering the overall question of what potential mediumistic readings have for bereavement healing. Further, answering these questions are essential to fully understanding the bereavement process.

To discover the realities of this, I compared the data from my study along with various other studies and theories from several different areas of psychology. When compared with these studies and adjoining understandings, there appears to be a hole or a missing link in the modern thinking of bereavement. The information leads me to infer, what could explain the interesting data and understandings found in the discussed studies and areas of psychology, is of a transpersonal nature. If this is the case, it potentially has huge connotations for the future of mediumistic readings and spirit communication in bereavement healing.

Exploring attachment to the deceased further, we find two main arguments, one by psychologist Freud, (1917) who suggested that the deceased person is so ingrained within the ego of the surviving individual, and upon being forced to give up a level of attachment, the mourner seeks to compensate by re-identifying with the deceased person. This can commonly happen through the clinging to, ruminating, and discussing memories associated with the deceased. In this way, the deceased is kept alive in the thought process or ego of the mourner. In these cases, this process appears to form a balancing of emotions and a balancing of letting go.

The other, by psychologist, Bowlby, (1977) who disagrees with the standard Freudian belief suggesting that attachment bonds are formed because of forces different from biological or libidinal-like drive needs being met. He referenced the work of researchers, Lorenz, (1935) and Harlow, (1958) suggesting each of them demonstrated in their work, that attachment occurred in the absence of these biogenetic needs.

Bowlby suggested in his thesis that attachment behaviour and feeling were connected to survival needs, and not the drives for food or sex. Instead, his theory focused on the need for support and safety. Specifically, if a human lost a person or thing they were very attached to, they became anxious and hysterical. This reaction was noted as being caused from feeling that without the support and feelings of safety from the person or thing in their life, they could not continue living their life.

When a loved one dies, this hysteria is exceptionally powerful, and the mourner seeks continual attachment in an attempt to feel as supported and as safe as they felt before the passing of the loved one.

However, in evolutionary psychology, it is thought that our minds have evolved from the beginnings of man to present day, much like a computer slowly changing its program to make the system more efficient as discussed by Crawford & Krebs, (2013). This natural selection goes back to the adaptive problems faced by our hunter-gatherer ancestors. It is a system designed to regulate behaviour so that these adaptive problems are successfully addressed. Crawford & Krebs, (2013) suggest that this continual evolution of the mind governs emotions that push us to have certain feelings related to all areas of our life, including kinship, and family relations.

Here, emotion is categorized as a superordinate program, whose function is to direct the activities and interactions of the subprograms governing areas like perception; attention; inference; memory; learning; motivational priorities; goal choice; categorization and conceptual frameworks; energy levels and effort allocation.

It is understood that within the mind there is each and every computational and functional definition of each emotion state, including how we respond to the death of a loved one and each emotion entrains various other adaptive programs, deactivating some, activating others, and adjusting the parameters of others, so that the whole system operates in a harmonious and efficacious way, when the individual is confronting certain kinds of triggering conditions or situations. The conditions or circumstances relevant to the emotions are those that:

- recurred ancestrally;
- could not be negotiated successfully unless there was a superordinate level of program coordination;
- had a productive and reliable repeated structure;
- had recognizable cues signalling their presence in which an error would have resulted in large fitness costs.

When a condition or situation of an evolutionarily, recognizable kind is detected, a signal is sent out from the emotion program that activates the specific constellation of subprograms. These subprograms are appropriate to solving the type of adaptive problems that were regularly embedded in that situation and then deactivates programs, whose operation might interfere with solving those types of adaptive problems.

Relating this understanding of the mind to modern attachment theory, continual bonding research and this study, a question arises - and I would suggest its answer is an important, if not integral next step in addressing bereavement healing: Why has our mind not evolved to detach immediately from the deceased for our greater good?

Doing so, this theoretically would increase our mental and physical productivity and chances of physical survival. It seems counterproductive and ultimately inefficient to experience all these emotional states and be driven to seek a persistent connection and bond with the deceased, especially if one has the conscious understanding that there is no life after death.

When approaching it from a purely practical and logical survival-based mindset, it appears to me that this behaviour is utterly pointless and it potentially greatly hinders our physical productivity and chances of physical survival after the death of a loved one. The thought that we remain attached for ego-based reasons related to fundamental human drives or survival needs or even to remember the lessons and knowledge we have gained from the deceased, and our experiences with them does potentially offer some form of explanation.

However, I do not feel they are adequate. In romantic relationships that have turned sour, we seem to be able to detach over time or sometimes, very quickly, without forgetting the lessons we have learned from our time in that relationship.

Logically, I can't see why we would need to do this differently with positive relationships to the deceased. It appears to me that somewhere in the computational evolution of the mind, it has been assessed that after death, we should behave in a manner as if the person is in some way missing instead of ceasing to exist. Thus, it appears to me, that a part of the mind either doesn't fully understand death or believes, at some level that in some way death is not the end of our consciousness.

If the mind understood death as a finite end of consciousness, logically, one would think that our minds would have evolved to experience all the emotions and drives only up to the point of death. That if death were a finite end of consciousness, after the death of a loved one, we would completely detach. This would be the most efficient thing to do; to totally redirect our attention to whatever was left in the now as quickly as possible.

It appears though that we don't and that in the case of positive relationships, we potentially never totally detach. Furthermore, our psyche drives us to "find" the deceased in whatever way we consciously are open to at any given time. Producing drives that appear to start subconsciously and gradually affect our actions.

If we were governed so strongly by our mind, as the discussed theories suggest, then surely, our mind would be powerful enough to shift our drives to feel very little for the deceased. Certainly, not continually distract us by going out of our way to make persistent connections with them.

This may be complex psychological forces clashing with each other. Potentially, the mind still is evolving and refining itself to be more efficient. I suggest though that we should not rule out a transpersonal related element to this phenomenon. If there is a form of afterlife then, logically, it would be very likely that some part of every person's consciousness would be aware of it at a subconscious level. This could offer an explanation as to why we appear to treat the deceased more as missing than ceasing to exist, and why even those who consciously disbelieve in a form of afterlife, still seek ways to form continual connections and bonds with the deceased.

Perhaps a part of all our minds knows that the deceased carry on? That even though we can't see them, we are aware that they are out there somewhere and the part of us that knows this drives us to reconnect with them.

More research needed

Whilst this is speculative, I believe research should take place in the future to prove if this theory has merit. The implications of this could prove greatly beneficial to bereavement healing and further demonstrates the potential of mediumistic readings in the process of bereavement healing.

If this theory were proven to be true, it would be quite apparent that establishing a transpersonal connection to the deceased would be integral to the healing process. What I also want to be clear on, is that I don't feel all Buddhist practice is unable to help symptoms of grief caused by bereavement in typical Westerners. In fact I have encouraged people to practise several forms of meditation that have Buddhist origin, in order to help them have better control over aspects of their ego and emotional hang-ups, along with releasing anxiety.

I feel the key here is detachment and potential closeting of emotions; our minds don't appear to want to detach and they don't appear to do well with emotional closeting. If a person were to practise Buddhism in a way that is not causing detachment, I feel it could be used very well together with mediumistic readings to those open to this particular type of approach.

In fact, I feel an ideal approach in those open to it, would be a mixture of mediumistic readings, counselling and meditation. I feel very strongly that research needs to take place looking to determine how effective these three are when used in tandem to treat symptoms of grief in the typical Westerner.

As we continue, I'd like to share with you two stories both from participants of my study.

TWELVE

Stories Behind The Study

•••••••••••••

Anne

The story to follow is that of a lovely lady who took part in the study. It is the story of a husband and a wife along with their sweet daughter. It is one that really pulls at my heart, having felt the deepness of the emotions involved. One that shows it's very difficult to know just what is round the corner. If it teaches us about something other than bereavement and mediumship, it teaches us that we must seize the moment and make it our own.

"When Ross asked me if I would tell our story, I was not quite sure where to start, so the beginning seems the best place. I met Richard when I was not quite 13, and he was 16. For the next 23 years, we were never apart for long. We had it all as far as I'm concerned: a lovely home, a beautiful daughter and each other. Who would have wanted anything more?

We had so many good times together as a couple and a family. We would go off rampaging, from camping to holidays in the sun, or off to London for the day. Even so, we were quite happy to snuggle up and watch a DVD, go on a bike ride or just take a stroll, as long as the three of us were together. Christmas was Richard's favourite time of year. Out would come the lights, Blackpool (a seaside town in England famous for its bright lights) had nothing on him.

On Christmas day, Rich would wake me up at about 5 am. 6 am if I was lucky! He would do this by just getting really up close and staring at me, and then he would be off to wake up our daughter, presents would be opened, whilst listening to Christmas songs. This was a tradition from when he was little. About 11:30 am both sets of our parents, and my brother would arrive, and the festivities would really take off!

He would be in his element. By 5:30 pm more guests would come. Most years, by the time everyone had come, it would be up to about 13 of us! He'd bring out the games, and we would have a good laugh. Rich was the best at dancing on the Nintendo Wii (games console), beating all young ones. Then again, he wasn't that old himself.

147

Richard loved to surprise us with little trips away. One time, we went camping for our daughter's tenth birthday with family friends. She wanted a barbecue and for us to all wear our onesies. So, all the girls adorned our onesies but unknown to Rich and our friend, we had also purchased them both one as well.

Richard's onesie was two-tone blue with feet and little babies all over the sleeves. When they were presented with their gifts, Rich was most pleased and jumped up to go and change. He appeared from inside the tent with the biggest grin on his face. He strutted around modelling his new gift with the most masculine of poses. He was so pleased with himself! We went camping only once more before he passed, but we will forever have our memories of Rich dancing around our tent. All of us doing a birthday conga.

We are lucky to have so many memories. I would love to share them all, but I'm afraid we would take up the whole of Ross' book. When it comes down to it, Richard was a great all-round man, partner, father, son, and friend. No one is perfect, but he was for us!

———

On Thursday, before the Jubilee weekend, I was tickling Richard when he said, "Ouch!" and when he felt his armpit, there was a small lump the size of a ping-pong ball, so we rang the doctor's, and he looked at it the very next day. Our doctor referred him to the hospital, but by the Jubilee Monday, which was just four days, the lump had grown to the size of a cricket ball. I took him to A & E, concerned it might be an abscess, but after an X-ray, we were told that it was not an abscess. They told us not to worry, as lumps that grow that quickly and also hurt are not suspicious.

Richard made an appointment for the hospital where we were told he would need a biopsy to be sure of what it might be. The doctors informed us of some possibilities, but they were only possibilities. Time seemed to drag, and every appointment took so long to come. Appointment for the pre-appointment for biopsy, then the biopsy itself, and then it was more waiting. It was so frustrating for all of us!

So much time seemed to go by with no answers until finally Richard was diagnosed with melanoma. He had the lump under his arm removed on July 24th, 2012. Then he had radiotherapy and chemotherapy. At no time were we told that the outcome would be the one we have been left with. We were always told the outcome was really positive, and we always believed we were going to win the fight.

When Rich went downhill really fast, it was such a shock. He had been so strong, upbeat and positive. It was heartbreaking. He was admitted to Southampton Hospital and on Wednesday, the 31st of October, we were told he had pneumonia, but he was reacting well to the antibiotics, and that he should be home by the following Wednesday.

On Friday, the 2nd of November, Rich sat on the end of his hospital bed making plans with my brother for New Year's Eve. That evening, my daughter and I gave Rich kisses and said goodbye a little early, as our daughter was off to Alton Towers with my family for the weekend. We said our goodbyes and Rich told Hope, our daughter, to have fun and that he was so proud of her. That would be the last thing he said to her, and I'm so glad that he did. Looking back at that time now, his words were a bit slurred, and he did say a few strange things, but Richard was on morphine, and it had that effect on him. I told the nurse, and she said she would keep an eye on him for me. I dropped our daughter off early the next morning with my family for the weekend and wasted a few hours until I could go back to the hospital.

As usual, I bent the hospital visiting rules and arrived early at 8 am. As soon as I saw Rich, I knew something was not right. He was very shaky, disoriented and when he tried to walk, he shuffled like an old man. He couldn't get his spoon to his mouth to eat his breakfast, and when he tried to take his pills, he kept dropping them but bless him, he still gave himself a shave, as he hated that 8 am shadow.

I kept telling the nurses who are so rushed off their feet and do such a brill job, that there was something really not right, but by 10 am I couldn't do it by myself anymore, so I called Richard's mum, who came straight away. She was so strong for both of us. At 12 pm, we were told that Richard's body was shutting down and that he had only 24 hours to live. What could you say? What could you do? We just couldn't believe it! How could this be happening?

We were told a little later, that the cancer had spread and was pushing on his organs. When he had his scan earlier that week, we were told his organs were fine. We didn't have much time to get our daughter back to say goodbye. That was the hardest phone call I have ever had to make in my life. She was amazing and still is. She is my hero. Sadly, by the time she got back, Richard could no longer talk, and he had to be sedated. I didn't leave the hospital, and neither did Richard's mum and dad, his aunties, his best friend, my parents and my brother.

Richard fought for three days, and not one of them left the hospital. We slept on the family room floor. Richard's mum, dad and I stayed with Rich and did not leave his side. Our daughter, who was only 11 at the time, came in and out. It was her wish, and she didn't want to leave, but obviously, it was a lot for her come to terms with. She bought him gifts that were dear to her and placed them in his hand, and then stayed with him to the end. Friends came in floods; even the nurses were affected and touched by the dedication of Richard's friends and family. The nurses had also become quite attached to our Rich. They said he was a star patient. He would help other patients by making them a cup of tea; have chats, even stopped one man from pulling out his drip.

By the night of Richard's passing, we all were so fatigued. I fell asleep on Richard's chest. Richard's mum gently woke me, and I could tell immediately it was time. It was like he had waited for me to wake up to say our last goodbyes. We told him how much we loved him and would miss him. Sadly, on the 5th of November at 10:59 pm, aged only 39, Richard lost his fight with cancer. After Rich had passed, I needed to leave the room knowing he was no longer there.

I had to keep my Rich in my heart and not add more sad memories that I did not want. I left Richard's mum and dad to say their goodbyes. I waited for them and then we made our way to the family room where everyone was waiting. More friends came, and we just sat for what seemed like forever, but finally it came the time when we needed to leave. I somehow drove myself and our daughter home, which I insisted on doing. I needed to take control, but I can remember thinking as we climbed into bed that night and hugged each other so very tight, how would we survive without him?

He was our everything. We had gone from three to two in days. Richard was my backbone. He was my right arm, my friend, my soul mate, and the father of my child. I had lived more of my life with him than I had without him and since the day we met I hadn't been away from him for more than a week, and now he was gone. He was the one who would comfort us in sad times. What could I do without him? It was at this time that I knew what the feeling of being surrounded by so many people but still being so so alone truly felt like. I hated it, but I had our daughter, and we had each other, and I would be strong for her even when it was hard.

~

My mind soon turned to seeking help from Ross, as Richard had had a reading from him a few years before and was blown away. However, I was advised by friends to give Rich time to settle in over in the afterlife. So, Richard's mum, auntie and I booked to see Ross in the following May. That way it would be six months after Richard's passing, and May was also the month that Richard was born.

The day of the reading seemed to take forever to come around, but finally, it was here. My mind was racing. What if Rich didn't make contact? How would we deal with it? It would feel like losing him all over again.

On our arrival, we were greeted by the lady of the house, who was very kind and showed us to a room that was very tranquil. This was where the reading would take place. We were offered a drink and then left to settle into our surroundings while Ross prepared himself for our reading. After a small wait, Ross entered the room and ran through everything, and then there was silence.

When Ross started the reading, he explained that an older man and lady were helping Rich come through because Richard had not long passed and needed a little help. It soon became clear from Ross' discretions that the older gentleman was Richard's granddad, and the lady was his Nan. Richard started on about the day of his passing and how he quickly deteriorated, and that he had drifted in and out of consciousness, being aware but not able to communicate. He had been aware that we were there and that I was talking to him, holding his hand and stroking his head. This made me feel better knowing he knew he was not alone.

Ross went on to explain that Richard was giving him a very sickly taste in his mouth. This would have been the morphine. Rich hated it so much. He always made sure there was a drink close to hand to wash it down with. Ross then went on to say that Rich was showing him his daughter and that she had bought some items that were dear to her and had placed them in Richard's hand, and that's where they stayed.

Ross later told us that Richard was aware that one of these items was left with him for his cremation, still clutched in his hand. This was amazing. Our daughter had brought two small toys to the hospital, one a bear called "Little Bear" that she had had since she was very small, and the other a tortoise. She had chosen the second toy as we have a tortoise that Rich would talk to every morning. Rich would greet him by saying, "Morning Sheldie boy!"

After Richard's passing, we gave the little bear back to our daughter, who still cherishes it, but the tortoise remained with Rich. Ross went on to describe some other objects that were also placed with Rich and that there were quite a few of them. Certainly everything Ross was saying was spot on! Richard then told Ross how we had been led to believe his illness was not as severe as it was and how the outcome was expected to be a much happier one and how it had been a shock to him, as well as to us when he deteriorated so rapidly.

—

Ross spoke about videos that were on Richard's phone and that they were taken on our last trip away together, and I had been looking at them recently, which I had. He also mentioned how Richard's voice was on this video, which was also true. The holiday was in Cornwall. It had meant a great deal to Rich and how much fun we had. This was incredible! There was no way Ross would have any of this information. Ross said Richard was showing him white flowers and that it had a recent significance. The flowers Richard's mum had given me earlier that day were a bunch of white roses. It was all mind-boggling.

He told us about how Richard's spirit was such a fun and charming one, how he adored his daughter and how close they were. I was so emotional, I could not stop the tears, and Richard's mother was welling up, too. She took hold of my hand, and I was grateful she was there to help me through the process. Finally, Ross asked if we had any questions; Richard's mum asked if he was happy. Ross was quiet for a little while. Then he told us that Richard was still getting used to things. He was not unhappy, but not happy.

He is with family, and they were looking after him, guiding him. He would grow stronger and become better at coming through, but he missed his family here so much and wanted to be with us here. Ross explained that sometimes it can take a spirit a long time to heal their grief of being physically separated from us here as well. Ross explained that the reading process often helps them just as much as it does us.

He also said that Rich watches over our daughter and us all. How proud he was of her and that he can see that she sometimes struggles with him not being here. He looks over her when she is at school and helps her to try her best. Ross even told us the name of the school she attends, and how they were having or had done work on the top floor of the school. I later asked Hope about the work at the school and she confirmed that there would be some building work taking place on the top floor and roof.

Rich managed to eventually get her name across to Ross though it did cause a little confusion to Ross at first, as her name has another meaning but he just came right out and said her name. He also mentioned that Hope and I were thinking about Rich recently, and it was somehow connected to a bird. For a school project, Hope was looking at poetry, and there was a poem about a crow. It was also about death and rebirth, and we both spoke about how it made us think of Rich. Ross left Richard's love with us and drew the reading to a close.

For me, the reading from Ross validated that Richard is very much around us all still. Not in body, but spirit, looking over us, and maybe at times guiding us a little. To know this means the world to me. It comforts our family and me and makes the loss bearable with help from Ross. I have been back to see Ross since our first reading and each time Richard comes through he is a little stronger and finding it easier. He also brings his humour with him, reminding us to laugh, have fun and that it is ok to do this.

He knows we will never-ever forget him. How could you? He loves that we talk about him, and to him, and even though we can't hear his answer, he is listening. This brings me peace of mind knowing Richard is ok. He is at peace and looking over us, and one day we'll meet again.

After the readings, Ross was very supportive to our daughter, Richard's family, and me telling us if we ever need to talk just to get in contact. So, I would like to say a big thank you from us all including Rich, and always our blessings."

I remember Anne's readings so clearly, Richard did stand out from all of the thousands and thousands of readings I've done in the last decade. Richard has one of the most genuine and kind-natured, caring souls I have ever felt. The love and appreciation I felt from those who knew him here and from him to those he knew, was also incredible. It is interesting when I read these stories back or listen to reading recordings, I often get quite emotional myself, having sensed the feelings and bonds of the people involved and the emotions feel very raw to me.

Anne's story is one of the stories I find myself getting most emotional with. Whilst I don't think I have ever told Anne this, I am sometimes asked how often I have come across people who have readings, where the person has found their soul mate – two people who really deeply care and love each other. The answer I tell them is not many. When I count up how many I have felt to be this way, Anne and Richard are always the first ones I count, as the feelings I felt in the reading were so intense, and in all ways so very real. I believe that the reading experiences have helped Anne move forward in her life but yet still hold an exceptionally loving continual bond with Richard.

Mentioned in Anne's story is a point rarely discussed and that is, that a mediumistic reading can have healing effects and be helpful for the spirit or spirits communicating. They have grief connected to their love for us, their desire to be with us and be there for us and they remain completely invested in our happiness or potential lack of it. They want to come through to let us know things that they may need to address or actions they did or didn't do, things they said or didn't say and events in the family before or after their passing.

They may wish to say sorry for something or clear the air over a negative situation. Sometimes, this can be very important for them on a karmic level and for their vibration and continual evolution in the afterlife.

~

Carol

Moving on to the second story, it again features another young male who chose to take his own physical life. Whilst it is clear that taking one's life has no impact on whether they go on to an afterlife, I am sometimes asked if that person is happier in heaven than they would be if they were still here.

That is always difficult for me to answer, but what I will say is, with the two young males who are featured in this book, who did take their lives, they were very sensitive. Sometimes, I feel in the long term, they can find much more peace and solace in their minds in heaven than they ever could here, certainly as things are currently here on Earth, and will be for some time to come.

What you will also see in this next story is that although the circumstances are similar, the people involved and their story is quite different. What you see with mediumship is how different people's lives are and how different people process grief. Even though parallels are found in people's lives, their lives are still quite different from each other. Each reading is most assuredly, quite different from the next.

"I am the mother of two children. My daughter Lucy was born in 1978 and my son Ben in 1981. Even though Ben passed away in 2010, I have never felt any less of a mother to him, so when the inevitable question comes from people I have only just met, "Do you have children?" I can only answer, "Yes, two." To not include Ben would feel as though I denied his existence. It would feel like a betrayal.

Ben was a very happy-go-lucky child. He made friends easily and was quite scatter-brained about his responsibilities. He'd wander off with friends after school without a thought about letting me know what he was up to, but he was always so full of joy about his adventures he was having with his friends that it was hard to be cross and anyway, he would have forgotten about it the next day! So, he bumbled through his early school days as if it was one long, joyful holiday.

When Lucy was seven and Ben was four, my marriage to their father ended. It had been a fractious relationship even before Ben was born and we finally decided it was time to go our separate ways. In some of my darker moments, I worry that maybe Ben's later difficulties were partly as a result of coming from a broken home, but we can only do what we think is the right thing to do at the time.

It cannot be right to bring children up in an environment of bickering and antagonism. Although Ben was a happy-go-lucky child, he was also very sensitive to other people's feelings and perhaps there were concerns stemming from his parent's separation that were running deep, only to surface later. If you lose a child to suicide you question every little detail of your life looking for the root cause, and you are left with a bucket full of 'what ifs', but no real answers.

Ben progressed through secondary school and college with much the same casual attitude that he'd had as a small child, but in primary school, he didn't achieve much academically. In fact, for a while, he was given extra tuition to bring him up to average. However, at secondary school, he began to excel. I asked him one day why he didn't do so well at primary school because he, obviously, had hidden talents. He said he had been bored at primary school. It's funny how children just accept the way things are. It obviously didn't cross his mind to question the education he was receiving and it never crossed my mind that he wasn't reaching his full potential. I was just happy that he was happy, and it never worried me that he may not be a high achiever academically.

Nevertheless, he did do well at secondary school and then progressed to college to take A levels. I don't think he made much effort to study, but he absorbed information quickly, and with little effort he achieved sufficient grades to gain a place at the university of his choice to study electronic engineering.

Ben was barely 18 when he left for university. He was so looking forward to going and, of course, I was thrilled for him and outwardly encouraged him to go, but inside I was broken hearted. I hated to think he was going to be a two-hour car journey away from me. I kept thinking about the mothers who waved their sons goodbye during the First World War knowing they were going to the front, and most likely they would not return home.

I think, at the time, I was trying to draw the comparison to snap myself out of self-pity. My son was going to university and was only two hours away. This was a good and positive thing and nothing like the farewells of those poor mothers, but as it turned out my foreboding was not as misplaced as I thought.

Ben did not take his life while still at university, but he came close.

Ben had a very gentle and caring nature and this applied to both humans and animals. He could not bear to see anyone or anything suffer and if it was in his power to help he would. When he was going to college, he would sometimes arrive with no money for his lunch because he'd given it to a homeless person on the way. When he left primary school, and the headmistress gave a little speech about each child, in turn, she said, "One thing to be said about Ben is that he can always see the other person's point of view."

I thought it was a beautiful thing to say about him, but I recall Ben being most put out. He was just eleven and said she had commented on other children's Math or English abilities, but not on the things he was good at. I tried to explain to him that what she'd said about him was the nicest thing she'd said about anyone, but Ben was just Ben, and it wouldn't have occurred to him that his empathetic nature was anything special. It was a true summing up of what made Ben who he was.

I remember once when the news broke about the abuse of Iraqi prisoners by American and British troops, I was expressing how appalled I was and how I hoped they would not escape justice and Ben said, "Mum, you just don't know how you would feel if you had witnessed the horrific deaths of many of your friends." So, he never did stop being able to see the other person's point of view.

—

Ben had a room in a residential block to begin life at university and made friends with others on his block. At least one of them stayed a friend for the remainder of Ben's physical life. Ben died at the age of 29. It seems to me, the road began to get rocky for him at university, but I only have very sketchy information about the issues that began to trouble him. He threw himself into student culture, and indeed, I know that socially that would have included quite a lot of drinking. Ben was not averse to excess drinking, as I knew from his pre-university days and I think this may have been something of a catalyst for the changes in him.

One day when still eighteen, he told me that he had attempted to take his life and had ended up in A&E. Because he was eighteen, he exercised his rights as an adult to refuse permission for anyone to call me. I knew nothing about it until he was out of the hospital and back at university.

He became very depressed and Ben's sister, Lucy, and I would have long telephone calls with him where he would say almost nothing at all, and we would make valiant efforts to lift his spirits. He didn't want to drop out of university.

He wanted to continue with his studies, at least for the time being and so began ten years of Ben battling depression, suicidal thoughts, going to counselling and numerous other therapies that he tried in turn.

One time when he was at home and had almost given up on going back to university, I persuaded him to go back. It was against what I wanted in my heart, but I was afraid for him that if he didn't go, he would regret it later. How I wish now I had just kept him home with me.

After Ben left university, and for at least his final year, he had been quite well and very positive about the future. He started working in London. For quite some time, maybe two years or so, he seemed to be strong and well and I really thought he had overcome the issues that had plagued him. However, I don't think there was ever a time when he wasn't on medication for depression, although he was not very forthcoming when I asked him about it. I think he probably thought he was protecting me.

Anyway, as a male in his mid-twenties, I wouldn't expect him to want to share everything with his mother. He was always quite a private person. I knew that he wasn't completely well, but I truly thought he was going in the right direction and that one day he would be able to leave his depression behind him, along with all the medication and therapies.

Then the blackness began to trouble him more, and he was once again looking for any new therapy or one that he hadn't tried before. There was more counselling, different counsellors and other therapies. The very nature of Ben's inquisitive mind would have led him to research his illness so that he probably knew more about it than some of the counsellors he met.

Ben would not suffer fools gladly, so if he didn't think they were up to the mark, he would go elsewhere and try somebody else. By the time he was into the second half of his twenties, he was also suffering from anxiety attacks and later agoraphobia. I have since learned that both these symptoms can be a side effect of antidepressant medication, but hindsight is a wonderful thing!

~

I wouldn't want to give the impression that all Ben's life at this time was doom and gloom. Far from it, in fact, it was ironic that on the surface, Ben lived a life that would be the envy of many. He was a young male adult living and working in London, surrounded by friends. His friends understood the difficulties he was facing and were there for him always, through the good times and bad. Sometimes during the worst of times, he would not even respond to their phone calls, but they never gave up on him and knowing that he was loved and *never isolated, or lonely was one of the greatest comforts to me after he had passed over.*

He had always been a music lover, and he explored all types of music. My partner, Tim, has also always been a big music lover and has a very expansive CD collection. Ben found his own tastes in music and when he came to stay with us, Tim and Ben would spend hours sharing new music they had found, swapping CDs and talking about new bands. I remember Ben, one day, joking that he was on a slippery slope now, as he'd developed a taste for Richard Thompson's music, one of Tim's favourite musicians, but hardly trendy! And he loved Bob Dylan – always a favourite of mine. Ben also learned to play guitar. My favourite photo, taken one Christmas, is of Ben strumming on a guitar while his little nephew, just two years old at the time, sat immediately in front of him totally rapt.

On the 8th of September 2010 at 1.30 am., our doorbell rang. Coincidentally, during the previous week there had been several rings on the doorbell in the middle of the night, but on looking out of the window, there had never been anyone there. This time, Tim looked out of the window to see a police car parked outside the house.

Having just woken up, but not entirely, I really thought the police had come to talk to us about the doorbells being rung in the middle of the night. I thought they could have waited until the morning, and then I heard the policeman ask if he could he come in. He wouldn't be calling at this time of night if it weren't important. I was fully awake then. Surely, it must be either a death or an injury to a family member. Please, God; don't let it be a death. I went downstairs to face the worst news I would ever receive in my life.

Sitting on the sofa was a lone, young policeman. I don't recall his exact words, but he had come to tell us that Ben had been found dead in his flat. He was found lying fully clothed in a dry bathtub with a pillow behind his head, a plastic bag over his head and a tube leading from a canister of helium had been taped to the inside of the bag.

He had left two notes, one to everyone apologizing for putting us through this, but saying he had wanted to take his life for ten years and had only put off doing so, for all this time, because he didn't want to hurt the people who loved him.

He also left another note for a friend who lived in the neighbouring flat telling her that he was taking his life, and by the time she read the note he would be dead. He had left the note in his friend's pigeon hole, knowing she would be at work all day, so by the time she got home, it would be too late.

So, he absolutely meant to die. There was no chance he would be discovered in time to save his life. He had asked her not to enter his flat herself but to call emergency services. He needed somebody to enter the flat because he had a cat and he didn't want it to starve. Ben would never overlook a detail like that. He loved his cat – he loved all animals.

She had a key and entered the flat anyway, but because he had been careful with his timing it was too late, he was already dead. She called emergency services and sat with him until they arrived. It was such a kind thing to do, she didn't need to stay, but she did.

I remember saying to the policeman, "This isn't just a nightmare is it?" Ever since the first occasion that Ben had attempted suicide, I had had nightmares, every now and then, that he was dead. The policeman, just quietly, said no. I asked whether there was any possibility that it was somebody else; he said no, again.

It is hard to absorb that sort of information. It's too much to really believe, and your mind plays tricks, offering other scenarios for you to clutch at. How could the policeman be sure it was him? It could be somebody else. He didn't know him, but even as I was thinking it, I felt guilty for hoping it was somebody else because then another mother would have to take on this pain.

When Bob Geldof commented on the loss of his daughter, Peaches, he said his family was beyond grief. It suggested they are experiencing grief beyond anything anyone else can understand as if to say everyone else suffers grief, we are suffering something else. It sounded arrogant, and yet, now I knew what he meant. We lose loved ones in our lives, grandparents, parents, and friends, even pets. I am in my sixties now and have lost many loved ones, but to lose a child takes you somewhere completely different. Through all the times of grief I'd been through before, I could not have imagined the pain I was now in or the terrible path I was now on.

If you lose a child to suicide, there is another dimension, the overwhelming guilt. If you lose your child to illness or accident, of course, the loss is the same, but if you lose a child to suicide it does not matter one bit what age the child was or the circumstances surrounding their death, you feel responsible. We are parents, our role in life is to look after our children, and you cannot fail in that more spectacularly than in failing to keep them alive.

The policeman left, and I rang Ben's sister, Lucy. I told her Ben was gone, and we cried together on the phone. She lives a two-hour car journey away, so

I could do nothing but leave her with this terrible news. After I had spoken to her, I began to pace the floor. I do not know why I felt compelled to do this, but I did. I walked up and down the room hour after hour. When morning came, I still paced pausing only to ring some people who needed to know that Ben had now left us.

I was filled with the conviction that as Ben hadn't been dead long, there must be a way we can reverse this. He had only been gone a few hours, somehow we should be able to reverse those few hours, and he'd be okay. I just had to work out how it was going to be done. I felt the answer was just a bit out of reach, but I'd probably get it in the end. I just needed to think.

The solution to all this must be there for me to take, but there was a sense of urgency about it too, I felt that we had to do this whatever it was, as soon as possible. If we let the time pass too far, it would be irreversible. This feeling that I could undo what had been done persisted for about three days before I finally understood that it was irreversible, and always had been.

I ate nothing, and the only thing I drank was black coffee, mug after mug of it. I continued to pace. At some point in the day, Tim called the doctor, and the doctor asked to speak to me. He asked if I was considering harming myself. I thought he wasn't making any sense. He was confusing me with Ben. It was Ben who had killed himself, and I didn't have time to talk to this idiot. I was still trying to work out how to bring Ben back. I handed the phone back to Tim and continued pacing and thinking, thinking, thinking.

At some point in the evening, I stopped pacing and sat for a while, as my hips were painful from all the walking. But I missed the pain. I wanted the pain, so I started again. The next night, the first one after we had heard the news, I didn't go to bed, and Tim stayed with me, although I did stop pacing to sit for a while.

I didn't want to sleep, the reality of waking up to this truth was far too painful, so I tried not to sleep at all. Of course, I could not help nodding off every now and then, but my fears were realized with the horror of waking to the reality of what had happened. It was just not worth any of the benefits of sleeping – even the little bit of oblivion that sleep gave me was not worth the pain of waking.

Tim dozed off for a while on the floor where he was sitting. In the morning, he told me that Ben had visited him in the night to say he was sorry but that he just could not carry on any longer. Anyone who knows Tim will tell you he is a very grounded, solid person who is certainly not given to fanciful thinking. So,

I believed him when he said Ben came to him. My strongest feeling though was to be upset that Ben had come to Tim and not me, and I was angry.

I was angry that Ben had struggled for years to get help for his depression but all avenues had failed him, and I was angry with him for doing this to me. A couple of years before he died, he had promised me he would never take his life after having attended a funeral of a friend who had died by suicide; witnessing for himself, the pain that his friend's family were in. I am not angry with him now. I understand that he had suffered far more than we ever understood and how can anyone know the dark places that somebody who feels driven to end their life finds himself, or herself, in.

Sometime during the first days, a doctor came to see me. I guess Tim must have asked him to come by and at that time, I was prepared to sit and talk to him. He was kind, and he asked how he could help. I told him there was only one thing I wanted, and that was Ben back, so unless he could do that for me, I wanted nothing from him.

I am by nature distrustful of medication and having seen Ben struggle through ten years of trying to battle depression, prescribed different drugs and various forms of counselling, I really could not see how in the end it had helped him. I wanted neither drugs nor counselling. What's more, I really would have welcomed dying, which in itself makes you understand the desperation of somebody who takes his or her own life. It is one thing though to wish you were dead; it's quite another to act upon that wish. In any case, I still had one child in this world plus a grandchild, so I felt as though I was sitting on the fence. Do I belong in this world or not?

I did, however, write myself a suicide plan, so that if the time came when I just could not continue, I would know exactly what to do. I wrote my plan out meticulously, down to the last detail about what I would wear and what to do in the event that I changed my mind at the last minute. My plan in very simple terms was to walk out into the sea; at a place I know which has strong tides and shelves away from the shore very steeply and very quickly.

The winter was ahead of us, which would be ideal for carrying out my suicide plan. The cold water would surely give me hypothermia, and I'm not a strong swimmer despite Ben's best efforts some years earlier to teach me to swim. The act of writing it all down eased my mind. I didn't have to think about it anymore. I had my notes that I carried around with me everywhere, and at a moment's notice, I could carry out my plan.

Grief made a prisoner of me. I felt as though I was at the bottom of a pit with brick walls surrounding me, stretching into infinity. Nobody could reach me and in this pit, there are no footholds to climb out. It is an entrapment. There was no future, no past, and I could not think about a future without Ben. Memories were just far too painful to recall, but this way of living is not sustainable.

I started to eat after four days because I knew I had to and I moved away from drinking coffee, which was making me ill, to drinking tea. I could not touch alcohol. I was afraid of where even the smallest amount of alcohol would take me. If I drank too much, which was certainly likely if I started on a bottle of wine, I would feel no better emotionally and would also have a hangover to cope with. I hated eating and even considered only eating cheese because I hate cheese so would not enjoy it. The guilt I felt for eating when my child was dead was enormous.

Having, at last, accepted that Ben's death was irreversible. I wanted proof that something of him, his spirit, the essence of him was still continuing. If I had to accept that I would not see him again in this life, the next best thing would be to know he is well and happy and that I will see him in another life one day. So, I started on something of a spiritual journey. I'm not religious. I wasn't brought up in a religious family, just a vaguely Church of England background requiring us to attend christenings, weddings, and funerals.

In any case, I have never accepted that the Christian faith is the only true faith. Locally, there was a spiritualist church that I had visited out of curiosity two or three times a few years previously. I had liked the simplicity of it, and I had liked the all-inclusive nature. It mattered not a jot what anyone's religion was or whether they had no religion; anything goes. I went along to it, and I also booked a private reading with the lady who ran the church and was herself a medium. The reading was very comforting.

She said she had sensed a spirit enter with me but could not sense whether the spirit was male or female as this spirit had not long passed over. To be fair, it really wouldn't have taken much to recognize I was suffering some extreme grief, so if she was looking for clues, there were certainly obvious ones for her to latch on to.

Nevertheless, I was open to accepting any hint that Ben was still there in some form, albeit one that was beyond my vision. She eventually settled on this spirit being that of a male and said that in life he had not believed in anything – but did now! This was perfectly true as Ben was an atheist.

She also recognized that he had taken his own life, which she could not have known. Still, most of what she told me was fairly generic and would not have been enough on its own to convince me that Ben had indeed been with us that day. I did not doubt the sincerity of the medium, but anyone who is so very desperate to know their loved one is still an entity in their own right is going to be very exacting about what they perceive as proof.

After the reading, even if I wasn't entirely convinced I certainly did feel a sense of calm, which I had not felt since before the moment I learnt of Ben's passing. I began to attend the spiritualist church regularly. When I first began to attend, I would become overwhelmed with my loss and sometimes, I wanted to get up and leave as soon as the service started. It was too much for me to sit still for so long and I also felt angry at some of the things that were said.

For example, most people have probably heard the theory that God never gives you anything beyond that which you can cope with. So where do suicides come into this? Very clearly, they have not been able to cope with what life had dealt them. It's obviously not true that God doesn't give you anything you cannot cope with or, the trials of life do not come from God or, this sort of God does not exist.

This kind of argument would go round and round in my head in the early days at the church. However, I would always leave the service with a sense of healing. Without fail, I would leave the church feeling lighter and with some little feeling of joy. This feeling would sometimes stay with me for an hour or two, sometimes into the next day, but it was certainly a healing of some kind, and without medication or counselling!

During the months following Ben's passing, I looked for signs from him. Since he smoked roll-ups, I would stand in the garden sniffing the air, hoping for just a hint of his tobacco smoke or I would look for things that maybe he had left for me to find. I did once find a tobacco filter for a roll-up on exactly a year to the day after his passing. It was in the middle of a doorway, on the floor, in the house. I still wonder... There have been other little hints that may or may not be to do with Ben, but there's always the possibility of coincidence. I wish there weren't!

Having found comfort, first of all, from the reading and secondly, from attending the dear little church, I wanted to explore further. I could only think this must be the way forward for me. For some people counselling helps, for some medication helps, and some look to formal religion, but whichever the way forward we are all looking for the same end result; for comfort and quite simply, a way to be able to carry on living.

I wanted to be sure that Ben was still a complete being and that he was happy. So I booked an appointment with another medium, Ross, who was recommended to me by a friend. Ross is based in Southampton, England, which is far from where I live, but because of that, I knew he would not be influenced by anything he might have subconsciously picked up from a local newspaper or general gossip.

I thought I might be apprehensive about visiting Ross for the first time, and since I don't like driving very much, especially if it's somewhere new that I don't know, I took the most relaxing option of travelling by train. Also, afraid that I might be delayed on public transport, I allowed far too much time, caught an early train and had a lot of time to kill in Southampton before my appointment.

By the time I needed to make my way to meet Ross, I was quite relaxed... until I got there! Then the butterflies started, and the fears of whether Ben would come through or whether he just wouldn't want to talk to me, or maybe I would receive a load of information which would mean nothing of any significance. For example, if Ross were to say your grandmother's here, fair enough since I'm in my sixties and even if one grandmother is still with us, there's little chance the other will be. If he tells me that you are working too hard, well, we all like to think we work hard, so that's a fair guess. What I mean is generic information. I wasn't looking for that.

—

As soon as Ross came into the room, I felt reassured. Here was a young man with a big smile, a quiet voice, and no pretentions. There are no bells and whistles with Ross, just a gentle, understanding way with him far beyond expectations in one so young. We talked briefly about what the process would involve, and he asked if I had any concerns before we started. I just wanted Ross to make a start. My concerns would only be addressed if I heard from Ben, and so I said no. Ross set a CD to record and began.

Ross said he was aware of three spirits, an older male, an older woman and a younger male. Did I know a male who had died of cancer? Somebody whose demise during the last three days was rapid. Somebody whose cancer was a factor but not the killer. It all seemed too vague to me, and I was floundering around in my memory to try to come up with somebody who could apply to that.

I had an uncle who died of cancer. He then said he was getting the name, John. My uncle was John, so that was kind of helpful; but still, John is a pretty common name. Having settled on these two older spirits being my uncle and auntie, Ross then said concerning the younger spirit, he was getting the name, Ben. I would like to make clear at this point that, when Ross gives a name, he gives it straight. He does not say, "I'm getting a name beginning with B, could be Bert, Ben, Brian..." When Ross gives a name, there is no messing about. When he said he was getting the name Ben, that is exactly what he gave me. I gasped and told Ross that Ben is my son.

Ross said he felt that Ben had died by his own hand, and then he told me from Ben's perspective what had happened on the last day of his life. I didn't know exactly what happened on that day. Nobody but Ben could have known, but Ross gave me some interesting information.

Ben had gone outside, but he was frustrated and angry over certain things. He then went into a building and up some stairs. He was thinking about a cat. This all made perfect sense. Ben was agoraphobic but was still working, so he had to go outside to get to work. He managed this most of the time, but sometimes simply could not make it and would stay at home phoning in sick.

Although I did not know whether Ben had been outside or not that day, it made sense that he could have been meaning to go to work but could not continue. When he returned to his flat, he would have had to go upstairs to get to it. Anger and frustration over his limitations because of his illness were common factors and the cat... Well, he had a cat, and he loved his cat dearly, and if, at that time, he was thinking of ending his life, he would have been thinking what he could do to ensure the cat was okay. I recognized these thought patterns in my son.

Ross said there was something wrong with the bed. I do not know if there was anything wrong with the bed. One day I might ask the people who entered his flat first, but I never understood why he laid down in the bath and not the bed to die. Perhaps there is a connection.

Ross asked if I had any questions and I asked if Ben visits us. He said that Ben visits somebody called Andy. Andy is Ben's father. Andy and I separated when Ben was four and he said he also spends a lot of time with Lucy, Ben's sister. He went on to name Lucy's son, who is my grandson and Ben's nephew and one of Ben's half siblings. He said that Ben spends a lot of time with his nephew and would continue to do so as he grew up.

By this time in the reading, Ross had given me several family names, all names that I knew and all given directly and fully without hesitation. Being given so many names clearly and in context was the most convincing evidence to me that Ben's spirit lives on, and was there with us communicating through Ross. Also, he had not given me any names that I couldn't place, so it certainly wasn't a case of running through a lot of common names until striking gold!

It was exactly the proof of Ben's existence that I needed. I was so pleased to hear that Ben looks out for my grandson. I could not wish for anything more –

except he hadn't confirmed yet that he visits me! I asked again, and the answer was that he visits frequently but that I know that anyway. Well yes, that's sort of true, but it's difficult to distinguish between a sense of something real and wishful thinking, so it was reassuring to be told my senses are correct.

When I left after the first reading, I was overwhelmed with the accuracy of everything Ross had given me. I knew as I travelled home, that I'd been connected to Ben, that there is a life after this one, and that Ben was happy and well. It was the beginnings of an inner peace for me. My visits to the spiritualist church had also brought me healing but despite all of my attendances, the mediums present left me far from completely convinced of an afterlife. However, I knew from this point on that it was true. I stopped remembering Ben as being unhappy, frustrated and depressed. I now had a powerful sense of Ben being happy and full of the humour that sometimes deserted him through his darkest days.

I went back to Ross for a second reading the following year. He remembered me and also remembered Ben was my son. It's a good way to start a reading. Ross had a memory of Ben's energy and connected with him quickly. I also think that Ben's progress in spirit helped; as time progresses, he appears to become stronger. Names were given to me as people that Ben visits and all that again made sense.

As with the first reading, Ross told me that Ben spends a lot of time with his nephew and plans to be a guiding force for him as he grows. It was nice to have this given to me again. I doubt Ross even remembered telling me this in the original reading. To be able to confirm something he had already told me was very significant to me.

Again, in this reading, Ross asked if I had any questions. He had asked this in the original reading, and I simply asked if Ben visits. In all honesty, it's pretty easy to guess what the answer would be, even though in my case, Ben did beat about the bush a bit, mentioning his father and sister before me, but I can't imagine anyone ever gets a message saying, "No, I never visit." This time, I was ready with a more challenging question. Every year somebody gives me something that is actually for Ben. Does he know what it is?

Ross did not answer immediately, but he kept putting his thumbs and forefingers together to form a circle. He said he thought it was something that fit into a very small container. Not correct. I asked if he wanted me to tell him what it was but no, he wanted to work on it a bit longer. He asked whether there was a card involved. Yes, there is. He asked if it related to a particular date. Yes, it does. Still he kept putting his thumbs and forefingers together into a circle, and he just said he kept seeing a small circle, and I told him I thought he had it, I should just tell him what it was. He agreed.

He was making the shape of a bracelet. Every year before he died, Ben's Hindu friend would give him a rakhi bracelet. This is a bracelet given by Hindu women to their brothers, once a year, or given to men who are as close as brothers. After Ben had died, she began sending them to me (together with a rakhi card), and I wear it for Ben.

Ross explained to me the way he received the information through images shown to him and that the image that he now knew was a bracelet was coming through a black and white outline. He couldn't see clearly what it was, and was thinking it was the outline of a circular container. He was trying to look into the middle of it but kept seeing nothing in it.

I think you would have to be very skeptical, indeed, not to accept this as evidence that Ben knew about the rakhi bracelet and card and was able to convey this through Ross. Of all the shapes Ross could have seen and made in front of me with his hands a circle, and to get that, there was a card connected to this item as well. That was definitely on point enough for me. Importantly, there is no way Ross could have known about this, and in any case, if he had, he would surely have given me a much straighter answer!

My second reading with Ross reconfirmed what I had felt with my first reading. This time, I felt far less that I was trying to verify Ben's continued existence, and more that I was checking in to say hello to Ben and get a bit of an update on what he was up to. It is an incredibly happy experience feeling that your child or any other loved one is progressing well, still loves you, is still with you and will never be far away.

After the second reading, I felt so comfortable with this knowledge that it began also to be a part of who I am. It's hard not to tell everyone that it's okay. I am still missing my lovely child, but I know he's doing well and actually, there's a good chance he's with me right now. I sense a closeness much of the time. Of course, I am naturally healing as time goes on, but the certainty of Ben's continual existence has taken away so much pain.

⌒

The third visit to Ross was definitely a "checking in". A "Hi Ben, how're you doing?" But, there was something that niggled me just a little. I couldn't help thinking of the possibility that Ross (and other mediums) are taking information from the recipient's mind. I don't mean deliberately but subconsciously so that the medium thinks they are getting information from spirit, but actually, it is coming from the recipient. Again, names were given to me of people Ben connects with, and this time, he mentioned a cat belonging to his father's family, and he named the cat. I did not even know they had a cat, but it turns out they do, and Ross had named it correctly. There went the theory that in some way the information is absorbed from the sitter's mind!

There was further confirmation of Ben looking out for his nephew, and it's great to have that re-confirmed, and a reference to someone's illness that Ben would not have known about before he died. Ross also told me that Ben was spending a lot of time with my father in spirit – a grandfather to Ben, who died before Ben was born. Ross named my father. He had not done this in previous readings.

Funny, just after Ben died, I remember thinking how well Ben and my dad would have got on. I don't know where that thought came from because it had never occurred to me before Ben died. However, in the very first reading I had with the spiritualist church medium and on two occasions with Ross, I have been told that my dad has been helping Ben progress in the afterlife. Ross also said they spend a lot of time together walking and fishing. My dad was a confirmed, lifelong fisherman! It made perfect sense.

———

I've only given a snapshot of the contents of the readings I have had with Ross. It would take too long to go into all the detail, but there are little things, like Ben mentioning something happening with the jumper I was wearing during my last reading. Yes, something did happen to it that morning – too boring to give the full details but significant because Ben must have been with me at the time to bring it through. I had also given something I had written about Ben to somebody that same morning and Ben made reference to that as well.

Ross is also happy to answer questions himself. Another thought that I had was, what if Ben reincarnated just before I die and we miss each other? Ross was able to reassure me by explaining that this wouldn't happen. He also assured me that I'm not the only one who has worried about this! We also discussed the concept of God never giving you more than you can handle. To which, Ross told me that such things are clearly not true and not logical and are made up by people with a lack of insight or people who want to make things out to be mystical when they aren't so mystical at all. This very much resonated with me and again, helped ease confusion in my mind.

I consider myself incredibly lucky to have found a way to connect with Ben. Connecting with him through Ross has brought much emotion to the surface *and many a tear to my eye, but it has all led to positive outcomes. I know my Ben is never far away. I know he's always going to be there for me. I know he listens to me, and I know I'll see him again. It is the next best thing to having him physically with me. I'm not afraid anymore that I have lost him forever.*

For anyone else looking for comfort and healing by connecting through a medium, I would just say that if you do not feel entirely convinced the first time or the time after, try other mediums. I was pretty skeptical to begin with and was very fortunate to find Ross so early on. There are plenty of well meaning, but not very good mediums, who will do their very best for you, but either consciously or unconsciously very much work on instinct and perception, so what they give you is pretty vague.

They may say things like, your mother is here; well for me, unless the medium can actually name my mother and tell me something that relates to her, like what she did for a living, I'm not going to be convinced. For me, Ross's readings have never been vague. For anyone who is skeptical and needs hard proof as I did, I would say keep looking until you find a medium who gives you so much evidence that there really isn't any room left for doubt.

It's not a belief, it becomes an understanding from the experiences, and there is a knowing related to this that I think can't be fully articulated."

Here we have another story that is always guaranteed to get me emotional. That said, I think all the ones I have used in this book evoke a lot of emotion in me. The interesting thing that also comes through is Carol's skeptical nature, which all mediums should encourage. Carol mentioned that the "knowing cannot be put into words", but what I feel she also highlights in her story is how aspects of powerful love and strong grief cannot be put into words. What we see here, again, is the power of Heaven Therapy to bring healing.

THIRTEEN

Rose With Thorns

•••••••••••••

How do mediums know they aren't just reading the recipient's mind?

Moving on, a very common question I'm asked is how do other mediums and I know we're not just reading the mind of the recipient? Firstly, that is something other psychics and I can do if we want, but generally to a more limited degree. The person, generally, must be singularly focusing on one thing quite strongly for the image to come through.

Disembodied spirits appear better at projecting their thoughts in this way than those still in body here on Earth. Subjectively, I feel I'm very aware of a difference between the two and I need to focus quite hard individually on one or the other for either to work. Further, mediums often come up with information that is not known to the recipient, and there are several examples of that happening in this book. This phenomenon indicates mind reading is not taking place.

Further, at times, mediums do not know exactly whom they are reading for. How could we possibly be reading a person's mind when we don't know whose mind we would need to read? Scientific studies have also taken place with mediums where they had no information on the recipient and had no contact during the reading with the recipient. The research demonstrates that mediums can obtain accurate information regarding people's loved ones who have passed. Studies at the Windbridge Institute like the most recent one of Beischel et al, (2015) are the best examples of this. I am fully supportive of readings that take place in a scientific setting, as I believe they can further validate the work of mediums.

Accusations of fraudulence

Scientific studies aside, of course, those approaching mediumship from a highly skeptical perspective will suggest that mediums employ all kinds of techniques to get information without using any psychic abilities, ie., cheating and being fraudulent.

I'd like to address this issue and what mediums are sometimes accused of. Firstly, let me say there have been many "mediums" that have been caught employing different non-psychic techniques and being fraudulent. I'm sure there are many others as well. Whilst, I cannot talk in a way to represent every "non-fraudulent" medium, I will talk from a perspective of what could be accused of me, some of my peers, and in some cases relate this to mediums in general.

The first thing mediums get accused of is using a set of techniques that involve getting information about the recipient of the reading from analyzing personal body language, clothing, manner of speech, age, etc. Let me tell you, I'm aware of aspects of these techniques, and if I relied on them, I'd be a very poor medium. If I were using such techniques, I would certainly, from time to time, get a fair amount of information very wrong! The expression "don't judge a book by its cover", rings true here!

Sometimes, I have had people for readings, and if you judged them based on these "cold reading techniques", you would have judged them so incorrectly that they would know a hundred percent you aren't doing what you claim as a medium. In my opinion, and the opinion of many academic researchers, cold reading studies have never been done showing that you can get names of deceased relatives and be able to put all the complex and detailed elements, common to a good mediumistic reading, together in a way that makes a meaningful and accurate reading.

There is information, and then there is precise information. Things like names, specific descriptions of events and things only known to the recipient of the reading or things not even yet known to the recipient, until an investigation takes place. The next common thing mediums are accused of relates more commonly to how mediums may get information about a person's deceased loved ones. It is called "hot reading" when a "medium" will research the recipient and their family background.

I know from personal experience from my family and friends, that at times, information is not recorded correctly, so again if I were employing this method, from time to time, I would get things very wrong and the person would most likely know you are not doing what you claim to be doing as a medium. Further, the practical element of this is time. Where would I find the time to be doing readings, public demonstrations of mediumship, replying to all the emails sent to me (which I do personally), doing academic work, writing books and be researching all this information on clients?

Not to mention, things like working out and spending time with friends and family, it simply would not be possible. Mediums do get accused of employing other persons to do this. However, with the expense that I would relate such an endeavour costing, I certainly would have no money left once I had handed it out to the people doing all this research work for me and paid all kinds of fees to websites and companies to provide me with this information.

At times, I'm reading for people in other countries, born perhaps in a tiny village in rural China. I think it would be extremely challenging to research any decent information on such people, if not impossible. Moreover, to read these people well through cold reading techniques, it would also potentially require a fair amount of knowledge on the custom, traditions and ways of the culture they have been brought up and lived in.

Even if somehow you were able to pull all this off, surely, there would be no way you could consistently hide this from a partner you were living with? They would have to be in on it; then I wonder what would happen when Mr./Ms. Medium and their other half – providing the other half isn't also a medium themselves – breaks up for some reason.

Undoubtedly, many a medium's "exes" would have pursued the ultimate spiteful form of revenge of speaking out and outing Mr./Ms. Medium as a fraud? The same would go for family members or friends you could have potential disagreements with and falling out. Indeed, this would have happened to all well-known and respected mediums out there who have ever lived with a partner who wasn't a medium, and the relationship went sour.

Perhaps, some of this could be achieved if I were extremely wealthy with some other source of income that covers all my bills and I have had no one close enough to see all this occurring. Well, I've lived with a partner before, now I'm happily married to a very observant wife, and if I was that wealthy, surely I would be on a yacht somewhere warm instead of writing this book and doing all this work.

I also ask people, who accuse mediums of fraudulence, a question in regards to "hot reading" people. What would happen, anytime a person with a common name like John Smith from a big city, like London, books a reading? Which is a fairly common occurrence. How would I have any idea which John Smith he is? There is simply no viable way I could consistently find out which John Smith is the one coming for the reading with me.

For public demonstrations, mediums are accused of having audience "plants". I certainly couldn't do this myself, as I would have to pay a lot of different people to sit there and agree to whatever I said. There would be no way I could use the same bunch over and over because people travel from all around to my events, sometimes attending several a year. It would appear very odd to such persons if they saw a person appear in one end of a country and also another and received a reading both times within a short period between events.

Further, what would stop such a person going to the press once I had paid them? Again, not plausible. Perhaps it could be suggested my wife does all this research, or other family members? Well, we all need to live and eat, so I would still have to pay them somehow or provide for them, which again would be way beyond most people's means. Aside from the fact they all have jobs themselves and several have children to look after. My wife has her job as well, and if it was her, what on earth did I do before I met her?

Even if all this were possible, I would either have to be remembering all this information to relay to the person in a private reading, or people in a public demonstration, or wear an earpiece, where someone spoke the information into my ear. In a private reading, I would certainly be close enough for a person to see such a device. And for public demonstrations, sometimes the front row is just as close as a person having a private reading.

Sometimes, I go out into the audience and give an audience member an item, shake their hand, hug them, etc. Further, whoever is speaking into my ear would have to stay well-hidden and, whilst my hair is long to one side at present, in the past I have had my hair very short, so again I would think, over time, I would have been caught out on this, at least, several times.

~

Someone could make an assumption that I do have the mental capacity to remember this information in sequence. For a public demonstration that would be somewhere around 20 plus first names, a handful of surnames, several road names and door numbers, at least one postal code (for the UK a postcode is a very specific set of numbers and letters that relates to a specific road or part of a road) around 20 memory links, a handful of passing circumstances, loads of personality traits and more, all in sequence for person 1, 2 all the way to possibly 8.

Let's say I do have that ability and no psychic ability, would I be using such a talent to pretend to be psychic and get all the complication and hassle that comes with it, or use it to do something much easier? Or lucrative? Or both? I think the answer to that is obvious.

Additionally, taking into account the next issue of somehow knowing where this person will be sitting, as, without that, it would again be impossible. Whilst some mediums offer information out, and hands are raised, I go directly to a person in the audience from the start and speak to them. There would be little chance for the person to signal me to them without being noticed.

I'm not sure how this information could be obtained especially at an event where a seat number is not assigned, which is very common. Even if it was the event organizer, who is another potential person who would have to keep forever quiet about everything that was going on, there is still very little chance of it being possible. I can tell you from experience that it's near impossible in a room, with as little as one hundred attendees, to know where someone is sitting.

In the past, I have tried to look and find where a family member or friend was, and failed to locate their face in the crowd. In some of the bigger venues I've done, I couldn't even make out if a person sitting a certain number of rows back is male or female, particularly if there are strong lights onto the stage and little or no lighting in the seating. This environment would also eliminate cold reading techniques.

Perhaps, if I had an earpiece, the "plant" could message the person who would be talking in my ear and tell them where they are sitting. However, as I said, I don't think a medium could get away with an earpiece for very long, certainly, not someone who does things like I do.

Taking it further to the extreme, if I had a device connected to say my leg, which through touch could transmit directions to a "plant's" location, I would still need to be having "plants" that, as discussed, is not plausible. To satisfy some, I have also allowed people from the audience to check me over for earpieces and any other device in front of the audience seconds before I start a demonstration of mediumship.

These audience members are chosen randomly, via a blind backward throwing of several beanbags by audience members. For these demonstrations, I also removed all items of jewelry, shoes, and socks so they could not be suggested to conceal a device. Additionally, cold reading techniques would also not be justified when I do telephone readings or Skype readings (no cam) where the recipient is in a different location, and often, a different country. From all of this, you can see that there is proof that mediums aren't all fraudulent.

At the beginning of my career, I started arranging readings with people through email, text or phone. At the time, I wouldn't even take a name, and if it were not by phone, I wouldn't even take a number. It wasn't the most professional or safe way to run a business in the modern world and that is why the process changed. Today the communication is (most often) exclusively through email. A form is sent by email to people who have distance readings (phone or Skype,) or for an in-person reading, they fill in the form upon arrival.

This form offers several things to protect the client and me. For instance, the form requires the person to confirm they are over the age of 18, not under the influence of drugs or alcohol, have no history of mental illness. It also ensures the recorded reading information is protected, etc. Running things properly, I should be able to demonstrate that a reading was booked for a certain person at a particular time and date. They turned up, and had said reading. Before even having the reading, they confirmed they were in a capable state to have a reading, and they left the premises at a particular time in a safe and content state.

Not only is this process professional, but also as a medium in today's times, you need to be very careful, particularly if you're reasonably well known. Of course, it's not good practice to try to deceive a medium you want to help you! For my part, there is some potentially important spiritual preparation that starts sometime before the reading. For instance, once they have told me their name, it goes into a book that I sit and pray and meditate with. I feel this builds a stronger link and energy for the reading that will take place.

As a particular person's reading gets closer, I will take the time to specifically meditate and pray for that person's reading. Whilst most mediums don't practise this and many others techniques I use, I credit this practice among others to being an important part of making my readings way above average in consistency, accuracy, and evidential quality.

This brings me to the next story I would like to share with you. It's a reading I did via phone, where unknown to me at the time, I wasn't even talking to the recipient at any point during the reading. I had no access to information relating to the recipient. False information was given on the form, and the person who spoke to me on the phone was not the person the reading was meant for.

This is a story, which I strongly suggest, rules out the possibility of any fraudulent means having taken place and clearly demonstrates that information was being received from the recipient's loved one. It also clearly demonstrates points I made earlier in this chapter, that issues caused by the physical body are no longer present in heaven, but issues related to the mind can linger on for a little while but with help become better and are overcome.

Rose

"My name is Rose. I was so delighted that Ross has asked me to write my story for his new book. My story must begin with who I am. I was born to an English father and an Indian mother. I was born, brought up and educated in England and later moved to India where I have lived for the past twenty years. My father passed away when I was three, and I have only a few blurry memories of him.

After his passing, my mother suffered from depression. Sometimes, she would go through phases of being happier, brighter and better, other times she could sink very low. My relationship with my mother was amazing, and I would often say that she was my heartbeat in life. I so loved her character, strong in heart, traditional in lots of ways, conducting herself in the role she played in the family; taking no nonsense from anyone. Tough love was her main trait as a mother, but she had a lovely soft side as well, particularly with me.

We were inseparable, and as I grew, we became the very best of friends. On odd occasions when a conversation escalated slightly, she would smile and tell me I could sometimes be a rose with thorns. That would always make me laugh, and we would give each other a big hug. As my mother aged, I was aware that she would sometimes forget a name or place. That can happen to us all and I did not put a great deal of importance to it. However, very slowly her memory started to deteriorate a little more, and I, together with all the family, became a little more concerned.

Looking back, I cannot clearly remember when my concern started to escalate. It was just a very gradual process, and there were the odd moments when her memory was crystal clear. The doctors warned us that there was a possibility that my mother may have the start of Alzheimer's. The thought of my beloved mother being unable to communicate properly and that physically she would slowly deteriorate, gave me huge concern. I spent as much time as I could with her hoping to encourage her to communicate regularly and sensibly. At a deeper level, I knew that there was little any of us could do.

As time went on, she also became unable to walk. I always felt somehow that she would go on forever, and here I had to face the death of the person

I loved most. Did people survive the death of the physical body? Surely, my beautiful mother could not simply cease to exist? Living in England for so many years, I knew mediums existed and that they purported to contact those who had passed over. I told her, in a moment when her mind was more aware, that if and when, she died I would try to contact her through a medium.

My mother was slowly slipping away mentally and in turn, my stress and general worry intensified. My grief brought constant tears, and I dreaded the day when she could not even recognize who I was. That day was closer than I thought possible. I would visit her, and she often wouldn't recognize who I was. She would get angry about sounds that were not there, these auditory hallucinations only seemed to get worse, and she would go on and on about odd smells, even though she never had any sense of smell from birth.

It was at that point that I felt she was lost to me. Each time after visiting her and her not recognizing me, I would go back to my car, and I would sit there for what seemed like ages and just cry and sob until I finally would gather the strength to drive home. I cannot even begin to explain the pain and anguish I felt when she finally passed away from a heart attack. I was inconsolable, and my pit of grief was so deep, I couldn't see any light. The funeral passed in a haze. I could not even think straight. My tears seemed endless.

<hr>

Eventually, I just had to get on with my life. I knew it would never be the same, and there seemed no way of dulling the constant grief. I thought once or twice about trying to find a reputable medium in England, but I did not know where to start. I had heard various stories about mediums, who were not very good, and there were some who would give vague comments based on the looks of the person being read, rather than bringing through loved ones who had passed over.

I could not bear the thought of raising my hopes and then receiving no validations or evidence that my mother was still alive in another dimension. I was lost living in India and finally had to put the idea of seeing a medium out of my mind. However, that tiny chink of light above my pit finally arrived when my friend suggested I read Earth Angel *by a young medium named Ross Bartlett. I loved the book and read it in a matter of a few days. I remember thinking how could a young man of nineteen or twenty possibly possess such a gift? It seemed far-fetched but how was I to know if the age of the medium is important?*

The stories in the book were astounding; so much evidence of life after death with loved ones coming through. The characters of those who had passed con-

firmed, so many names given, so many validations, it all seemed too good to be true. Somehow and at some deep level, I felt that if anybody could help me, it could well be this young man.

Perhaps, he could prove my mother was alive, that she knew what was happening in my life and could give me the evidence I desperately needed to heal my grief and change my life. I needed a plan that would leave no doubt at all that the information was coming from my mother. This plan had to be foolproof, and I had an idea how to develop it.

My good friend Beth, in England, would be the one to help me, and it would give me another opportunity to visit the beautiful county of Yorkshire where she lived, and that I became so fond of during my time in England. Beth was more than pleased to help, especially if it meant helping me to come to terms with the death of my mother. She agreed to book a telephone reading with Ross in her name and through her email address.

She would be the person talking to Ross, whilst I was in the same room listening through the loudspeaker, and I would let her know if the information coming through was correct or not. I thought there was a possibility that Ross may naturally psychically link with Beth's relatives rather than to my own.

I didn't know enough about mediumship to know if what I wanted to happen was even possible, but that was a chance I had to take. Ross, of course, would not know I was in the room, he had never met me, did not know my name or anything at all about my family or me. I have no presence at all online and have never joined any social media sites like Facebook or Twitter.

The perfect plan, but would it work? Beth made the booking with her own email address, and I flew from India to be with her. This was around two and a half years after my mother had passed. On the day of the reading, to say I was anxious would be a complete understatement! I felt this was my one and only chance, so failure would mean living with my grief for the rest of my life. I remember a tear or two falling from my eyes as the call was made.

Ross began talking to Beth and stated, "I am aware of a lady wishing to make a connection who had developed Alzheimer's in her later years. There were heart complications, and a heart attack was the final reason she passed. Do you understand this information?" I swallowed hard and nodded vigorously even though Beth knew the information was correct. Oh my goodness, I thought, how amazing is that?

What followed were sensational, clear and concise details of my mother's character: very strong, traditional motherly role within the family, very loving but firm with a gentle and softer side. I kept agreeing, and Beth kept saying *yes, as the tears welled up in my eyes. At first, Ross, I suppose understandably, believed this communicator was Beth's mother and said that you were insepa-rable and best friends, impeccably close.*

He then validated the area where my family grew up in England. Ross spoke about a long road with terrace housing, and the house on the corner had a post box next to it. This was the very house I lived in for so many years! I was elated and crying at the same time. Then he mentioned connections to India and the name of Rose being important. I was astounded.

Shortly after this information Ross asked if the name of Amrita was im-portant and the name seemed to be connected to the communicator. My jaw dropped in amazement. This was my mother's name! I smiled for the first time during the experience. It was as if a part of my being was jolted back into life and the relief was exhilarating yet somehow calming.

What then followed was a description of her illness, what she went through and conversations that took place around her bedside. All were correct, including one just before she passed, where I talked about a memory of riding with her on a bus and the bus broke down. Even Beth didn't know I had talked about this to my mother when I thought she was sleeping. Beth didn't even know that event hap-pened and didn't know about many things Ross mentioned.

Ross explained that my mother had absorbed some of this information said around her bedside and remembered when her mind was back to normal after passing over to heaven. The other information was passed on to her through my father, who would visit us from heaven and sit with us each time I visited my mother. He went on to say they were back together, and very much in love. I was so happy to hear this as my mother never remarried. She always used to say, "I still love your father just as much as I did the day he died. Why would I go looking for anything else when my heart is already taken?"

Ross continued saying that she had suffered from depression, and my moth-er told him that it was so ingrained in her psyche that when she got over to heaven, she was still a bit up and down sometimes, but it wasn't too long until she was completely cured of the depression. He said that the depression was related so much to my father's passing and a deep missing and longing for him. Therefore, when they were reunited and spent more and more time together, the depression naturally began to lift. Patterns connected to the depression were something she sought help for in heaven and through psychotherapeutic techniques, all aspects of the depression were removed from her mind.

He continued to say my mother was unable to walk later in life, but that she said she was dancing in heaven all the time now. When my mother was younger, she loved to dance. Ross continued saying she no longer heard things that were not there. This, of course, made sense to me. Then he said something that had me open-mouthed again: "She had a problem with her nose, she couldn't smell things, but she is saying she can now in heaven." Beth just kept saying, "Yes, yes, I understand."

I just nodded my head crying uncontrollably, but not making a sound so that Ross would have no indication. The whole reading, I was holding a cushion in my hands right up to my face, curled up with my knees into my chest on the chair, crying silent tears in the cushion.

Then Ross talked about me. He said Amrita stated Rose's personality was a bit like her with some tough love and a sharp side at times, that he was seeing images that suggested Amrita thought of her as like a rose with thorns. Beth replied that she was often called by that name. I just could not believe the incredible evidence coming from my mother through Ross. Beth started to tear up as well and was holding her hand over her mouth when not replying to Ross. I felt it was so much better and clearer than I ever imagined possible!

That Ross had said the very personal words my mother would call me! It was way more than chance. The only people on Earth, who knew this information, were Beth and two family members. None of which Ross had any previous contact with.

Ross then said there is a male here with the name Benjamin. He was Beth's uncle who had passed away around five years previous. Ross asked if Beth knew who Benjamin would be and naturally she replied, "Yes, he was my uncle." Ross proceeded to describe to Beth how Benjamin suffered from lung cancer and how he fought right up until the end. Beth was never very close to her uncle, but she did know about his illness and passing.

Ross told Beth that her uncle was watching over her and wanted to let her know he is very fond of her, having gotten to know her more as a person since he had been on the other side.

It was then that Ross said based on the feelings from Amrita and Benjamin, it was as if Amrita was actually not connected directly by blood to Beth. He continued saying Amrita kept relating and showing him thoughts connected to Rose. Well, of course, whilst it was clearly a bit confusing to Ross at the time, it made perfect sense to Beth and me. By the end, my handkerchief was wet through, and my vast grief had been lifted away, or perhaps I was being lifted out of it.

Sometime afterward, I communicated directly with Ross and told him that throughout the reading I was in the room crying nonstop, trying to remain composed but failing! I told him that the reading has changed my life and helped me to go beyond the grief and bereavement of losing my mother. I described the whole experience as a journey from the deep grief that I had fallen into and could see no way out. Now I feel like I'm back in the world again. I explained to him what Beth and I had done. Whilst I can imagine he would have preferred me to be upfront with him from the start, he seemed understanding.

He did explain that the reading might have been stronger, again, if I was more upfront, as it would potentially have allowed for more energy to be generated for the reading from his practices and techniques leading up to the day. Ross explained further that everything aside, as long as the people connected to me in heaven knew what I was doing, it could always potentially work. Ross said, that ultimately the success of a reading done like this very much hinged on him not getting confused by some of the references, images, and feelings that were related to me and not Beth. Thankfully down to my mother, Ross and Beth's uncle it worked out better than I hoped.

What I learnt from this incredible experience is that I now know my mother is indeed as alive as she ever was, and that in due time we will once again be together. I now know that we survive the death of the physical body and that communication between heaven and earth is perfectly possible. I'm completely puzzled why this knowledge is not more widely known. I do know that my intuition was right about Ross and that he is exactly what I hoped he would be.

I am now very aware of the healing power of mediumship to deal with grief. I do know I owe a huge debt of gratitude to the friend who gave me Earth Angel *to read, and to Beth for her wonderful friendship and her willingness to help me uncover the truth about my mother, and of course to Ross.*

Do spirits wait for their lovers or do they get into other romantic relationships?

As this reading was not long ago, I remember it quite vividly. I feel that there is a lovely message within a message here. When two people who love each other tremendously, in other words, true lovers, are separated by the death of the physical body, if their love is true enough and they are soul mates or soul twins, as I prefer to call them, and they wish it, they can both wait, and when reunited in heaven their loving and romantic relationship continues.

In the meantime, the one on the other side never truly leaves the side of their lover who remains on Earth in the physical dimension. Of course, there are many examples of people here getting into other relationships after their lover has passed on and I have never known a spirit be unaccepting or unsupportive of this. They will then also pursue other romantic relationships in heaven. The spirit ultimately knows and understands our thinking process and wants us to be happy.

Perhaps, it was even always best for both persons to pursue other people romantically. Each situation is different just as each couple is different and through this, each bond in a romantic relationship is different. If the couple are soul twins then I'm sure each will wait. If not, I'm sure each will move on to another relationship. It doesn't mean they didn't care very deeply for each other or that they no longer do. It simply means in the long term, it wasn't meant to be. It was not the right blend of souls. We can be very close to a lot of people but it doesn't mean we are all soul twins to each other.

As a whole, Rose's reading was certainly a very interesting reading because of the blind and detached conditions under which it took place. Whilst I certainly don't recommend people doing this without the medium being aware of it, due to the complications that can arise regarding misinterpreting elements of the reading and the possibility of spirits also wanting to come through for the actual person speaking with the medium, this reading demonstrates that it can still work.

It does bring up potentially moral and ethical questions about how one should approach a reading and how one may approach it to give it the greatest chance of success. In the past, when I have told this story to others, I have been asked how much did it potentially affect my process of spiritual preparation and does deceit actually detract from the energy built?

In terms of it affecting the process, the process is that I pray and meditate first for the communicating process itself, between this world and the next that the person (in this case, Beth) would be involved in, specifically that it will go well. This is what I always pray on. So, what happened did not necessarily have a negative impact this way. Further, I pray that the person would find the healing they seek. The healing Beth was seeking was to see her friend Rose healed.

So again, it did not necessarily have a negative impact on the energy I was trying to build. It's not hugely uncommon for spirits to come through in readings, when they didn't know the recipient, and are wishing to have a message passed on through that recipient to another family member or friend, or the recipient that the spirit did know. Sometimes, the spirit is desperate to get a message to someone they care about and using the recipient of the reading, as the medium's medium might be the only way for them to do it.

Is a lack of openness and deceit ideal for readings? Certainly not. I can say things would likely be more potent with being able to think and pray directly for the actual recipient who is having the reading. Further, that if the person having the reading is only open and gives love in the way they approach the reading, it will be better than the reverse. That being said, early on in my career, I have given great readings to drunken men in pubs that have been dragged along by their wives and girlfriends, where they then have been in floods of tears by the end of the reading.

I've also given great readings to people that our society would deem are of not such great character. A good medium can work with very poor energy and make it good. However, for great consistent results, the more openness, the more respect given to the spirit helpers of the medium, and the medium themselves, the more consistent and direct positive and loving energy that is put into the communication from both sides and therefore, the easier it will be for the medium to get great consistent results. Anything less, and those results become more at risk of taking a decline.

I knew before Rose's reading began, that something was up, but I went ahead anyway, as the feeling was not too bad. I was not going to accuse someone of something without actual proof. It wouldn't have been good for the potential reading either, so in that way I put Rose first.

How did I feel when she admitted the process she set out? Well, I wasn't happy, but I was sympathetic. It is not the first time someone has done something like this and also, put potential traps in place trying to catch me doing something I'm not doing, or trick me in some form. It most likely won't be the last either. Whilst I'm trying to promote mediumship more and more as a spiritual practice, a serious therapeutic practice, that works well in that context. Some people just aren't ready mentally, one way or another, to approach a reading in a way that makes for the ideal conditions, but I can certainly sympathize with the suffering that has them that way.

Something I always recommend is that the recipient on the lead up to the reading, sends out as many thoughts to their loved ones, on the other side, to come through as strongly as possible because help and healing is needed. This is also a huge help in building the energy for the reading.

Overall, mediumship readings are most powerful when they are conducted in as spiritual a manner as possible, in a sacred manner. It has and always will be at the base a sacred practice – not religious but sacred and spiritual. This is a sacred practice that needs to be treated with the upmost respect, a sacred practice that can be utilized as a very serious and powerful means of therapy and a massive part of the continual spiritual evolution of humankind.

Yes, there is some place right now for entertainment-based mediumship on TV and on stage. However, when you are dealing with people's lives and emotions so intimately, consistency is critical.

The internet problem

In the modern world, every medium faces what I like to call the "internet problem". This is when after a reading the recipient, for certain psychological reasons which I will address in more detail later in the book, goes away after the reading and tries to find out how easy it may have been to find the information conveyed during the reading. This can, at times, be very problematic, as some people today feel a need to post everything, or a lot of the significant things that happen in their life, on Facebook or other social media and don't have their profiles on private settings.

A person may go and find that much of what the medium said can be sourced from social media accounts. The medium can only pass on the significant information he or she is given and able to understand from the spirits communicating with him or her. If you have a large portion of significant information on your personal social media sites, then I would advise you to ensure they are on a private setting before you book a reading. However, as I have said, if you look at things rationally and with a certain amount of understanding and perspective related to what I have discussed earlier, one can conclude that a medium, like myself, is not getting information from people's Facebook pages or any websites.

Speaking overall, 99 percent of the time, with a good medium there will be information conveyed in a reading that someone would not be able to find on any website. You may also have cases where the medium may get a name or piece of information incorrect and he or she has misinterpreted something. As an example, it just so happens that the name he or she mentions is the name of a person who used to live at your address before you moved there, but is incorrectly still listed as living there along with you.

This may happen because the medium may see an image of his or her uncle that can naturally make him/her think of another uncle of his/hers and the medium is aware that the spirit is trying to tell him/her that one of their uncle's names is significant to the person receiving the reading. Unfortunately, the medium's mind has gotten in the way a little, and now he/she isn't sure which is the right uncle. Perhaps, they pick Uncle number one's name when, in actuality, it was Uncle number two's name that was significant. It could happen that Uncle number one's name is the incorrect name on the census or land register, etc. This can also happen with a surname.

These types of incidences are extremely rare, but if you do enough readings, it will happen! When these occurrences did happen to me, each time I replied to the person and highlighted certain things and explained how this happens and happened in their case. Where necessary, I have offered a free complimentary reading to address what was wrong and for the spirit to evidentially clear up the matter at issue.

The broader issue

This is something that all mediums should be prepared to do if this is brought to their attention. However, if the recipient of the reading looked at things, taking into account everything I've discussed so far within this book, they would find a lack of logic in their issues with the reading. Sometimes, these occurrences can happen when there may be complex psychological needs of the recipient that are not adequately met during the reading process. Also, on occasion, if aspects of the reading that addressed the psychological needs of the recipient, are strongly challenged after the reading.

From Rose's reading, if I was reading the mind of Beth that would not explain the pieces of information which came through relating to Rose and her mother that was not consciously known to Beth at the time. Information in Tanya's reading was conveyed that she didn't know, and had to validate. How could I have read that piece of information from her mind, if she didn't know that particular piece of information? There are several stories in the book that show similar occurrences, including the one about Jessica on page 87.

Jessica had two relatives come through whom she knew nothing about, not even their names. In fact, no one on Earth knew her great-great grandfather's and great-great uncle's names. It wasn't until she researched the family tree that the information was verified. This is not an uncommon occurrence in mediumistic readings. Sometimes, the spirits communicating will specifically mention something not known to the recipient, so that the recipient knows the medium is not reading their mind, and the information is truly coming from them.

In the Windbridge Institute studies I mentioned, information was passed to the person speaking to the medium on behalf of the recipient, information related to the recipient that the individual had no conscious awareness off. Sometimes, before a demonstration, spirit helpers of mine will tell me a name of a spirit who will communicate later in the demonstration, or even a whole address that I will need to mention, postcode included. I would suggest that this all rules out mediums reading the mind of the recipient.

How do mediums know they aren't getting the information from God or some universal consciousness?

Another common question is, how do other mediums and I know we aren't just getting information from the infinite, universal consciousness, Great Spirit, God, etc.? I touched on this whilst discussing reincarnation. To elaborate further, firstly, let me say that this would still relate to using psychic ability, and if that were possible, surely, an afterlife would also be very likely and far from impossible.

Again, other psychics and I can get information this way, subjectively to me, that is a very different approach that requires me to direct my mind in a different way. This is very similar to me asking you, how do you know when you're talking out loud in a room to yourself or when you are talking directly to a person? You know because you're speaking out to the world and you're not aware of anyone in the room, and in the other, you are aware of someone through your senses, and you choose to talk directly to them and receive an answer you perceive as coming directly from them.

When you send direct communication to the infinite, the answer doesn't come from any exact place, it comes more from deeper inside yourself. There is no changing personality and feeling as such, unlike when talking to an individual spirit. The two are very different experiences that feel and work differently and involve a different process.

Physical mediumship phenomenon that involves various physical manifestations of spirit that many others and I have witnessed has demonstrated individual consciousness survives physical death, and no physical manifestation of a spirit though this means has ever suggested it is not individual consciousness mediums communicate with. In fact there are accounts of spirit manifestations validating mediums do get information from individual consciousness.

I will discuss physical mediumship later in the book. The OBEs (Out-of-Body Experiences) suggest survival of individual consciousness and again certain accounts have suggested that mediums do get information from an individual's consciousness. OBEs are also far more common than most think. The data available suggests around one in ten people have had an experience that they consider to be an OBE.

Additionally, unassisted spontaneous ADCs that happen to regular people suggest that individual consciousness survives physical death, and further, humans can psychically experience information from these spirits. Overall, asking this question to a medium is just as logical as asking how do you know that we are not all a part of an advanced computer program, or that everyone and everything aren't just a projection created by our minds? Or how do you know you're not in a coma and will one day wake up? I can't say for sure that I'm not in a coma and one day will wake up to a real world, but what I can say is that this is far from the most logical train of thought, based on my experience.

How do mediums know they aren't getting the information from the Devil or demons?

Another common question is how do we know we aren't talking to the devil or demons who are trying to manipulate people's feelings and maybe move them away from God, etc.? This question follows no real logic, and my response always is, if their God does nothing for all these people in such pain and grief and their devil and his demons help heal so many people and help guide them to being better people, perhaps you need to rethink who they worship and who is positive and who is negative.

Further, with experienced mediums, there is no way to hide what sort of entity you are, regarding being more negative or positive. The spirit could talk a good game, but as an experienced medium, you feel the soul of the spirit on the deepest of levels. There really is no way for them to hide from me or me to hide from them, what is within the soul; either positive or negative will be felt, it can't be masked from a strong, experienced medium.

Do angels and demons exist?

Something I do get asked is, do angels and demons exist? Well, I'm certain they do, as based on my understanding of the reality of what I've termed the multiverse that is within the void; there is an infinite amount of creation and the beings we call angels would be one of them, as would the beings we call demons.

Having said that, I'm very skeptical of anyone who claims to communicate regularly with angels. Angels are not something you will ever normally hear mediums talking about. It is only in recent years, communicating with angels and angel readers have become much more of a thing, and it seems lots of people have jumped on the angel wagon, so to speak. No reputable medium that I'm aware of claims to communicate with angels on a regular basis if at all.

There are several very good reasons for this, angels are nothing like humans, their vibration would be much higher than ours, they are said to be creatures of purity, endless love, compassion, incomparable virtue that have never been in a physical body, a messenger from high realms of heaven. Mediums find it challenging enough connecting with and communicating with your grandmother, much less an angel. Their vibration would be so way above ours, from my perspective consistent mediumistic communication, would be extraordinarily difficult, if not impossible.

In many religious scriptures, communication from angels is not a regular occurrence, and when it happens, it is often short and often reserved for the saintliest of people and only happens when there is a very important spiritual reason. Not what is going on with a person's physical work, or their relationship, or their finances, or if they are going to buy a house.

In fact, besides them being compassionate, I see no reason an angel would ever want to be anywhere near here. A lot of people here think the world is not such a positive or nice place. Imagine how an angel would feel? Ultimately there is very little proof available that those who claim to talk to angels, and get accurate information, aren't just picking the information up psychically from the recipient of the reading or the infinite.

I've never heard of an angel manifesting during a séance to validate anything. I can also tell you from experience several well-known angel whisperers are far from angelic. Whilst my autobiography is called *Earth Angel*, it is saying I'm a messenger for people here, for the regular folk. I wouldn't ever claim to be of a vibration where I could communicate with such highly evolved beings with relative ease on a regular basis.

However, I'm not saying it never happens and that all people who say they communicate with angels never do. I'm suggesting it's a lot less common than it's portrayed to be. I suspect that sometimes people are having experiences of their own ancestors and mistaking them as an angel. If you were to pray to angelic entities, then I'm sure they would receive your thoughts and potentially use their power to help. That is a different thing again and should not be confused with regular angel communication.

About demons, they would basically be the negative angelic counterparts. Their vibration is again so different to us they aren't going to be able to hang around Earth all the time looking to cause trouble. Demonic possession is, in my experience, an exceptionally rare thing and is not what is actually going on in nearly all reported cases. This is the same for reported hauntings. Real hauntings are exceptionally rare.

As for Satan or the Devil as it can be referred to, did it exist, well if it did, I can't really say for sure as I've never spoken to it and why would I have? Do I know a spirit who has said they have seen or communicated with it on the other side? No, and this again would make sense as they would be on such a different vibration to us.

I'm again very skeptical of anyone who claims to communicate with either the Devil or on the reverse side of the coin, Jesus, regularly. Once again, I'm not saying it has never happened. If a medium ever claims they have communicated with Jesus, I feel they should be expected to do something world changing, as it wouldn't make much sense for him just to pop in to say "Hi" or just nudge them in the right direction in their life or even help them to nudge someone else in the right direction.

Surely, his efforts would be better used making a larger difference to the world. Specifically, bringing a clear set of messages that could drastically help humanity. He wasn't here for mundane things when he was incarnated, so why would he be now? Even if Jesus did communicate with me on a regular basis, I wouldn't say it until I had done some great things to show I have such an importance to the world and justify such an audacious claim.

What I have just explained also stands for other potential forms of life from other religions and philosophies, examples of these would be fairies and elementals. The closer the vibration, the better chance of easy communication, and the more different the vibration is, the harder it would be.

FOURTEEN

The Future of Heaven Therapy

The next big question in this book is what is the future of Heaven Therapy and mankind communicating with heaven? Is it going to change the world? And if so, how?

Are other ways to communicate with spirits useful?

I'm often asked if I feel other ways to communicate with the spirit world that have been used in the past are of use in the future. There are three main areas to consider, the first being dowsing and Ouija/spirit boards and the second, trance mediumship, and the third, forms of physical mediumship.

Dowsing and the Ouija/spirit board

Dowsing to communicate with spirit often uses a pendulum and Ouija/spirit boards are very well used. Whilst some people assert that spirit directly moves the pendulum or the planchette that is, in my opinion, simply not true. Scientific tests like that of Burgess et al, (1998) have shown that ideo-motor activity causes the glass to move, meaning the participant or participants whose fingers are touching the pendulum or planchette move the item subconsciously. This is sometimes referred to as the "carpenter effect."

This happens through a thought or mental image causing a reflexive muscular reaction, often of minimal degree. However, many minimal movements very easily add up to big movements of the pendulum or planchette. In essence, it is an automatic muscular response caused by a thought held within the mind. Therefore, the participants are not consciously trying to move the dowsing item, it happens subconsciously and whatever is held within the subconscious areas of the mind, or even the conscious mind of the participants, can and does easily affect the movements of the dowsing item.

To many scientists, this completely debunks the phenomena. I would suggest it doesn't have to mean that this is never a genuine means to communicate with the spirit world. Some people profess to have had amazing experiences using these methods, and accurate information was conveyed that could not have been known to anyone who was touching the glass or anyone in the room. However, I'm not aware of any tests under scientific observation and structure that have yielded such results.

So, how can it still potentially be a way that spirit has seemingly communicated accurate information (albeit, apparently very inconsistent)? Well, I suggest that just like with other areas of mediumship I've discussed, the spirits would work through the mind of the recipients. In this case, influencing their thoughts from within the participant's subconscious through into their conscious minds as well to produce the correct information. This could explain why some people have apparently seen interesting results that suggest spirit communication.

It could also explain why at times the information is completely incorrect. If the participants are not skilled at mediumship, their subconscious will very likely not register and channel through the correct information. Hence, it will be information created in their minds, by their thoughts and subconscious gobbledygook. The chances of, say, five Ouija/spirit board participants all being good conduits is pretty darn slim.

Normally, it is people with no mediumistic ability that practise and certainly not mediums who have proved themselves under scientific observation. This was also the case in all the scientific tests that have addressed the accuracy of the information conveyed. Of course, even if three are good mediums but two aren't, the planchette will be affected by the two who aren't and, at times, be guided off the correct direction.

An experiment using genuine extremely gifted mediums, who have been scientifically tested previously and shown to receive accurate information, could be interesting, and I feel could produce some positive results. However, I would expect at least some inconsistency in the phenomena due to the nature of the process.

For the dowsing pendulum, you typically have one person using the item, but again, if they are not a good medium it will not work well at all. I have seen fascinating results, first hand, when a capable medium is using a pendulum to acquire information from spirit. The issue is these practices have been detached from how they were practised in previous cultures, where they were most often practised by mediums who knew what they were doing, not the average person.

The Ouija board, in the incarnation we are familiar with, was produced as an after-dinner board game. Yes, a toy and is actually a trademark of Hasbro, Inc. Today the process is implemented more commonly using an upside down glass on a common table and is often referred to as a glass table-top séance.

Similar methods are table tipping and standing human pendulum techniques. The table tipping is just what most would think. The participant's fingers are laid on the table and the table moves and tips in a direction to indicate a response. The human pendulum is a lesser-used technique that involves a person standing, being subconsciously influenced, to lean or swing in a direction to indicate a response. These methods should also not be practised by untrained individuals.

Whilst the Ouija board itself and these methods carry no power with them and are certainly not evil, if you don't know what you're doing and don't have the right intentions, you can potentially attract more negative energies from the afterlife.

Trance mediumship

In trance mediumship, the spirit seeks to blend and connect on a deeper level with the medium. There are several levels of trance mediumship. During the lighter stage, the spirit seeks to influence the medium's thoughts and through them, the spirit will speak. In this method, the medium will not say, "I have a spirit here by the name of George, and he has come to talk with you"; the medium will say, "Hello, my name is George, and I have come to speak with you." It is the spirit speaking in the first person through the medium.

At this level, the medium is conscious to different degrees and will often be aware of aspects of/or all of what is being said. I've seen a lot of this and when it's come to channelling ordinary spirits like loved ones who have passed it's certainly not as reliable as mental mediumship. During the deeper stage, the medium moves into a state of somnambulism, where there is seen to be zero influence from the medium's conscious mind and the medium will awaken after the process is over with no memory of what was said through the medium's vocal cords.

This process is a form of extensive spirit possession where the spirit extensively merges with the energetic matrix and biological system of the body. In my opinion, most likely through the microtubules of the medium strongly enough to completely take over the medium's body for the space of time.

In this deep state, it has been known that the medium's voice could change from male to female or have accents or even talk in other languages depending on the spirit being channelled. Although, the latter is not considered to have happened adequately under scientific observation.

This is potentially an excellent means of communication, if it ever did exist. I've never seen consistent somnambulistic trance mediumship. I have potentially seen glimpses of it, but nothing anywhere near efficient enough to be used as a means for someone to sit down and receive a message directly from a loved one or some pertinent piece of information that could help humanity. For this reason, I don't see it as having much direct value to mediumship and Heaven Therapy moving into the future.

Physical mediumship

Physical mediumship is the manipulation of physical matter from spirits. Ranging from levitation of objects to knocking on objects, to apports, which is the dematerialization of an object from another space that is then materialized in the location of the activity. Additionally, direct voice, which is when the physical voice of a spirit, is projected in the location of activity. If it were my grandmother, who was communicating through direct voice to me, then everyone in the room would be able to hear her voice, providing they are in earshot. No form of physical mediumship happens telepathically in a person's mind. It is all physical vibration phenomena.

The last forms of physical mediumship are partial materialization, where the hand of my grandmother may appear in the space of activity. It may come to me and hold my hand or in the case of transfiguration, a specialized aspect of this, it is the face of the spirit communicator that is supposed to appear over the face of the medium. There is also full materialization, where the spirit momentarily fully appears back in physical form.

In such a case, my grandmother would appear fully in the room and providing there was enough light, everyone in the room could see her. This form of mediumship is again very rare. I have experienced aspects of the above, some of these experiences I capture in my autobiography. Some of the experiences happened without a claimed physical medium present. These experiences have completely convinced me of the reality of these physical phenomena and physical mediumship in general.

I have also attended séances by physical mediums from different cultures. The majority of them, unfortunately, I have been very unimpressed with. Most are not doing exactly what they say they are doing, and most likely are completely fraudulent, and with others, there may be problems of consistency. I believe any person who claims to be a physical medium in the Western world should put themselves forward for extensive scientific testing. With the ones that have been tested in more modern times, the research from my perspective has been inconclusive. In the past, a large number of physical mediums have been tested, and the results by some of the mediums suggested the phenomena were taking place.

If someone is a real physical medium, the testing should likely reveal this quite easily. There isn't much grey area with this sort of mediumship. It either happens, or it doesn't. It's not as subjective, as it is objective. Such mediums should not be anxious about just doing an ok session and not a great session because even an ok session would lead to amazing results. This should lead anyone to question either how inconsistent some "physical mediums" believe themselves to be or why else they appear worried and not wanting to share the amazing abilities they claim?

The only other reason would be fraudulence, and decent scientific testing and observation should easily discover that. It is very well known that a high amount of fraudulence has taken place with this form of mediumship, particularly in the Victorian era. In many ways, it is quite easy to try to fake this to persons who don't know enough about mediumistic phenomena, or lack enough logical thinking and convince them of mediumistic activity.

⁓

You also get people who actually imagine things that happen in the séances that didn't. I've seen this happen many times when attending séances and talking after to attendees who claim to have seen physical phenomena happen that myself or my friends did not see or hear, even though we were sat closer to the medium.

For example, they say an object was levitated out halfway down the room, when in reality that object never went a quarter of the way down the room. It appears to me these people imagine these things to try to reassure certain beliefs in their minds. This is not helpful as these people often will talk about the séance and the medium to many people and give this amazing glowing report that was actually nothing like what happened.

I certainly know if I could consistently produce physical mediumship, the first thing I would do is take it to parapsychologists and say watch me do this. Parapsychologists aren't all cynics, as people sometimes portray them. Some aren't even skeptical about the afterlife, perhaps because of an experience they may have had or due to certain research results, they have an understanding of an afterlife.

Several have seen my mental mediumship work to date, and each has been very positive regarding it, to the point that they have suggested that I do appear to be getting accurate information about a person's deceased loved ones. Most parapsychologists are more than happy to observe and work with mediums of all kinds, in a fair way.

Some shamanistic practitioners, whose practices feature physical mediumship, may not wish to put themselves forward for testing as their culture is different than modern Western culture and they feel their ways must be kept amongst their people and are sacred. Their methods are different. Indeed, some fear if they were to take these outside of people who are invited into their tribe and culture, moving it away from the sacred and showing how the power has been built and created through their cultural practices over hundreds or thousands of years, it could potentially lead to the practices no longer working.

This might be the case. I can see how that might happen but it also very well might not. Again, it's all about energy and how they use it. It is difficult to explain without being around the people, the culture, their spirituality and their spiritual practices and methods of creating the mediumship. Though many may think this an excuse to hide some fraudulent behaviour, and in certain cases that is very true, from my experiences, I certainly can understand why, at least, some who are potentially completely genuine could feel very hesitant about trying to share their practices.

The development of this form of mediumship also takes many years of dedication and sacrifice, much more so, than mental mediumship, which if done properly also requires extensive dedication and sacrifice. With Spiritualist forms of physical mediumship, often you will also need a number of people dedicated to helping you develop, to sit with you and help the process along.

These people need to be very unselfish and patient, and perhaps, have as much dedication to the process as the medium. These types of qualities I find very rare in our world today. Therefore, for these reasons, I don't see it making a big difference any time soon, even though it could have the potential to be a game-changer in the world. However, in the near future, I do have it in mind to further explore physical mediumship and its potential use for Heaven Therapy, as well as the world in general.

I hope to do so through scientific experiments and to try to continue to develop and perform these mediumship techniques consistently myself. So far, I have only been able to perform some on extremely rare occasions. This may be because the method I'm using is flawed, or I need more time and effort into developing the approach to create more consistency. Perhaps, other unknown conditions at that specific time caused the phenomena to be able to take place, or it could well be a mixture of all of these.

Poltergeist activity

Many people may have heard of the terms, poltergeists and poltergeist activity. Poltergeist activity is a physical phenomenon that happens because of a spirit, but it's a term used more often for hauntings, where the activity is often unwanted and often more negative or mischievous in nature. The term is never used within spiritualism. Such activity would be labelled as physical phenomena of a more negative or mischievous nature produced by a spirit.

Many parapsychologists have been convinced that poltergeist activity is real. One of the many well-known examples of parapsychological investigators believing a haunting was real was with the Enfield poltergeist. The activity took place at a council house in Brimsdown, Enfield, England from 1977 to 1979 and appeared to centre around two young girls whom were sisters, aged eleven and thirteen at the time. Whilst it is thought that some of the activity may have been staged by the girls for a number of potential reasons, there are several researchers who still believe at least a portion of the phenomena was really spirit activity. This is just one of many famous cases and there are many more that are not as famous and are often only described in the books of parapsychologists or, at times, only discussed in private to those they trust.

It's worth highlighting further here, that many parapsychologists and transpersonal scientists, who study spiritual and paranormal phenomena have been convinced by certain findings or a mixture of findings and their personal experiences.

Many also feel mediumship, the afterlife, and other psychic abilities are very real. In fact, it's not uncommon at all. Some have even professed to have some level of psychic ability themselves; perhaps the most well known example of this was a parapsychologist by the name of Alex Tanous.

Meeting a fair few people in this field, I've found many academic persons will claim to have had experiences often taking place at a location of a paranormal investigation that they cannot explain away to this day.

Paranormal investigations

On that note, paranormal investigations could one day produce a piece of footage or recording or an image that substantially adds to the proof of transbodily consciousness. There are already interesting examples of these out there that have not been explained away. However, it is not like what is often portrayed in TV shows, where there is so much great activity happening in the first half-hour of getting to the location.

Most investigations last for a whole evening, or even a full day and night. Favourable activity and interesting results are rare. The chances of the general public experiencing any strong physical phenomena or seeing a ghost or spirit during a public investigation are extremely low. It's something more for the professionals and dedicated knowledgeable enthusiasts who are willing to give up much time to it.

Whilst I have heard people saying really interesting activity has occurred to them, maybe once or twice during investigations, these persons have normally been on hundreds of paranormal investigations. You certainly won't normally be communicating with your relatives on such events. So here again, this isn't accessible to the general public unless you're doing a more serious investigation in a small group, under the guidance of people who know what they are doing.

I have also found, when I have been invited to do these sorts of events at certain well-known places often thought to be the most active locations, there is often absolutely no activity, at least, not what people say goes on there. I find that the locations that no one has heard of or ever investigated are often the most active. That is not the case all the time, but it seems to be the majority of the time.

Psychokinesis

The physical phenomena described above should not be confused with psychokinesis, sometimes referred to as telekinesis. This is the manipulation of physical objects through the mind of a person who is in a physical body. This is commonly exhibited in the bending, spinning or pushing of an object. Individual studies have taken place where scientists have been convinced by the phenomena.

With all of these phenomena, you need to sift through the fraudulence. It is because the exceptional is the minority. Four research papers here, five research papers there, may show some proof. However, ten say no significant results were found. In recent times, the Institute of Biosensory Psychology in St Petersburg, Russia has claimed to have had success with developing psychokinesis in ordinary people. Whilst I have not been there and seen the phenomena, several scientists have mentioned to me that they visited the institute and were impressed by the phenomena displayed, suggesting what they experienced was proof that psychokinesis is very real.

Spiritual healing

I am also asked if I consider forms of spiritual healing to be forms of Heaven Therapy? Yes, I do find some forms of spiritual healing to be forms of Heaven Therapy, specifically the ones that involve channelling the energy from spirits to help the process. Many different psychologists, Harald Walach to name one, have conducted multiple studies that produced results that suggested that spiritual healing is a real phenomenon and the results are not due to the placebo effect. Walach et al, (2008) is just one study example.

There are also countless phenomenological accounts of spiritual healing working. That being said, it doesn't appear to be a consistent phenomenon regarding the power of healing received. For instance, I know of several spiritual healers who seemed to, at times, perform healing that really did work. Yet, they were, unfortunately, unable to heal a close loved one from cancer.

It appears it can work but it's not always consistently strong enough and with practitioners today, the power appears limited. I'm not aware of anyone in modern times who is said to miraculously have healed the blind to see again, but I am aware of people seemingly healing illnesses like HIV, cancer, meningitis, brain and neurological diseases, along with many other diseases. It appears to me from the results of various studies, that the greater the amount of healers performing the healing, either in person or projecting from a distance, the stronger the effect is.

I feel experiments conducted in the areas discussed could potentially aid the understanding of consciousness, and if done properly, may bring evidence to support transbodily consciousness being a reality. Certain forms of physical mediumship even have the potential to conclusively prove the existence of transbodily consciousness. However, the methods in their current forms won't ever be accessible to the general public and also may not be available to the scientific community.

Perhaps, with breakthroughs in other areas of consciousness these techniques can be refined and made consistent. However, in the next chapter, I will address better ways in which I think we could move things forward and get conclusive objective proof of the existence of transpersonal consciousness.

FIFTEEN

The Future of Heaven
Therapy Continued

. . . .

One of the most important things that I discovered in the study, MSc, is if a person's psychological needs are not met by the mediumistic reading, the symptoms of bereavement can get worse, and in some extreme cases could be enough to potentially cause the person to end their physical life.

I would propose that at the very least, a study must be done to determine in greater detail what a person experiences when these specific psychological needs are not met through the reading. This would help to further understand the potential risks involved and potentially may also shed further light on how, as a whole, healing is experienced through this approach.

Personally, it is because of the above that I try to discuss the psychological needs of the recipient whenever possible, at various points, before the reading begins, as long as the person is comfortable with this. I feel mediums should make the recipients aware of potential adverse effects of the process if their psychological needs are not met. It's all about being professional and taking better care of your clients.

I suggest my fellow mediums and those who would like to venture into this area, research and understand aspects of psychology that relate to these areas, with a particular eye on therapeutic approaches, transpersonal and otherwise.

The more you understand where your clients are in their bereavement process, what their needs are, how their needs of healing may be fulfilled or how things could be made worse, the better equipped you are to help.

I have seen and heard of many "mediums" who do more psychological damage to their client because they have no concept of various things discussed in this book, much less extensive knowledge. Sometimes people are in very fragile states. They could have heart conditions; in particular, the elderly need to be handled with great care. Not knowing what you are doing and not being able to handle different situations could even be fatal for the type of person I've just mentioned. I've seen myself how fragile individuals can become ill, very quickly, just by having a mediumistic reading.

For instance, I was giving a demonstration around three or four years ago, and I went up to an elderly lady in the audience. When I started talking about her father who had passed away she became exceedingly emotional. You could see all the anxiety connected to the bereavement was being brought to the surface, and there was a lot of it.

Seemingly, far too much for her to be able to handle. She began to shake, and hyperventilate, started clutching her chest and complaining of feeling pain in her chest and heart and a feeling of dizziness. It was pretty clear to me that this lady was having an anxiety attack. Whilst I could see she was emotional, the change from just showing emotion to these symptoms happened very fast, somewhere between three and four sentences of information that I passed on. This all probably happened in about 30 seconds to about a minute. Some of this time, I was not looking at her as I was focused on the communication.

Thankfully, I was able to recognize what was happening and was able to take control of the situation. I quickly came down off the stage, went to her seat in the audience and using hypnosis techniques, I was able to calm her down to a point I could continue to talk to her about the spirit communicating and what they were saying to me.

Now, you might be thinking why didn't you calm her down and just leave things be? Yes, I could have done this. However, we were mid-point in the reading, and I had just brought a whole load of anxiety to the surface, I didn't want her going away with all this unresolved stress related to the passing of the spirit communicator. I worried that if unresolved she could experience another attack later that evening when she may be on her own.

In the process of my calming her down, I had also asked her daughter, who was sitting next to her if her mother had a heart condition, and if she was in general good health. To which her daughter replied, no heart condition and yes, her general health was good.

Think of this as being in a storm in the ocean and your ship is half-way up a wave, you're worried about the wave breaking on your ship before you get to the top, but you're half way up now and if you were to turn around, it could be just as bad or worse. So you're sort of stuck, needing to stable the ship and continue up and over the wave to pull through the storm. What I had tried to do was calm the storm, and make the wave as small as possible, and when I felt she was calm enough, I made the decision to continue to give the message, holding her hand with her looking right into my eyes.

As I continued, she calmed down a little more and a little more, and by the time I had reached the natural end of the reading, I was happy with the state she was in. My hand hadn't fared too well in the process of her vice-like-grip; bless her, but she was now fine. I told a steward to get the lady a glass of water, and I told her daughter to alert the nearby steward if she became dizzy again or was experiencing any problem.

She sat there fine for the remainder of the demonstration, and I made sure to keep as much of an eye on her as possible for the remainder of it. The lady and her daughter came and spoke to me after the reading and thanked me for everything, especially for making her feel better physically and continuing the reading. They also told me that her life had been changed by the messages. She would not forget what I said and did and the things her father had told her, how he had shown her he was still very much alive in heaven and watching over her.

What would have happened that day if I didn't know what I know and had the training I did? One could only guess, and this is just one example. So, I think you can see why I advise a certain level of knowledge and training in relevant areas is important. Overall, I believe this is important in establishing Heaven Therapy as a more recognized alternative means of treating grief due to bereavement and potentially integral for it being a successful one.

Taking the above into consideration, it does need to be said, that for some people a reading via phone or Skype, where the medium is not there to help, should the person experience anything like what I've discussed, is something to be avoided and can be potentially quite dangerous. This is something the medium should endeavour to explain before the reading is booked.

In an ideal world, every medium would have to have a certain level of knowledge of psychology, hypnosis, even CPR and of course Psi phenomena and specifically bereavement, perhaps as much as a Ph.D. Of course, this is not going to happen anytime soon. Mediumship is not policed, in any form, and I also can't see that changing anytime soon. We may not too far from now, even need mediums anymore. I hope that will be the case and it is something I will discuss shortly.

Validating transbodily consciousness
and mediumship

I believe what would be helpful to mediums in the future, are further well carried out studies regarding testing the reality of Psi phenomena and mediumship. As mediums, further scientific authentication that we are receiving accurate information regarding a person's deceased loved ones would only benefit us. The same goes for all forms of psychic ability. There is a bit of a debate on how to best do this, where some feel the best way to prove this is to use the general population to test if psychic ability exists, and others believe studies should be focused on persons who are considered exceptionally gifted.

From my perspective, using the general population does have some merit. However, I suggest, the focus must be on the extremely gifted category. I would say the general population is not gifted or trained enough to produce a consistent result needed for science. At times, studies would indicate psychic ability but many, perhaps most, won't. Currently and not surprisingly, that is very much what I have found when reviewing the data.

Whilst studies on the exceptionally gifted category have certainly not always produced results that indicate psychic ability, I would argue that perhaps the psychics used may not be as gifted as they were made out to be or thought they were. I think the best approach would be to test exceptionally gifted mediums, under controlled conditions and first whittle out any that don't make the grade. Hopefully, you will be left with a small group of genuinely, exceptionally gifted individuals who could consistently produce results that indicate psychic ability.

This is the type of approach that the Windbridge Institute has taken, and when reviewing the data, it is these studies where the results appear to consistently suggest mediumship is a very real phenomenon.

Personally, I feel there is a strong need for more statistically based studies that quantify facts to demonstrate a psychic phenomenon is occurring. Ultimately, mainstream science and the world as a whole, pay more attention to such experiments and results as opposed to just subjective-based experiences.

For instance, a group of fifty individuals suggesting they have had an out-of-body experience. This is compelling and may even indicate transbodily consciousness being a reality. However, if thirty persons from a group have out-of-body experiences, in a controlled setting, and during that time they access information they wouldn't be able to know otherwise, this would be very different.

As an example, if the word cupcake is placed on top of the cupboard, and when the subjects are back in body they remember and speak the word cupcake, this would be amazing and would scientifically highly indicate transbodily consciousness is a reality. We need more studies like this. If results were consistent enough, it could prove transbodily consciousness is an absolute reality, and this very well may be the way it is proven to be the case.

In the meantime, there are also many possible ways to conduct a similar experiment to prove psychic ability. For instance, I was doing some taster filming with ITV Studios a couple of years ago, and they asked me to go into a storage container yard and pick the container where they had hidden a person. All I had was this person's watch to psychically pick up on their energy, and then match that energy to an energy I felt within one of the containers.

There were ninety-eight storage containers in this yard, so I had a 1 in 98 chance of getting it right the first time through with what we would call chance. Well, it took me around 20 minutes to narrow it down to the container I felt was right, and thankfully, I was correct and picked the very container the person was in.

As you can see, these types of experiments done in a controlled setting could greatly help validate psychic phenomena. This isn't to say the study of phenomenological subjective experience doesn't have merit, because it does. We wouldn't be at this point today without it. However, it's not the long-term answer to faster global validation.

The real main issue with validating transpersonal consciousness is that we have no means to objectively detect consciousness outside the physical body through a device. The scientific community as a whole is not even sure what consciousness exactly is and how it is created. If there were a way that could be devised in which an objective measurement, of what appears to be consciousness, outside of a physical body could be taken, this would be the Holy Grail, so to speak.

This would not be a person's subjective experience but a device that would seemingly pick up on the consciousness of a disembodied spirit, and if this could be done consistently through a device, this should provide conclusive proof of a form of transbodily consciousness, specifically the quantum soul.

Depending on how the experiment was done, it could also potentially prove the eternal existence of the quantum soul. If such data could be incorporated with other connecting research, then, I feel we would have definitive proof of transbodily consciousness and the afterlife.

Perhaps in time, the method could be developed and refined to allow for objective communication between this world and the next, where spirits would be able to communicate messages through the device. In this way, Heaven Therapy for the world could begin. Perhaps even in time, all persons could have such a device in their home and mediums would no longer be needed. I hope this is the future for Heaven Therapy, as this is something I wish to work towards as my career continues.

The importance of transpersonal science

More people are looking at consciousness and particularly the potential transpersonal aspects of it – researching it from all angles. Which is why I feel transpersonal science is critical. It seeks to take into account all perspectives and believes that spirituality and science can potentially have the same understanding.

From my perspective, mainstream science often limits itself when it comes to consciousness by continuing to have a narrow viewpoint. You see, many people are trying to put together a jigsaw puzzle. They are attempting to match pieces of the puzzle together to reveal the overall picture. However, the mainstream is not concerned with what is considered transpersonal and paranormal phenomena and as such, they don't figure it into the puzzle. Whereas someone like me seeks to find how my pieces of the puzzle fit in with the mainstream and how it can potentially reveal the overall picture.

Mainstream scientists have yet to prove aspects of their jigsaw puzzle, and I think there will always be missing pieces in it. The problem, of course, is not science, that I want to make clear right here. The problem is close-minded scientists. Science is just a method of investigation, a tool for testing ideas.

It is the mainstream scientists that I feel generally are not using the tool to its full potential, as generally they aren't interested in looking at filling those gaps with pieces that go beyond how they have set out to fit their puzzle together.

I think it will be someone or more likely several people who look outside the mainstream box, who end up connecting all the pieces together and revealing the overall picture of consciousness and life. This is a picture that has already begun to take good shape and one that, from my perspective, includes the eternal existence of the human soul.

What mediumship and Heaven Therapy certainly don't need are genuine mediums faking the odd thing. What might be going through your mind is… but Ross, why would genuine mediums fake stuff when they can perform mediumship? There are several reasons this can happen, and I suppose one could say that one way or another, they all come back to the human ego.

A genuine medium may fake something because they want to be seen as the best medium and perhaps aren't talented enough. They may fake something because they have performed a certain level of mediumship or feat of mediumship in the past, but aren't capable of doing it consistently. However, that level may now be what people expect from them on a regular basis. Also, they may fake something because they are run-down and need a break, and know they can't perform the mediumship expected of them all the time, but they have no way out as a full-time medium.

If they were to say sorry, I need a few months or even a few weeks, they won't get paid the money they may need to live. They may even fake something because they want to help someone or a set of people, but feel they can't perform well enough at that time for whatever reason without faking certain things.

Think of it like a soccer player who scored a free kick five weeks in a row, the sixth week comes round and he thinks, I can't do this again. He wants to be as good as the player who did it six times, or the fans expect that of him because he did it the last five times.

Knowing this, he wants to please the fans, and is worried if he doesn't please the fans enough then some of them might suffer greatly because of it, even take their own life, or he might crumble from the pressure and will be without a job, and he can't live without the job.

If a soccer player could press a button in his pocket to somehow cheat and make him score more goals, with the thought that it's unlikely for anyone to find out about this, how many soccer players do you think would not push the button ever? That being said, such occurrences will only come back to hurt mediumship and Heaven Therapy in the long run.

We need to try to support mediums, so they can feel more comfortable with not being perfect. Raise awareness of the mediumship process to ensure people are more understanding and also don't put everything on the line on the outcome of one single reading. This is very difficult, but if we can make any difference in these ways, we must try. In this way, I hope mediums can also support each other more to help each other cope with the pressure.

Sadly, many mediums see each other as competition. Being a medium and a spiritual person does not automatically go together. There have been plenty of people with different levels of mediumistic ability who aren't spiritual people by most people's standards at all. This often surprises many, but as I have highlighted, mediumship is a natural ability that can be developed in a number of set ways.

Also, the spirit world doesn't have enough mediums to be too choosy in who to help. If that person has not-so-great intentions and spirituality, but they can be used to do good, the spirit world will still help them develop also in the hope that the practice will help them in time become more spiritual. That being said, as my spirituality has grown, my mediumship has become stronger from it. I teach that the two complement each other.

However, a person could be very spiritual but not very much mediumistic, at all. They may not have developed that aspect of themselves yet and they may find it very hard to do so due to how their mind is and many other factors.

Thankfully, more people are becoming interested in studying the areas I've discussed, particularly connected to consciousness. Also, thankfully, some of these people are very intelligent, and very experienced in certain areas. What I feel I do have on my side that other scientists, academics, researchers or whatever you wish to call them don't, is my connection to the afterlife and the universe at large through my psychic abilities.

Through my mind, if I can understand the direction given by the spirits, I can follow their guidance to the answers and methods to what I have just discussed. Perhaps it will take someone with the right mixture of intelligence, experience in several areas and ability to connect with the transpersonal through psychic ability to be able to figure things out and do what needs to be done. Who knows who that might be; I certainly don't at present. I just plan on doing my bit, however small or large that may turn out to be. I hope more and more people will come along and want to do their bit, with a transpersonally minded approach to solving the puzzle.

In order to take the first steps towards this, we will need more scientists standing up and saying they feel that a transpersonal existence can be or is a reality. It is great when a scientist, who doesn't believe in an afterlife, has an experience that convinces them of it and instead of keeping it to themselves, they talk about it with the public.

A recent example of this is American neurosurgeon, Eben Alexander and his bestselling book. Alexander, (2012) published *Proof of Heaven* detailing how his experience connected to neuroscience did not allow for a belief in an afterlife, but how his stance changed when he became gravely ill with meningitis and became comatose. He suggests while in the coma that he experienced a set of visual experiences and feelings that due to the state of his brain at the time, he should not have experienced or remembered when he awoke from the coma.

Whilst his book and experience has received criticism, this again, is nothing new. Scientists are always criticized by other scientists, especially if a scientist is saying something the other doesn't believe is possible, or goes against their research or outlook based on their understandings and beliefs.

Whilst I do find some of the apparent transpersonal and transbodily experiences Alexander describes to be a bit odd, it remains a good example of a very qualified man of science speaking out about how he feels the transpersonal is very real, based on relating his apparent transpersonal experience to his understanding of science.

Some criticisms are more justifiable than others. Sometimes it can simply come down to a person's word as to who is being honest or who isn't. If Eben's experience was real or not, that is just one experience that indicates transpersonal consciousness, out of countless millions. Mainstream science can't simply explain them all away, but they will certainly have a good go at it, and rightly so. If they didn't, they wouldn't be doing their job nor being true to themselves and their views from whatever their experience is.

Overall, I will suggest that the puzzle, riddle, and mystery that consciousness has been, in regard to how it's created and what properties it has, will definitely be solved in the next hundred years. It very likely may even be solved in the next fifty to sixty years and possibly may very well be solved somewhere in the next forty years. Maybe even as soon as the next ten or twenty years, depending on how fast certain events and breakthroughs happen.

From my perspective, what will be proven is consciousness is transbodily and those who have left their physical bodies behind live on eternally in the afterlife. As I have touched on, there are thousands and thousands of sensible, respectable and scientifically minded people with the same view, who are becoming more interested in exploring consciousness and the transpersonal in a more disciplined way. Some would like nothing more than to show the world that what I discuss is true, and these passionate people won't stop until everyone knows what they know.

SIXTEEN

Completing The Puzzle,
Making The Circle Complete

• • • • • • • • • • • • • •

The future of humanity

Now, we are here near the end of the book. If you are still reading, it shows you have an open mind, open heart, and want to learn and grow. Thank you for putting up with me. I'd be interested to know how you have found the content of the book. Perhaps the last big question I'm often asked is how I feel about the future of humanity, and the direction things are going.

Well, in just the immediate future much change is on the horizon and not small change, big change. To the point, in 30 or 40 years the world will be so different in so many ways! We, who are here now, will have trouble recognizing it. Cars will likely be driving themselves, prototypes for these already exist. Some scientists predict medical science will be at a point where it can halt and, even reverse aging indefinitely, stop us from getting infections of all kinds, and cure all known diseases.

Some scientists predict artificial intelligence will have well surpassed that of humans and eventually robots will take over nearly all of our manual labour. Eventually, we certainly will end up having household robots to help around the home. Many predict we will know the reality of consciousness and all these things have massive short-term and long-term impacts. For instance, if we stop aging and dying, the world may well end up mostly or exclusively vegan, as it may be necessary to support the population and the environment.

We will be going further and further out into space and may have begun to colonize other planets. If we have been able to establish objective communication with the afterlife through a device during these years, that would open up infinite possibility. Some of this seems hard to believe, but these are all things that can happen.

And in some cases are very likely to happen in that time frame; some may happen sooner than thought and some a touch later. Some of it may still be hard to get your head around and to picture and imagine, but think about it, 60 years ago, the first mobile phone wasn't even made. Skype would have been completely out of this world. Computers, in 20 years' time, will make our current ones seem like we were living in the Stone Age. There should hopefully be more people studying aspects of spirituality and transpersonal phenomena and hopefully, all of this together can usher in a more spiritual age. Everything is moving on so rapidly now, it's like a snowball effect. We are now a huge snowball that has started to gain momentum, and will only increase more and more, faster and faster.

All this will bring further challenges for us on Earth. Challenges that I'm sure our loved ones in heaven will need to comfort us on and give us guidance. Overall in the long run I feel these things only stand to make the world better. In some ways, it is a very exciting time to be on this planet. Whilst some seem to feel that spiritually we are going backwards, this, in my opinion, is absolutely nonsense.

If you actually look at the history of man we are more spiritually evolved as a whole than we have ever been. Don't get me wrong, we have a very long way to go, but we are entering deeper and deeper into our spiritual potential, now moving forward at a better rate than we have ever been before. Huge shifts don't happen overnight so things may seem to drag on, but I can assure you the process that will cause an enormous change is happening.

All of the above and the content of the book as a whole may have raised certain questions in your mind, and if that is the case, I talk about all these things in lectures and workshops, where people can ask whatever question they like. So, if you have questions or are just interested in learning more, come along and find out more and even ask a question.

Of course I would love to have it so spirits could directly explain everything to you through a device, they would be able to do it better than me I'm sure and it would also save me an obscene amount of time writing books like this, but until that technology is available, you will have to put up with me and others like me for a little while longer.

When it comes to this book, some would argue that where I have related to science, I'm discussing concepts that are pseudoscience. I would argue that with certain studies I have mentioned that is far from true. Regarding the rest, I would say everything is considered pseudoscience until it's proven to be true.

It is worth mentioning, at this point, that science is not concrete and understanding is always evolving. There is a concept known as "the half-life of knowledge". The half-life of knowledge is the amount of time that has to elapse before half of the knowledge, in a particular area, is superseded or shown to be untrue. Scientific knowledge is suggested on average to be growing by a factor of ten, every fifty years. This means that half of what scientists may have known about a particular subject will be wrong or obsolete in 45 years.

Of course, every field is different, and there are different opinions on exactly what the half-life of knowledge is for each field. For the area of psychology, some theorize it to be as little as five years. How crazy is that? Will this rate slow down? Perhaps, in some areas of science, it will, as we get to points of being completely spot on and knowing all there is to know about that particular subject. However, in some fields, I feel the rate is likely to sooner or later increase before it really slows down, that is if it ever does.

———

Academically speaking, it could certainly be said that a book could make more of a point and stronger case if it were to explore the potential of transpersonal consciousness and the afterlife by simply exploring the reality of Psi or mediumistic phenomena. If it is also done in a more pragmatic way along with a much more rigid scientifically minded structure that may give it more credence in certain people's minds. I certainly would agree, but that is another book entirely and one, which I may write, come the completion of my Ph.D. and further research that I hope will shed light on potential ways to detect the disembodied consciousness of spirits through a device.

By then, maybe the Holy Grail of scientific evidence of transbodily consciousness and the afterlife may have been found and could even be the defining factor of that book. Further, if I had followed such an approach for this book, I would not have been able to discuss nearly any of the major questions I'm often asked and covered. Questions that people clearly want and need answers to.

Some may suggest that other aspects of this book could be considered largely philosophically based, and that is fair. However, most importantly, it's a philosophical perspective based on real extensive experience with the phenomena, and connecting that phenomena to scientific study. The essence of this book always was to be a large focus on the phenomenological experiences of mediums, everyday people and myself.

These experiences are relayed in a light way to modern scientific theories, concepts and studies. They are conveyed through a thinking process that although in many ways, is transpersonally inspired, I feel it does not lack a good amount of logic and healthy skepticism. I feel the thoughts are far more disciplined than you will find in the average book on spirituality.

Many books on spirituality, I feel, are written in a way that exemplifies that their enquiry into spirituality has been very undisciplined and potentially influenced by some things that in no way can be proven or the average person here could never relate to. They often lack any scientific understanding and it doesn't appear they have a desire to explore spirituality in a more down to earth, tangible, and disciplined manner.

Much logical thinking doesn't seem to ever take place. I mention this because I hope my more disciplined and rational enquiry into spirituality is something that is, at least, somewhat reflected in my writing, in order to help form a good overview of a potential point where science and the concepts of spirituality discussed in this book may meet and in my opinion already are.

Science and religion are not so different

At the end of the day, science and religion aren't all that different either. I can feel the heated glares from mainstream scientists already for saying such blasphemy... but I feel it is true. To explain, religious leaders follow a set of procedures that are sacred to them, that have been passed down and potentially kept the same or adapted over generations and generations. They are seen as sacred because they are viewed as understandings and procedures that hold answers, bring truth and form the right path. Religion serves as a process and tool to investigate ideas and the world. Religious persons often take things in faith, for instance that a religious figure:

a) Did have said experience;

b) Really did exist;

c) Really did perform said miracle, etc.

They may not have been there at the time, but believe what has been passed down. These are understandings based on what was available to them at the time and current day people then try to relate these to the world and their personal life as it is now.

Scientists also follow a set of understandings and procedures that have been passed down and adapted over generations and generations. They too, follow these, as they are a process and tool seen to bring truth and hold the answers, and form the right path. If there is such a thing as a secular form of sacredness, the scientific method is very sacred for scientists.

They also, at times, have to follow some premises with a little bit of faith. They will need a certain amount of faith that previous research they base their understandings and work around, was done well and is correct. Further, that their research and theory is even on the right track and they aren't barking up the wrong tree, so to speak.

With certain areas of science, it is very difficult to provide conclusive proof. It can be mostly just theories, grounded guesswork based on what is scientifically measured and observed at this time. As you may know, the world's most famous scientist still in this physical dimension, Stephen Hawking, is the Director of Research at the Centre for Theoretical Cosmology within the University of Cambridge. The keyword here being theoretical.

Mainstream science believes x, y, z about consciousness but they don't know for sure. They have faith that their thoughts are correct, but not solid proof. Scientists do have their methods to try to make sense of the world, and from these methods and their personal experience they form certain understandings about the world. However, really they are more grounded beliefs when you scale it back than solid understandings. More grounded than general religious beliefs? Yes certainly. However, still beliefs.

The more these beliefs can be proven, the more they are commonly referred to as understandings. In a similar way, people who receive evidence from mediums and paranormal phenomena, can reach a point where it's not a belief, but in their minds, a grounded understanding gained from experience. It becomes a knowing, not a faith.

A knowing that often has a transpersonal element that comes with it. An understanding, coupled with a feeling that is so deeply rooted in one's self and beyond oneself that it transcends the physical and transcends their very being. Through these processes, it is as if their minds have awakened to a level of perception where one knows of an afterlife intellectually, but also understands and feels it on a transpersonal level.

Yes, a person could argue that religion is false and has been used to control people and that religion is all about control. Firstly, that's not true for the majority of religions. Yes, some certainly but not all, and the problem is sometimes not with the religion, but with some of the people who claim to follow it. The religion could be anything, but that doesn't mean people have to follow it or all of it. It was a person or set of people who also invented religion in the first place. It didn't just invent itself. Further, a person could argue that science has also been used to control people in plenty of ways throughout history and they wouldn't be wrong, either. The world is still full of it today. However, again it's not the science that is the problem, it's how the people have used it, and in certain ways continue to use it.

In my opinion, it is important to remain as well disciplined as possible and to follow as much of a scientifically sound method as possible. Otherwise, much could potentially be mistaken for truth. This process, hopefully, leads to a decently grounded understanding, where the process of duplicating results eliminates faith from the equation more and more.

The good thing is, the more we advance technologically, the more we can do certain experiments, form particular measurements and gain a greater understanding of the overall picture of reality. That being said, when you pull everything else away, there always has to be some element of belief based on experience.

~

Ultimately, everything comes back to belief, no matter what you follow. This is a belief based on your experiences, your observations and your observations of other's experience that you relate to yours. Again, this is what science is at the core. Science is about observation, and from that, conclusions are made on what appears to be true based on these sets of observations. Through scientific study, we can seek a more grounded conclusion. We can make the information as objective as possible. However, we can ultimately only settle on the conclusions from within ourselves.

Again, I could relate here to something I brought up earlier and ask you how do you know, as you're reading this book, you aren't actually reading a book at all and you are in a coma, and eventually you will wake up to the real world? You could reply, "Well, that doesn't make sense," and based on your experiences, it would be very improbable and in many ways illogical.

Though, you could still not provide yourself, or me, with a hundred percent proof that you are not in a coma. This is the same for me asking how do you know you aren't just a part of one highly advanced, by our current standards, computer program? That the real world as we think of it, is not our world? Again, you could say that is not logical and I would agree with you, but you couldn't provide definitive proof that you're not part of a computer program. Thus, you can see that ultimately everything relates back to an aspect of belief based on your experience and observations.

Scientific method has its pros, but I also feel it has its cons. Often, it limits itself by its procedure. The strength in true spirituality is that it doesn't limit itself. It's not afraid to go beyond convention to explore and find an answer and to dive down the proverbial rabbit hole without obstruction.

However, as suggested, if this is done in a completely undisciplined way then it can certainly lead to mistaken truths and that is clear to see from the history of man. What I see, though, is that the two approaches can combine together and make up for each other's weakness. These together can then move us on faster than either of them could on their own. This is the reason I did my Master's of Science degree, and ultimately will look to assist in a merged approach between spirituality and science to put the final nail in the coffin of the riddle of consciousness and the afterlife. Pun very much intended.

The fault in many mainstream scientists

As I have discussed, what the world needs is that stronger objective proof of transbodily consciousness and the afterlife, to cause a paradigm shift. That Holy Grail must be found. We, however, must also be ready to believe the proof when it arrives. If a means is discovered there will be some who still won't want to believe it. Those people, who have certain beliefs greatly ingrained in their egos, would say perhaps that it is demons pretending to be other spirits or that it's just plain lies by the government.

Their egos will not allow them to accept the truth they would be confronted with. Their ego would be afraid of letting go of a belief system that challenges aspects of their perception of existence. There are also some scientists who are very prone to being stuck in their ego. At a recent lecture I attended, the scientist speaking mentioned reincarnation and that if more proof became available, he might change his mind to believe in it. He followed to say, then again, he might not.

Some very well respected scientists make statements that in many ways are unscientific. Examples are statements similar to, "I have found no evidence in the universe of God through studying how the physical universe works, therefore, I don't believe in an afterlife." Many mainstream scientists have come out with comments similar to this. These types of comments I see as being flawed in conception and flawed through hypocritically unscientific assumption.

Firstly, most, if not all, of these scientists are relating to God in a very different way than I have related to God. They are relating to God as more of an unnatural force that shapes our universe and controls our lives, perhaps one that is more of the standard parochial conception of God. Secondly, they haven't found definitive evidence of God through studying the physical universe, and even when studying things that could be understood as unphysical they proceed only to relate these things wherever possible, and however possible, to just the physical universe.

Well, pardon my language but no brown mucky stuff. Of course, they wouldn't have found definitive evidence of God this way. One would never find conclusive proof of God through studying just one type of manifestation of God through limited measuring tools. They are missing the main conceptions of what God is, and the various properties attributed to God. If God is also ultimately outside time and space, unless your conscious mind is also outside time and space and infinite, then good luck with trying to find a conscious way to measure God.

To find, in any form, a merger between the physical universe and its processes, with something that is the most "un-physical" thing possible, requires someone who better understands the infinite, God, and the afterlife. They would need to try to break down the various manifestations of such things philosophically and then relate this to science and the physical.

I have tried to follow this very method through this book. The best way to find the connections and, in my opinion, the truth, is not by looking at the physical and then trying to relate it to the spiritual, the best way is looking first at the spiritual and then try to relate it to the physical.

You see, I, and others like me, are not so different than the mainstream scientists when you scale it right back. They are looking for the natural within the universe. So are people like me, the difference is that we have seen the natural in the mystical and the spiritual. Another thing I have noticed so many mainstream scientists do, is if they haven't found evidence of the conception of God in the physical universe, they then make an enormous assumption that there is no afterlife, without researching and investigating if there are natural processes in the universe that lead to and facilitate a form of afterlife.

Sadly, they simply believe this is impossible. What an enormous ungrounded assumption, and key word here being belief, that is. In reality there is more proof of an afterlife than there is of there not being one. There is already enough definitive proof out there. Unfortunately, you can bet most scientists have never really delved that deeply, and certainly never investigated it in a scientific or spiritual manner. Yet, somehow they feel they know the answers.

Of course, most people scientific and otherwise would rejoice, and great healing would be found in further objective proof of an afterlife and all the things I've discussed in this book. Depending on how it comes, it could even lead on to this physical world becoming much more Utopian. Orch-OR theory and studies that appear to validate it, however, are not the only lifeline. It could still be that the integral piece of the puzzle that demonstrates transbodily consciousness is still missing.

Quantum brain dynamics is another theory that I would suggest could include transbodily consciousness being a reality. The theory itself has evolved over the years from a collection of ideas and research. Jibu & Yasue, (1995) put them together well in the book "Quantum Brain Dynamics and Consciousness". They discuss the theory that the electric dipoles of the water molecules of the brain constitute a quantum field, referred to as the cortical field. Whilst proponents of the theory differ slightly as to the way consciousness arises in this system, I would suggest that if this theory were to be proven true, that the thoughts of Jibu and Yasue, (1995) are correct in that consciousness, as we know it, arises from interaction between the energy of the quantum field and the bimolecular waves of the neuronal network.

Further, I would suggest that the information that forms our personality, memory and self is stored within the electromagnetic quantum field. That it is this field that interacts with, and at least in part, controls the neural network in the brain.

Some proponents of this theory like Ricciardi & Umezawa, (1967) have suggested that long-range coherent waves within and between brain cells are key in memory retrieval. In various ways, quantum brain dynamic theories are very similar to Orch-OR. I suggest Orch-OR and these other theories can co-exist and even complement each other in forms. I'm sure if there is a further integral missing piece of the puzzle, it will be found sooner rather than later.

From my perspective, Orch-OR theory is currently a tremendous avenue to follow and the first theory in science that I feel can be married exactly to my phenomenological experiences and that of countless millions. Quantum brain dynamics currently coming a close second, in my eyes, but it is perhaps just as valid as Orch-OR and no less promising when connected to the transbodily phenomenological experiences.

I plan on doing research looking at the potentials of electromagnetic transbodily phenomena, as I believe it could potentially produce fruitful results in detecting human consciousness outside the physical body, through a completely objective measuring device, specifically, the consciousness of disembodied spirits. If such a process was consistent, then it might even be able to be refined to establish direct objective communication with heaven through the device.

—

In a way, spiritualism and mediumship have always looked towards a merger between spirituality and science. These seek to take the spiritual and bring forth as much scientific proof as possible. That provides evidence that can be processed both subjectively and objectively. I know what I have said in this book will stand the test of time. That not too far in the future, what I have discussed in the book, will be considered by the majority as the truth.

Science is catching up with these particular truths, which humans have known about from the beginning of our existence. I feel it is only the lack of knowledge regarding the spiritual, transpersonal or paranormal that causes a potential continual stumbling block. As I have suggested, many scientists with opposing opinions on the possible reality of afterlife, most likely, have never studied or immersed themselves in the paranormal and transpersonal. Therefore, it's impossible for them to have a well-rounded, and grounded take on these subjects.

Unfortunately, too many currently do comment, and there are many that listen to them. It's rather like asking a physicist their opinion on whether you have a certain disease, instead of asking a doctor of medicine. Two different areas of science, which study two different parts of reality. One could tell you how your body works on a particular level and the other can tell how it works on another. However, only one of them through their methods and experience will have the knowledge and the experience to form the right answer regarding whether you have that particular disease or not. In this case, it would not be the physicist.

I do believe we are now on our way to fully illuminating the truth that has always been right in front of our faces and from that, changing mainstream understanding. This is the truth that is known to many through their experiences and from certain scientific studies. From these experiences, this very same truth has already been demonstrated over and over again and is constantly being re-validated. It is the powerful truth that we all have a trans-bodily quantum soul that lives on eternally.

Further, that one day, sooner or later, we can spend eternity with our loved ones in heaven, and we can find greater peace and harmony than we find currently on Earth. This truth tells us all is not lost in the physical dimension's bitter sands of time and that love always lives on within us in heaven and love most assuredly does conquer all.

What inspires me

Love is what all this is about at the end of the day, for what would life be without love? It is love that has most likely brought you to reading this book. People sometimes ask me what keeps you going doing the work you are doing? What gets you through the challenges? What inspires you? The answer is simple. Pain, grief, and love inspire me.

The people featured in this book inspire me because I know the pain, the suffering, the grief that is in our world today and that which I have experienced in my life and have felt through communicating with the spirits, and felt from their loved ones who remain on Earth. I've seen this pain over and over, and that is what leaves me thinking, I have to keep going, I have to keep trying to make things better, try to do whatever I can to end so much of the pain and suffering.

My hope is that I can keep attempting to make more and more of this circular puzzle complete. I feel you can never accuse a medium, like me, of not caring because if we didn't care, care a real lot, we wouldn't keep going through the challenges our life and work brings. We wouldn't do half of what we do if we didn't care. Some care more than others, of course, but what I care about is just doing whatever I can, however, small or large. As I have said, that is no easy task. One that comes with many challenges, but one that I will keep trying to fulfill.

Before the book closes, it is important to highlight that nobody can receive information from his or her loved ones on the other side twenty-four hours a day, seven days a week. Or anything like this. After we have received evidence of the afterlife, we need to embrace it and allow it to calm our soul to the point that we don't need constant validations of our loved ones being around us or even feel the need for regular communication.

This part of the process is not about letting go. It's about embracing change and continuing our lives. Our loved ones will always be there is what is shown in the readings and other forms of proof. It's about being comfortable with that, without needing more. People get hooked on it and those are the people that go round and round their whole life seeing different mediums. Some go to spiritualist church every Sunday in hope of a top-up message.

I don't need to have messages from my grandmother ever. Not because I can talk to her all the time but because it's actually harder for me to talk to her than it would be a spirit I don't know. I just don't need it. I talk to her and I know she hears it. I know she visits. Not because I sense her presence all the time but because why wouldn't she, given everything I know about her and the afterlife? I don't need to hear from her on any level because I already know she is there and I know what she would think because I know her.

I'm sure she also has much she is up to. I don't need to know what that is all the time because I will find out when I get over there and have a big catch-up or when a device is invented here where I can talk to her with ease; like a spirit phone or email system. This is something that I plan on researching as part of my continual academic experience. It is something that I feel can fall into place once we have a device and method for detecting transbodily consciousness.

In the meantime, I honour my grandmother by being happy and living life. Not by being upset. Someday maybe signs of her presence will come but if they don't they don't. It strikes me when people often long for more and more messages, at times they doubt the connection they had with their loved one here. People shouldn't because if the spirit came to them in a reading, it shows they love you with everything they are today. Just as you loved them the same and they know that. Never doubt this. They often say it, again and again, in readings.

Of course, you weren't perfect and neither were they. That's life here on Earth, not love. Don't confuse the two. Be at peace with yourself and you can find greater peace with living life in a happier way without the need for continual top-up messages, validations and reassurances.

If right now you need that personal proof and healing to get to that point, go out and book a reading with a good mental medium. Try not to be too discouraged if the first experience doesn't go so well. Remain calm and try again with another medium. Sometimes, it can be hard to find a very good medium. Even if other people feel they had a good experience, it may be their expectations and needs are lower than yours. Or the medium you see has an off day. When you find the right medium it will lead to very powerful healing.

A client of mine described this experience as:

"With some mediums it's like having an old phone but when you find a really great medium it's like all of a sudden you have been given an iPhone that works so much better and can do so many things the old phone can't do. You perhaps couldn't even imagine when you had the old phone what an iPhone would be like. It's the iPhone medium that has the ability to give you the benefits that you always needed with the old phone."

The very last question raised in this book, and so far left untouched, is did Tanya ever receive from Jack the nickname he called her by? Well, just as the information in this book demonstrates that life eventually comes round full-circle, and we will be reunited with our loved ones in heaven, and those who have passed over long ago, let me bring this book to a close by making the circle of the book complete.

Tanya

"When I went back to see Ross, I asked him the very same questions you find in this book. Getting the answers really helped me understand everything on a deeper level, Ross' answers made logical sense to me. They weren't too out there or ungrounded. It wasn't about mysticism it was about real life, real love and real happiness. I know he is going to go on to bigger and bigger things, because I believe the world needs his message.

The world needs his insight to help more things go in the right direction and bring people the healing they so desperately need. I have had several follow-up readings with Ross. Each one has brought new relevant information to me and demonstrated my amazing son is still so close to me.

After Ross had gotten in touch with Jack, he said if you give the spirits time, it doesn't matter how much trouble they have or how complicated the infor-mation is, providing the medium is good enough, has enough experience of the thing the spirit is trying to communicate, the spirits will find a way to get the message across to them in a way their conscious mind will recognize, and that could come in a number of ways.

So, I received a message one day from Ross saying that Jack had visited him during meditation and reminded Ross of something he saw the day before: a young girl in a park who looked somewhere around five years of age had fallen over and was screaming out Mumsieeeeeeee! Ross then asked me if there was significance to the word Mumsie and me.

As I read his words, I burst into tears for that was the nickname Jack called me. I was always his Mumsie. Ross said it made sense to him now why he was seeing lots of images relate to his childhood and his mother, something he did mention when he told me it wasn't coming through in a literal way. He explained how his mind must have been processing it as meaning mum, which made him think of his mum and his childhood. He explained it was right in front of his face but his conscious mind would have been dismissing it. Wanting to perceive any word that didn't have mum in it. It was the simplicity of it that made it difficult in this case. It is so close to something that is so generic with just the smallest twist to it, to be personal, but easily missed amongst the generic aspect.

I asked Ross if it was luck that he was in the right place, at the right time to hear that, so Jack could then empathize with him the connection and to tell me. Ross said no, we have our free will, but mediums should be in touch with the spirits and the Great Spirit, that infinite flux of energy and information, God, if you wish to call it that. If you are in touch, let them guide your actions, give into the flow of their direction, and then they will steer you to where you need to be. The issue is most people aren't in touch in this way.

As Ross explained that to me, I thought to myself, I suppose that relates to the question I asked him about why some mediums are more accurate and evidential than others; some are more in touch with heaven and the universe than others.

The world certainly needs more mediums who are really reallyyyy in touch with the afterlife. I suppose this also shows that someone, like me, who was looking for proof also need to be patient. Ross told me sometimes people are not patient, if all their psychological needs, as he called them, aren't met right away, their ego can get the better of them, betray them and guide them away from the healing they are looking for. He said when he sees this happen, it saddens him greatly, because he knows if they were a little more patient and aspects of their ego were a little more calm on certain levels they would receive the healing they need.

I also think that is such a shame because then they may not ever find the healing they need. Just as I needed it. Surely, they will go through the rest of their earthly life suffering without that healing. If that had happened to me, I know I would no longer be here on Earth. I had planned to kill myself if the first reading with Ross didn't go well enough. I had everything planned out in my mind and suicide notes already written from long ago.

I knew, eventually, I also needed to hear that word Mumsie, come through Ross from my son, and sure enough with a little bit of time and a little bit of patience it did. I just needed to listen to a medium like Ross and let him guide my healing journey.

So, I have Ross, the spirits that help him and my lovely Jack to thank for stopping me from causing further harm to myself. I cannot begin to tell you how the validation of receiving the nickname has brightened up my life again, and brought me peace. I certainly knew from that point on, Mumsie and Jack would always be close, but wait, there is more.... in my last meeting with Ross, he told me Jack had brought him and me a packet of Jammie Dodgers.

They are a particular brand of biscuit, for those who may not be familiar with it. Whilst Ross said he was unsure of the significance, I knew exactly what Jack was referring to. He had a nickname for me, but I also had my nickname for him too, and that nickname was Jammie Dodger. Oh, what conclusive proof that is of my beautiful son's continual and eternal existence, and our continual connection!

Mumsie and Jammie Dodger will always be close; one day, one way or another we will meet again when the time is right. In the meantime, as I continue to move forward in my life I'm sure I will continue to receive messages from my Jack, periodically through one means or another. Messages that will bring a smile to my face again and again, not because it will reaffirm he is close to me because I know that now, in fact, in some ways, I feel closer to Jack now than I ever did.

The messages and love that will come will be for Mumsie and Jammie Dodger, to continue in our own way to have that special connection we always shared and always will."

You see, you are never alone, your loved ones and the Great Spirit will be with you always.

Ross

References

Alexander, E. (2012). *Proof of Heaven: A Neurosurgeon's Journey Into the Afterlife*. Simon and Schuster.

Batalhão, T. B., Souza, A. M., Mazzola, L., Auccaise, R., Sarthour, R. S., Oliveira, I. S., ... & Serra, R. M. (2014). Experimental reconstruction of work distribution and study of fluctuation relations in a closed quantum system. Physical review letters, 113(14), 140601.

Beischel, J., Boccuzzi, M., Biuso, M., & Rock, A. J. (2015). Anomalous information reception by research mediums under blinded conditions II: Replication and extension. EXPLORE: The Journal of Science & Healing, 11(2), 136-142. doi: 10.1016/j.explore.2015.01.001

Beischel, J., Mosher, C., & Boccuzzi, M. (2014-2015). The possible effects on bereavement of assisted after-death communication during readings with psychic mediums: A continuing bonds perspective. Omega: Journal of Death and Dying, 70(2), 169-194. doi: 10.2190/OM.70.2.b

Boss, P. (1977). A clarification of the concept of psychological father presence in families experiencing ambiguity of boundary. Journal of Marriage & the Family, 39(1), 141-151.

Boss, P. (2012). Resilience as tolerance for ambiguity. In D. S. Becvar (Ed.), Handbook of family resilience (pp. 285-297). New York: Springer.

Bowlby, J. (1977). The making and breaking of affectional bonds. II. Some principles of psychotherapy. The fiftieth Maudsley Lecture. The British Journal of Psychiatry, 130(5), 421-431.

Brown, A. S. (2004). The déjà vu experience. Psychology Press.

Burgess, C. A., Kirsch, I., Shane, H., Niederauer, K. L., Graham, S. M., & Bacon, A. (1998). Facilitated communication as an ideomotor response. Psychological Science, 9(1), 71-74.

Cooper, C.E. (2012). Telephone Calls from the Dead. Old Portsmouth: Tricorn Books.

Crawford, C., & Krebs, D. L. (Eds.). (2013). Handbook of evolutionary psychology: Ideas, issues, and applications. Psychology Press.

Currier, J. M., Neimeyer, R. A., & Berman, J. S. (2008). The effectiveness of psychotherapeutic interventions for bereaved persons: a comprehensive quantitative review. Psychological Bulletin, 134(5), 648.

Evenden, R.E., Cooper, C.E., & Mitchell, G. (2013). A counselling approach to mediumship: Adaptive outcomes of grief following an exceptional experience. Journal of Exceptional Experiences and Psychology, 1 (2), 12-19.

Feynman, R. P., Leighton, R. B., & Sands, M. (2013). The Feynman Lectures on Physics, Desktop Edition Volume I (Vol. 1). Basic books.

Field, N. P., Gao, B., & Paderna, L. (2005). Continuing bonds in bereavement: An attachment theory based perspective. Death studies, 29(4), 277-299.

Freud, S. (1917). *Mourning and Melancholia.* Standard edition, 14(239), 1957-61.

Hameroff, S., & Penrose, R. (1996). Orchestrated reduction of quantum coherence in brain microtubules: A model for consciousness. Mathematics and computers in simulation, 40(3), 453-480.

Hameroff, S., & Chopra, D. (2012). The "Quantum Soul": A Scientific Hypothesis. In Exploring frontiers of the mind-brain relationship (pp. 79-93). Springer New York.

Hameroff, S., & Penrose, R. (2014). Consciousness in the universe: A review of the 'Orch OR' theory. Physics of life reviews, 11(1), 39-78.

Harlow, H. F. (1958). *The nature of love.* American psychologist, 13(12), 673.

Jibu, M., & Yasue, K. (1995). Quantum brain dynamics and consciousness: an introduction (Vol. 3). John Benjamins Publishing.

Jung, C. G. (1936). *The concept of the collective unconscious.* Collected works, 9(Part I).

Lethbridge, T. C. (1961). *Ghost and Goul.* Routledge and K. Paul.

Lorenz, K. Z. (1935). Der Kumpan in der Umwelt des Vogels. Journal für Ornithologie, 83, 137–213, 289–412.

Ricciardi, L. M., & Umezawa, H. (1967). Brain and physics of many-body problems. Kybernetik, 4(2), 44-48.

Stevenson, I. (1980). Twenty cases suggestive of reincarnation. University of Virginia Press.

Stevenson, I. (1987). Children who remember previous lives. Charlottesville: University Press of Virginia.

Walach, H., Bösch, H., Lewith, G., Naumann, J., Schwarzer, B., Falk, S., ... & Tomasson, H. (2008). Effectiveness of distant healing for patients with chronic fatigue syndrome: a randomised controlled partially blinded trial (EUHEALS). Psychotherapy and psychosomatics, 77(3), 158-166.

Watson, J. B. (1930). *Behaviorism,* revised ed. University of Chicago Press.

Wilber, K., Enlger, J., & Brown, D. (1986). Transformations of Consciousness. Conventional and Contemplative Perspectives on development.

Worden, J.W. (2008). Grief counselling and grief therapy; A handbook for the mental health practitioner (4th ed.), New York: Springer.

~

For more information on Ross Bartlett and to contact him please see his website: *www.rosswbartlett.com*